Praise for Wicked Times

I loved the man and his poems. He was the revolutionary angel of American poetry.

—PETE SEEGER, folk singer, activist

Wicked Times is a collection that inspires both admiration and gratitude in a reader. The neglected poet Aaron Kramer was an artist of considerable substance, and this volume performs an invaluable service to U.S. cultural history by restoring Kramer's work to print in a form that showcases the breadth and depth of his achievement.

—ALAN WALD, professor of English at the University of
   Michigan and author of *Exiles from a Future Time*

In his poem "Indigo," Aaron Kramer says that it was rage that summoned Mrs. Chiga, revered Japanese artist, to devote her life to making blue cloth. From his teen years into his seventies, something very much like rage—rage at human evil, rage at an America where justice is blind—drove Kramer himself. He saw in the daily news a flotilla of horrors that had to be sunk, fathomed, and sounded in poetry, poetry that an America still in progress might find of use. Yet he feared the "Muse of politics" had misled him artistically, that he had not "broke[n] through again and again," as he says Paul Celan, for one, had. But *Wicked Times* proves him a poet of relentless integrity and moral fervor. May his unfashionable example inspire poets to come.

—WILLIAM HEYEN, author of *Erika: Poems of the Holocaust*
   and other volumes

Political poets are seldom given enough credit for the pleasures they derive from writing. Aaron Kramer sang (to paraphrase an old review) because for him singing was one of the joys of living. He was a generous, spirited person. He wrote diverse poems, some of them angry, but all shaped by the joy of singing. To be sure, he had his low moments. In 1954, not long before the scheduled release of the anti-McCarthyite *Roll the Forbidden Drums!* his publisher actually returned the galleys with apologies and a frank admission that Kramer's name in 1954 would make it suicidal for it to give the book its imprint. But Kramer wrote on. In 1950 his embattled work as bookkeeper and office manager at Local 16, UOPWA in New York, which was fighting against the widespread removal of Communists from union leadership, caused him severe bleeding ulcers. But he wrote more poems. Now many of them are gathered here, and now the real joy Kramer took from poetry can finally be shared by his readers.

—ALAN FILREIS, professor of English at the University of
    Pennsylvania and author of *Modernism from Right to Left*

In discovering the beauty and breadth of Aaron Kramer's life work as a writer of passion and social conscience, I feel I am finding a kindred spirit.

—BARBARA KINGSOLVER, author of *The Poisonwood Bible,*
    Prodigal Summer, and other books

Wicked Times

Aaron Kramer at about age thirty

Wicked Times

SELECTED POEMS

Aaron Kramer

*Edited and with a
Biographical Essay by
Cary Nelson and
Donald Gilzinger Jr.*

UNIVERSITY OF ILLINOIS PRESS

URBANA AND CHICAGO

The photographs in this book appear courtesy of the family of Aaron Kramer.

Library of Congress Cataloging-in-Publication Data
Kramer, Aaron, 1921–
Wicked times : selected poems / Aaron Kramer ; edited and with a
biographical essay by Cary Nelson and Donald Gilzinger, Jr.
p.   cm. — (American poetry recovery series)
Includes bibliographical references (p.) and index.
ISBN 0-252-02918-6 (cloth : alk. paper)
I. Nelson, Cary.
II. Gilzinger, Donald.
III. Title.
IV. Series.
PS3521.R29A6   2004
811'.52—dc22   2003021629

For
Paula Treichler
Carol Gilzinger
and
the Kramer family

Contents

Aaron Kramer: American Prophet
Donald Gilzinger Jr. and Cary Nelson

Open the Book of Time, if you have eyes;
turn to your page, and know it.

Suddenly, poet, your season of brooding is ended.
The egg, secretly guarded, is hatched. Now high over
your countrymen's heads, on wings that are splendid
the swan of your sorrow and theirs is beginning to fly.

We offer *Wicked Times* as evidence that the American poetry establishment
has long neglected one of its most compelling and accomplished poets.
Perhaps no other American-born poet of the last century has so success-
fully adapted traditional forms to the combined projects of progressive
social criticism and historical witness. He sought in the music of poetry not
only cultural knowledge but also incitement to change. Through much of
his career, Aaron Kramer (1921–97) was a recognized figure in Left literary
circles. For a number of years he also had a devoted following and a notable
presence in the New York area, especially among those who attended his
readings or listened to his radio broadcasts. Yet Kramer himself despaired
of ever reaching a broad national audience and ever receiving wide criti-
cal attention. The venues that reviewed him early on largely abandoned
him as he matured. All this is the subject of one of his mid-career poems,
"To Himself" (1964).

Even if Kramer's poetry had been more widely reviewed, however, it
would not have been easy to become the widely read people's poet he
sought to be. What does it mean, we might ask, to be a people's poet here
or elsewhere in the world? It is not, to be sure, a universal concept, for to
be a people's poet in Moscow in 1917 was not the same as being one in
Madrid in 1937, let alone New York in 1957. It is a question not only of the
mechanisms for publishing and distributing poetry and of the character of
the different audiences for that poetry but also of the social roles poetry
plays here and in other countries. An extensive national following outside
the often more limited audiences for books of poetry would probably have
required newspaper syndication and broad dissemination of a significant
number of Kramer's poems. Given Kramer's political commitments—he
was, after all, the poet who promised in "Oh How We Suffer: Song of the
Masses," published in the *Daily Worker* when he was but fifteen, that work-

ers would "rise from bondage" to carry "the flag of the slaves" and "march with it over the rulers' graves"—that was not simply unlikely; it was impossible. From being published in newspapers across the country, he could have evolved into a poet with a large national audience, especially in the decades when dozens of American newspapers had staff members writing book reviews. It has happened before to other poets, though more often in the nineteenth and early twentieth centuries than in the decades—from the 1930s through the 1990s—when Kramer was writing. Yet one can certainly argue that Kramer was producing poems Americans needed to see, poems about work and race and political repression, among others. Meanwhile, the literary establishment, which sometimes offers a potential trickle-down route from celebrity to popularity, denied him any visibility at all.

Yet even the *Daily Worker* did not quite know what to do with him at first, sometimes publishing him on its "Junior America" page and sometimes elsewhere. Kramer in fact started out as a child proletarian poet, at a time when his fellow proletarian poets—all a few crucial years older—effectively belonged to the previous generation. Kramer published four poems in *New Pioneer* in 1934, when he was only twelve years old. Here is the opening stanza of the third, from August 1934, "We'll Fight for Our Cause!" casting a cold eye on the sort of patriotic militarism that led a generation to die in European fields two decades earlier:

> For thousands of years, you've called us to war,
>> With many a high-sounding phrase
> You've lured us with wonderful tales galore
> You've not told that innocent blood will pour
>> You've blinded us with praise.

And here is the first stanza of "To Angelo Herndon," from November, dedicated to the young black Communist who helped organize a 1932 interracial hunger strike in Georgia and was charged with the capital offense of inciting an insurrection as a result. Kramer draws out of Herndon's case another broad lesson:

> You youthful proletarian,
> Of an oppressed and starving race;
> Your hardships are the hardships
> That all working youth must face.

In three years Kramer was publishing in the *Daily Worker.* Langston Hughes was also publishing revolutionary poems there, but he was born in 1902 and had published his first book in 1926. Edwin Rolfe, born in 1909, published his first *Daily Worker* poems in the late 1920s and was already in Spain with the Lincoln Battalion by 1937; his first book had been reviewed in the *New York Times Book Review* the year before. Muriel Rukeyser, shortly to issue her first book from Yale, was born in 1913. She was barely eight years older than Kramer, but it was enough to make her a young adult when he was a teenager. All these writers gained their first visibility in the infamous red decade when alternative radical publishers briefly flourished and establishment venues occasionally took notice. By the time Kramer became a young adult the moment was over. Yet even on the Left he was too young for anyone to notice that, still at age fifteen, in his 1937 poem "The Shoe-Shine Boy," he had written one of the definitive vignettes about class. The poem is a successor to Thoreau's "I Am the Little Irish Boy," which Kramer would later praise in his *The Prophetic Tradition in American Poetry, 1835–1900,* and the political equivalent of Countee Cullen's 1925 "Incident." Kramer's speaker reports seeing "a child whose shoes looked old / Shining another's, till they shone like gold." "From that day," he tells us, "I could not understand / Why this is called a great and noble land."

The poem also shows how early Kramer mastered traditional meters and developed a critical relation to them, for "The Shoe-Shine Boy" is a deliberately ironic use of heroic couplets. The decision to take on traditional forms—using them, altering them—would characterize his whole career. Much like Claude McKay and Edna St. Vincent Millay, who took over the sonnet and reinvented it earlier in the century, Kramer adopted traditional meters—favoring iambic trimeter, tetrameter, and pentameter—in part to install a radical politics within inherited rhythms. He wanted to radicalize root and branch of our literary tradition, not to abandon it for alternative forms. Nor was he alone in having such impulses. Most famously, W. H. Auden reworked traditional rhymed forms for political ends in the 1930s and 1940s. Our devotion to experimental modernism has unfortunately led us to underestimate the transformations most of these poets, Kramer among them, effected.

Meanwhile, the American Left was mostly ill prepared to read Kramer with the care he deserves. Many of the poets of the radical, Communist left of the 1930s thought their natural lineage was the free verse tradition that began with Whitman. Many of the poets and critics who would have been most capable of appreciating Kramer's craft, ironically, were cultural conservatives who would have found his politics offensive.

If Kramer was poorly served by both the timing of his birth and the literary establishment, however, neither his frequent publication in fugitive chapbooks nor his chosen subjects helped him gain mainstream attention either. What national newspaper or magazine would have dared—at the height of the American inquisition—to review a collection of poems that savaged McCarthyism, Kramer's 1954 *Roll the Forbidden Drums?* Two years earlier he had issued *Denmark Vesey and Other Poems.* The poem sequence, about an aborted 1822 slave revolt in Charleston, South Carolina, that gives the book its title, is one of the most ambitious and inventive poems about race ever written by a white poet. Though "Denmark Vesey" was widely performed in an oratorio version, it has left few traces in literary culture, the most notable being Alan Wald's important comments in his 1994 *Writing from the Left.* Kramer would eventually go on to write moving and powerfully reflective poems about family life, aging, and death—topics more easily assimilated to mainstream culture—but his other lifelong interests did not closely match the taste of those defining the modern American canon. Worse still, Kramer devoted himself to poems about the ironies of work under capitalism and took the stance of the loyal opposition during decades of American political life and international adventures.

Kramer was also aiming for a broad popular audience. From the outset he felt no temptation to write for an elite coterie. Superficially, at least, his poetry is immensely accessible, but the social and political messages he puts forward require complex cultural negotiations and a willingness to entertain alternative bodies of knowledge. Much the same can be said of Langston Hughes, who also mounted a radical critique of American culture in language often deceptively simple. Formally, Kramer's poems seem easy as well. His lines are often relatively short, his stanzas regular, his rhyme schemes often straightforward, though Kramer does tend, for example, to loosen formal verse with anapests and feminine rhymes, thereby adding extra syllables to some of his lines. Yet Kramer's poems also relentlessly test and challenge the relationship between traditional forms and subject matter. Written regularly about the last two hundred years of signal violence, the poems press against the limits of what traditional forms—especially those with rhymed and metered lines—can handle. Can one write rhymed verse about the Holocaust? Kramer did.

While so many other modern poets distrusted convention itself, Kramer instead explored its limits and possibilities. We have gathered together here those of his experiments that we think succeed, but one can readily find poems elsewhere in his books and pamphlets where he perhaps risked everything and lost the wager. But he also often seems to know instinctively where traditional forms should perhaps be wary of going. His rhymed Holocaust poem "The Thunder of the Grass" gives us a narrative of Nazi violence in the Warsaw ghetto. Years later he returns to the subject to say that even after decades "The Rising in the Warsaw Ghetto" defines the month of April:

We define it now by those
who, from Warsaw's frozen ground,
like a great green field arose
in a burst of fatal sound.

One feels here the poignant tension between the poem's nearly impossible subject—which contradicts every consolation and empties every aesthetic tradition of its confidence—and the regularities of the verse echoing through years of literary history. The rhymes and the rhythms evoke pleasure and the memory of pleasure, yet Warsaw's burst of sound was fatal. Unease thereby permeates everything the poem would celebrate. And that unstable balance works. The Holocaust surfaces again when Kramer travels in Europe and commemorates the invisible dead who crowd its architecture and its public places. And he marks its memory again when Kurt Waldheim wins approval in an Austrian vote. Yet he does not try to render into rhyme the very heart of the death camp experience. For that, regular rhythm and rhyme will not do.

To have followed Kramer's history of responses to the Holocaust, along with the other continuities of his career, however, would have taken a fairly devoted fan. It would have meant acquiring all twenty-eight of Kramer's poetry books and chapbooks. Many of his poems were scattered in self-published or small-press collections unlikely to be in bookstores, let alone widely reviewed. Others remained uncollected in magazines. Never in his lifetime were all of his best poems collected in one book. That is what we have sought to do here. We have included as well a detailed account of his life and career, information that cannot be found elsewhere.

The date after each poem title in the table of contents refers to the first date of publication, whether that was in a journal or a book. The notes to the poems give additional publication history. Kramer frequently published individual poems in response to current events, then later included them in a poem sequence. We have felt free in such cases to reprint either the individual poem or the later sequence, whichever best served this selection of his poems.

The arrangement of the poems here is topical, a pattern Kramer himself followed in *The Burning Bush* (1983), the one partial career overview he published. A number of his chapbooks, written amidst the fires of history, were also effectively topical collections. Yet we have the luxury of following his interests over a lifetime. The result is not only a portrait of change and development but also a record of continuity and commitment. His first Spanish Civil War poem, "In the Land of Olives"—never included in any of his books but reprinted here—was published only a month after his sixteenth birthday. His final group of poems about Spain and its 1936–39 civil war dates from 1991, fifty-eight years later, and there are Aaron Kramer Spanish Civil War poems from most of the intervening decades. The poems we reprint in opposition to American imperialism and our experiments in national thought control span exactly the same years. His first poem attacking the political forces that would later become codified as McCarthyism, "The Soul of Martin Dies," dates from 1940. "Called In," a requiem for a generation's political anguish at enforced political testimony, comes from 1980. His poems on Jewish topics run from 1940 to 1985. He wrote elegies about friends and public figures, as well as poems about African American history, for over fifty years.

There are equally powerful registers of commitment in his more temporally concentrated interests. His remarkable travel poems mix intricate observation with sharp social and political commentary. He travels simultaneously to places and through history. Indeed, Kramer cannot simply travel in space because space for him is layered with time. Everywhere he looks the past breaks through the phenomenal veneer of the present. What might seem obsessive, however, is leavened by a continuing reflexiveness about his own determination to read the present historically. He is as much an inwardly bemused traveler as an historically attentive one. And that is because he recognizes the social incongruity—for an American, in a country often heedless of the past—of his insistence on the historicality of lived time.

Of course, neither Kramer's interests nor our section divisions are mutually exclusive. Some of his poems on Jewish themes could as easily go into the section of travel poems, as could a number of the poems burdened with the Spanish Civil War. While the groupings here thus allow us to foreground his key commitments, they also intersect and overlap in interesting ways. The thematic groupings also help readers see the connections between Kramer's poetry and that of his contemporaries. If his lyricism and his metrics sometimes set him apart from many of his fellow poets, including most left-wing poets of the generations in which he wrote, his main subjects link him with many other writers. In pursuing a lyrical politics he certainly belongs in Edwin Rolfe's company. Both Kramer and Rolfe wrote regularly about the perils of capitalist labor, and both did important work about McCarthyism. They are also among those American poets who returned again and again to write about the Spanish Civil War. Whether haunted or inspired by that last great cause of the 1930s, Aaron Kramer, Edwin Rolfe, Muriel Rukeyser, and Norman Rosten were among the American poets who wrote poems about the Spanish Civil War throughout their lives. Philip Levine has now taken up their mantle.[1]

Levine, notably, like Kramer, writes just as often about the American workplace. As one recognizes these shared interests, a cluster of progressive commitments begins to define a community of poets who worked through the last century. Yet Kramer also has strong links both with those poets who have written about the Holocaust and with those who are devoted to African American history. Some of the colleagues to whom we have showed "Denmark Vesey" assumed that Kramer was black. Kramer's career repeatedly testifies to commitments that render readers' expectations about racial identity unreliable.

Wicked Times, a title adapted from one of his fugitive chapbooks, offers readers not only an impressive corpus of such work but also a fundamental challenge to our ingrained assumptions about modern poetry. Now that the full range of Kramer's work is available in one place it may prompt us to rethink the possibilities of rhymed, metered verse in regular stanzas as a form of historical engagement. It has been that before, as any reader of English ballads or the poetry of William Blake will know, but we had perhaps set aside awareness of that possibility over much of the last century. That is a history Aaron Kramer would have us revisit. His poems in four- or five-beat quatrains are interspersed with occasional sonnets ("The Count") and near sonnets ("The Shoe-Shine Boy"), twelve lines in iambic pentameter. Throughout his career, he rings changes on the ballad stanza. The first section of his 1943 poem "Natchez," for example, which he titles "The Ballad," turns the ABAB ballad quatrain into longer rhymed couplets; the form is thus different to the eye but the same to the ear. "In my own work," he writes in a September 14, 1949, letter to the editor of the *Daily Worker,* "I have decided to reject the experimental forms, feeling that they would hamper my effort to reach a large audience." Yet, "how quickly," he adds, "our leading experimentalists return to the old ballad form when they are most anxious to create 'effective impact.'" "Denmark Vesey" mounts variation after variation on the ballad in a tour-de-force formal experiment. And then these transformed ballads carry history with them into the present, making witness link lamentation with a will to change.

The ballad has, of course, been both metrically regular and rhymed, along with being highly political for centuries. Its history encompasses several related aims—elevating individuals to heroic status, establishing a generalized class or ethnic protest, celebrating historical events that an audience is ready to commemorate. And its influence has spread beyond the ballad form itself. So Kramer can write a 1943 rhymed paean in a bracing iambic trimeter to Paul Robeson, a man who reached heroic stature early in his life:

Tonight Paul Robeson sings.
His feet are enough of a stage.
His voice is a hammer that rings.
His voice is a bull in rage.
Tonight Paul Robeson sings.
His eyes are enough of light.
His smiles are eagle wings.
A tree of steel is his height.
Come out of your room, your cage!
Come out to the Concert Hall!
Here is your waiting's wage.
Here is your chance to grow tall.

Even here, the insistent beat is complicated by anapestic feet substituting for iambic ones. But everything—including the lovely interlocking rhyme scheme (ABAB/ACAC/BDBD)—combines to give us a sounding board we can use to celebrate the heroic stature of a Robeson performance. There are among us, Kramer repeatedly shows, worthy subjects for the ballad and its allied forms. By the time Kramer wrote his 1937 rhymed tribute to Tom Mooney, the labor leader had been imprisoned for two decades and was already a legendary martyr.

Yet political rhyme, to take but one feature of Kramer's practice, is also often inherently self-conscious. It can install self-recognition in the reading subject, urging participatory assent, not just neutral observation. Often it evokes a collective voice. To read a political poem appreciatively is to join a group. The rhymed political poem is thus a form of public discourse. While it can be a terrain for private contemplation, it will likely make other claims on us as well.

Of course political satire has also been metrically insistent and rhymed for centuries. In Kramer's "The Soul of Martin Dies," a poem about the first chair of the House Committee on Un-American Activities, Dies remarks, "My hair turned grey / with worry for the U.S.A."; then Satan in turn invokes the expertise of another of Hell's residents in judgment of Dies himself: "William Randolph Hearst, / has told me why you should be cursed." Here too, then, Kramer exploits the capacity of meter and rhyme both for formal certification and for readerly participation. *Wicked Times* opens with rhymed satire in the poems of "A Consumer Culture," moves to the celebratory rhymed carnivalesque of the poems about New York, and continues with the generalized rhymed protest of the poems about exploitation in the workplace.

A satirical politics underlies several of the rhymed poems in "The Loyal Opposition" as well. Kramer's aim is never to have the poetry's political judgments simply permeate the memory of events but rather to register the moment of truth and to credit political difference and opposition. To savor the meter and the rhyme is thus to savor the recognition. There is no need for the rhyme to be suppressed, to be traversed without pause or emphasis. There is thus no reason to prefer enjambed lines in political poems. Kramer mixes end-stopped and enjambed lines to combine ongoing motion with repeated emphasis. In a series of poems in "The Loyal Opposition"—beginning with "Have You Felt the Heart of America?" "The Breeze," and "May First 1940"—Kramer punctuates the poetry's political assertions with rhyme. Yet he is also willing to use meter and rhyme to evoke the counter-song of the oppressor. Here are the opening lines of "Loyalty March":

> You should have heard them holler KILL!! You should
> have seen them lunge by dozens from the line
> of march, and fall upon a lad who stood
> among the crowd, and kick his skull, his spine
> because he said that killing wasn't good.

The formal elements here mix satire with condemnation, mimicking fascism's nightmare marching rhythms. Much the same effect dominates the opening stanza of "All-Star Neutron Day":

> The mouths of Auschwitz's unholy pillars
> sent sacrificial incense toward the skies.
> Now men ask: From the womb of Bachs and Schillers
> how could there be a leaping forth of killers
> without one gasp, one turning down of eyes?

The sequence "pillars," "Schillers," and "killers" meets W. K. Wimsatt's definition of a complex rhyme that deliberately crosses categories, creating aberrant and disruptive linkages that forge meaning through the marriage of sound and sense. If the second rhyme is a lightly irreverent response to the first, it is still within its world of meaning (the Bachs and Schillers of our day are pillars of the community), but this only sets up the startling new link with the third rhyme, which now turns revelatory.

Kramer's skill and inventiveness in negotiating the political relationship between form, sound, diction, and meaning becomes still more impressive in one of his major achievements, the twenty-six-poem sequence "Denmark Vesey," privately printed in 1952 and unavailable since then. There the first poem offers a hint of internal rhyme in Kramer's riveting definition of plantation agriculture—"acres rooted by uprooted hands"—and then gives the first full rhymes to slavery, as the founder of the middle passage gets the inspiration to kidnap African men, women, and children, then sees the idea become a thriving business:

> That inspiration swiftly turned to gold.
> The first shocked screams were muffled in the hold
> of ships—and there in chains the kidnapped lay
> while those who loved them wept, a world away.

Interestingly, the opening poem is partly about hearing and listening—about whether any of the slavers either heard or cared about their captives' cries of agony—and thus the rhymes *we* hear reinforce the narrative's ironies. Then, in a typical Kramer strategy, the hint of internal rhyme in the first poem is fulfilled in the second: "*The sobs and moans cut through my bones.*" This line, as it happens, is from one white resident who *does* hear, the wife of a slave owner or auctioneer. This poem, "Auction Block," is a brilliantly executed dialogue between her and her husband, with their respective statements differentiated in italics and roman type. The poem reinforces what will be a constant theme in the sequence, that white civilization is grounded not only in its indifference to the suffering it imposes on its darker brothers but also in a suppression of its own humanity, a pattern that Kramer intensifies as the narrative progresses. "*Not right, not right! a dreadful sight!*" the wife cries out, the break in the line not so much effecting a pause as creating two rapid-fire segments. We first think the lines move quickly because the woman is so intensely horrified, but at the end we know that they move quickly because the man wants to get the whole experience out of the way without thinking. The uncomprehending husband wonders what could be wrong? After all, the sale went "smooth and clean." Once he realizes at least dimly why she is distressed, his response is precise and telling:

> You like a rug in every room;
> diamonds in your hair.
> Without those blacks to bend their backs
> your wrists would soon be bare.

He closes with a demand that reinforces the sequence's thematics: "let's hear / no more of what you think." Next the third poem gives full voice to slavery's victims. "Plantation Song" combines blues repetitions with echoes of spirituals:

How many days will it be,
oh how many days will it be?
I'll count them, Lord, I know how to count
until my hands go free.

In an effort to lend material difference to the cultures of the decaying elite and the rising folk, Kramer gives the ruling whites (but not the sailors) voice in off rhymes and runover lines, while his black speakers are dramatized in strong rhyme and repetition, though not in dialect. His black characters also find their experience coalescing in concise symbols—like Vesey's hammer, which the whites, later in the sequence, will hear as drumming a lullaby shoring up their privilege while the blacks hear it as nailing down the boards to "make slavery a coffin"—while white culture spills over in shapeless waste:

Through Col. Prioleau's majestic shutters,
music like wine poured into evening's cup,
until it overflowed along the gutters
where greedy coachmen stooped to lap it up.

These lines are from "Minuet," the tenth poem in the sequence. Meanwhile, anticipating what will happen in the United States, the poems following "Plantation Song" give several perspectives on a slave revolt in Santo Domingo, with Kramer creating different forms for each speaker. Except for the following stanza, "Revolt in Santo Domingo" uses an insistent AAA rhyme: "They crushed the whip that they'd been baptized with. / They broke the harness they had bent beneath, / and kicked it back into their masters' teeth." Then "Song of Returning Sailors" shifts to a ballad in the mode of oral history:

We bring forbidden tidings
from harbors far and near—
and some will dance who hear it,
and some will die of fear.

Two poems later, in "Refugee Relief," Kramer recounts the indulgences of Charleston's white culture in runover pentameter lines—exemplifying the measured confidence of their presumed cultural supremacy. But an undercurrent of violence rewrites their version of high culture in brutal terms: "the loudest orchestra they could assemble / would lash the night with waltz and minuet." He then offers a song measure for Denmark Vesey, awarding him by contrast him an uncompromised music: "they hired his hammer but night after night / he hammered their chains into dust."

All this is building toward a climactic moment in the sequence. In "Refugee Relief," "Charleston Nocturne," and "The Minuet" Kramer has progressively drawn out the careless indulgence, wasted wealth, violent repression, and fundamental exhaustion of white culture. "The Minuet" ends by showing us the generational decline of white privilege:

> But they were pale, for all the pirouetting;
> haggard and hushed, for all the boasts and toasts.
> Even the young: past grieving, past forgetting,
> performed their fathers' graceful dance like ghosts.

Then we get "Vesey's Nightmare" in off-rhymed five-beat couplets, an astonishing poem in which white cannibals and vampires feed on black bodies and decorate themselves with human trophies—like ghouls elevated to positions of social prominence: "Instead of an ordinary meal, they had / young Negro bodies, baked to the bone . . . The lovely brocade their ladies wore / had once been Negro grandmothers' hair." In "Vesey Speaks to the Congregation," a poem that fuses lamentation and solidarity, we get Vesey's testimony of his bodily identification with the oppressed in rhymed couplets:

> My leg is weak from the chains you wear;
> my shoulders break at the load you bear;
> my back is marked by your masters' whips;
> and from your wounds my own blood drips. . . .

The reaction of the whites to intimations of revolt gets its own distinctive rhythm. In "The Legislators Vote" the relentless, lurching rhythm perfectly instantiates the legislature as an institutionalized lynch mob:

> "A law! a law! let's pass one now!"
> "A Santo Domingo we'll never allow!"
> "Look out for whisperers!" "Fine them!" "Jail them!"
> "Bind them!" "Starve them!" "Brand them!" "Flail them!"

In the next poem, "A Meeting at Vesey's," Kramer takes these very rhythmic effects and gives them a hushed but incantatory twist:

> All through the cotton from row to row
> whisper, whisper the word!

Wherever the whip has worked its woe
whisper, whisper the word!

In poem after poem, Kramer invents new stanzas and rhyme schemes, always finding fresh ways to embody the developing content. In "Ned's Silence," the rhymes let the slavers celebrate the way they torture a potential informant:

We held a lantern to his eyes;
we kicked him out of sleep;
we told him that his son would die,
and still he did not weep.

Later his confession comes in blank verse, granting him a certain formal dignity despite the forced betrayal, followed by off-rhymed four-beat couplets. "The Sentence Is Announced" returns to a ballad form, but "The Hanging," when Vesey is found out and punished, adopts long, funereal seven-beat couplets: "And when the moon herself was hanged while rolling down the night, / the slavers locked their windows, and the doors they bolted tight." But the final poem, "The Hammer and the Light," is devoted to echoes of the blues, a form, as Kramer pointed out in a 1994 letter to Alan Wald, "Langston Hughes taught me to love as a child." The final poem offers us what Kramer would call "symbols too of a resistance tyranny could not crush." It is, he asserted, "as much about 1952 as about 1822."[2] "The Sentence Is Announced" was performed at West Coast rallies for Julius and Ethel Rosenberg. "Every word in the entire book, and the private printing of the book itself," Kramer writes, "was an act of defiance. That year I was on fire." Finally, the balladic base of "Denmark Vesey" helps transform the story into legend, lifting the force of the narrative out of the vicissitudes of continuing historical debate about Vesey's real intentions and establishing it on a plane of wider testimony. Whatever happened in 1822, the story of what many believed to have happened has been repeatedly retold. That narrative has its own historical life. Among the retellings, Kramer's may be the most notable. It speaks not only to one revolt but also to the whole history of race relations in America. Its rhymes offer inspiration to resistance now and in the future.

Indeed a pattern of interlocking sound and thematics testifies to the poem's contemporary relevance. "When will we see you, Sun—in what strange land?" ask the kidnapped men and women on the middle passage. "How many days will it be, / oh how many days . . . until my hands go free" ask the slaves in "Plantation Song." "Too long we are forgotten—too long we wait" answer the black parishioners in "Sunday Offertory Prayer." And of course readers are to recognize they are waiting still. The only answer is to act.

For "Denmark Vesey" repeatedly makes it clear that the slaves can only look to themselves to gain their freedom. In the opening poem, Kramer poses the necessary human challenge for the crew of a slave ship: "If sometimes a shrill cry upset the air / and reached the state-room, did the captain care . . . ?" The answer is indirect, but more powerful for that:

> Perhaps the free winds and the unbound waves
> rendered the lamentation of the slaves
> in language that the sky might understand. . . .
> But from the sky's red mouth no answer came.
> —The port was reached; the cargo seemed quite tame. . . .

If the middle passage is rendered here as a violation of natural law, it is also brutally clear that nature does not care; hence, the appalling figure of the sky's unspeaking red mouth, with its implications of impending violence and imaging of throttled anguish. Several poems later the religious component of a plea to the heavens becomes clear. The slaves offer a "Sunday Offertory Prayer" and then in "Vesey Speaks to the Congregation" he responds with a couplet that echoes the I.W.W.'s famous dismissal of pie-in-the-sky patience: "You look for freedom in the sky? / Then chained you'll live, and chained you'll die!" But Vesey is only making explicit what the meticulously analytic prayer makes evident the slaves already know. No passive plea to values human or divine will carry any weight. The revolt fails, but the poem keeps resistance alive as an option. As Kramer constructed his intricate and mutually reinforcing collage of sound and sense, segregation was in full force across the country. The McCarthyite witch hunts were well under way. "Turn all your sobs to battle-cries," Kramer urges through his African American persona, "cry freedom! freedom! and arise." As the poem turns the lessons of history into song, its lyric politics rises to all oppressive occasions. Reading Kramer, listening to Kramer—here in the presence of one of the masterpieces of American modernism and perhaps the single most ambitious poem about African American history ever written by a white American—requires attention to all these implications. And none of this would have the force it does without Kramer's inventive mix of traditional forms and meters, which gives the poem drama and counterpoint, granting performative integrity to the individual poems and a rich play of difference and similarity to the sequence as a whole.

But nearly a half century after composing "Denmark Vesey," during the winter of 1996/97, while he was hurriedly copy-editing the three books that would soon comprise his posthumous publications, Aaron Kramer had become convinced that, following his death, all his work would be forgotten and disappear. He was tormented by the prospect that his family and friends would throw out the many cartons of manuscripts, correspondence, newspaper clippings, and scrapbooks he had carefully collected and arranged during the course of his life and which were now stashed in his Oakdale, Long Island, home's many closets and basement. Even the establishment between 1994 and 1996 of an Aaron Kramer archive in the Special Collections Library at the University of Michigan, Ann Arbor, as well as earlier, smaller dedicated collections at Harvard, Brown, SUNY Buffalo, and SUNY Stony Brook, did little to dispel his fear that he had vanished from American literature. For a man who in his youth had been used to extensive public acclaim as a people's poet, favorable reviews in important periodicals, and a steadily growing reputation as a translator of German and Yiddish poets, the decades of critical silence following the McCarthy era had been abrupt, painful, and complete, akin to a biblical fall from grace. As he neared his death in April 1997, Kramer despondently declared his conviction to one of us that his life's achievement would soon be neglected and lost forever.

❖ ❖ ❖

Aaron Kramer was born at home, a cold-water flat, on Williams Avenue in the East New York section of Brooklyn on December 13, 1921. The son of Hyman and Mary Click Kramer, he had an older sister, Regina, born three years earlier. Hyman, an immigrant from Ukraine, was a low-waged bookbinder. Sometimes he attempted, unsuccessfully, to establish his own business, for example as an occasional proprietor of a small-goods stall in Union Square, Manhattan. Mary, an immigrant from Poland, had done domestic and cafeteria work. The Kramers were among the working poor. The parents' immersion in the socialism and communism of Eastern Europe and their membership in the Communist Party in the United States shaped young Aaron's sociopolitical consciousness.

The Kramer family moved to Bensonhurst in Brooklyn in 1934, where the reality of Depression life often burdened them with limited family income. Not having a room of his own, young Aaron slept in the kitchen. Not until after 1934 was there a telephone in their home; family calls were made and received at the corner candy store's public phone.

Kramer's poetic talent manifested itself early. He began writing poetry while attending PS 174 in East New York. An admittedly unruly student in Miss Pearl Bynoe's first-grade class, he often ignored her assignments and

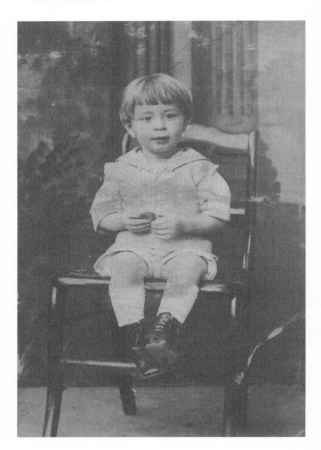

Kramer in 1925.

daydreamed instead. One day he began to write his first poem, "something about a man asleep in a haystack." Instead of scolding him, Miss Bynoe (as Kramer would always refer to her) read his poem aloud. Miss Bynoe then asked him to try to write another poem. Her affectionate encouragement and the class's applause caused him to become her "best scholar." At the end of the school year, Miss Bynoe gave him a gift of several pieces of oak tag on which she had written out his poems. Kramer cried.[3]

When he was just twelve, his first published poem, "Milk," appeared in a local newspaper. "Milk" includes these lines (which his daughters incompletely recollected):

Milk the purest food
The drink of health
. . . The fluid stands on the table of wealth . . .

Better than all foods compiled
What is better for a child?

In 1935, while in junior high school, Kramer declared himself a "people's poet." He was already publishing poetry in *New Pioneer;* for example, his uncollected "My Song" appeared in the April 1934 issue, also when he was twelve. After a dispute with the editors of *New Pioneer* in August 1936 over a misprinted line in "The Statue" (the young Kramer was adamant that his lines appear without typos, transposed lines, or other errors—a trait he would manifest throughout his life), Kramer began publishing in the children's section of the *Sunday Worker.*

In 1936, Kramer entered Abraham Lincoln High School in Bensonhurst. Because of his intellectual ability, he skipped grades and graduated in 1937 at the age of fifteen. While there, he published in the school literary magazine as well as continuing regular publication in both the *Sunday Worker* and the *Daily Worker,* which printed poems such as "Ballad of Tom Mooney" (September 26, 1937) and "In the Land of Olives" (January 16, 1938), among others. During this time, he became a member of the Young Communist League.

In 1938, Kramer and his future wife, Katherine (Kitty) Kolodny, then fourteen, met at the secular, socialist *Yiddishkeit* bungalow camp, *Nit Gedayget* (Camp Not-to-Worry), near Beacon in upstate Putnam County, New York. The young woman from the Bronx utterly fascinated Kramer, who was on summer break after his first year at Brooklyn College.

By that same year, he had written such a considerable body of poetry that Hyman Kramer encouraged him to publish a collection in a volume. Kramer's first book, *The Alarm Clock,* appeared in April 1938, sponsored by local branches of the International Workers Order and the Young Communist League of Bensonhurst and partially underwritten by his proud father. *The Alarm Clock* includes an introduction by Mary Mack of the *Sunday Worker.* In poems such as "Thought on a Train," "The Shoe-Shine Boy," "Have You Felt the Heart of America?" and "Smiles and Blood," Kramer demonstrates his engagement with the fundamental social issues like labor, racism, and class struggle that would concern him for the rest of his life.

Kramer started attending Brooklyn College in the fall of 1937. He usually walked the four miles to the campus from his home on Twenty-ninth Street in Brooklyn because he could not afford the nickel for public transportation. During this time, he began studying German, among other reasons so that he could read Heine and Rilke in the original. As a member of the Young Communist League and the American Student Union, he was also intensely involved in political as well as literary activity on the campus. However, he soon discovered that the young communist and labor writers on the college literary magazine, deeply influenced by Modernist poets like W. H. Auden, who was then teaching at Brooklyn College, scorned the rhymed poetry Kramer was writing as old-fashioned and outdated. He had already begun experiencing a similar resistance to his lyric poetry from the Young Labor Poets group whose workshops he attended in Manhattan. In a 1981 article for the *Brooklyn College Alumni Literary Review,* Kramer recalled that "[t]here began a titanic, if secret, struggle within me, which has even now not entirely been resolved, between the role of 'people's poet,' spokesman for the 'voiceless millions,' in traditional stanzas and accessible language, and the yearning to master 20th century techniques, to win acceptance by all my older staffmates on *Observer.*"[4]

The Molotov-Ribbentrop Non-Aggression Pact of August 22, 1939, engendered Kramer's early doubts regarding the Communist Party, USA. Like many other American Communists, he was embarrassed by the CPUSA's willing accommodation to the betrayal of its principles represented by the pact, even though some considered the pact necessary for the survival of the Soviet Union. Instead of being an antifascist force, the CPUSA, commencing with the pact, now championed American neutrality toward Hitler and the fascists. Kramer's relationship with the party would become increasingly troubled until his complete break with it in 1955.

During this period, Kramer issued his second volume of poetry, *Another Fountain,* privately printed in May 1940. *Another Fountain* focuses on a range of social and political issues: the Spanish Civil War in "Sunlight" and "Dave Duran," Chinese resistance to Japanese aggression in "The Ballad of Two Heroes," racism in the United States in "Summer," and an early criticism of the House Committee on Un-American Activities in "The Soul of Martin Dies."

In 1941, Kramer graduated from Brooklyn College at nineteen with a B.A. in English. Since poverty was still an issue, he could not even afford to buy a copy of *Broeklundian 1941,* the college yearbook. Kramer had wanted to become a teacher but was advised that because of his slight lisp, in actuality merely a strongly sibilant New York accent, he would likely never pass the New York City Department of Education speech test. Several months later, he was drafted. When his physical examination revealed an ulcer, he was excused from active duty.

Early in 1942, Kramer left New York to find work in Washington, D.C. Jobs were still scarce at the close of the Depression and the beginning of World War II, but he was able to get a clerk's position at the War Department. Shortly thereafter, he wrote to Kitty proposing that they marry. Kitty, then eighteen, agreed and traveled to Washington to marry Kramer, then twenty.

THE VOLCANO

Under a mountain that grows no trees
cringe ~~the~~ women and men I know,
who stumble ~~on~~ over each other ~~and look with their hands,~~ hearts
for the ~~eyes have nothing~~ eyes to see.
They ~~are~~ Afraid to dream, ~~and~~ they have forgotten
the meaning of ~~prayers;~~ dawn now ~~and~~ love
is dropping out of their lives, and laughter
knocks loudly, but runs away.

Who ~~can see~~ believes that under a mountain
a whimper has been entombed,
that those I love have lost their faces
~~weary of searching~~ jumbled so long in the dark?
Who ~~can see~~ believes that under a mountain
~~there~~ is a fire that somehow grew,
~~there is~~ a wild and steaming liquid,
rising, ~~and~~ demanding room,
of the blood that ~~creeps~~ from hearts and fingers,
of the tears, that ~~are~~ were never lost?
Who ~~can see~~ believes that a raging cauldron
is under the hill without trees?

I will make songs for the ones I love,
out of their ~~pain~~ madness and storaged ~~hate~~ woe,
to lash the ~~ceiling~~ top of the giant tomb
until it trembles ~~in terror,~~ mute and bursts like a toy;
'til ~~the~~ hope and the ~~fury~~ are flung up high
and ~~the~~ lava pours down the cool white day,
and those I love climb out of the mountain
where eyes ~~have~~ nothing to see.

Kramer's revision of a poem in his copy of *Another Fountain* (1940).

Both sets of parents went to Washington to attend the wedding. Kitty was soon working, too, as a typist for the War Department.

By 1943, Kramer was publishing in *New Masses*. Because of an incident at the War Department, he vigilantly began to hide certain aspects of his life. One day, a coworker warned him that a political file establishing his CPUSA association existed and that his supervisors would fire him shortly. Realizing he would be exposed and foreseeing the inevitable, Kramer resigned from his job, and he and Kitty, who was pregnant, left Washington to return to New York City. Their first child, Carol, was born in Manhattan.

Later that year, Harbinger House published *'Til the Grass Is Ripe for Dancing*, which expands upon issues explored in *Another Fountain:* American racism in "Natchez" and "Paul Robeson" (part 3 of "The Steel and the Eagles"), family life in "The Rockabye Love" (part 1 of "Love Poem for My Parents"), and fascism in "France" and "Song of Lidice."

Kramer found employment as a bookkeeper, first for the United Office and Professional Workers of America, Local 16, on Twenty-ninth Street in Manhattan, then for the Mandel Motor Truck Exchange, a used-truck company in Long Island City, and later for a Fifth Avenue importer of Japanese goods. He would continue to work as a bookkeeper until he began his student teaching in 1959, but he would always dislike the work. He felt that

Kramer in 1943 with his infant daughter Carol.

most of the companies that employed him existed only to make a profit and exploited their workers. Kramer seethed at this kind of work and dreamed of becoming a teacher; however, he was aware that required loyalty oaths and background checks might expose his political affiliations thus preventing him from working as an educator.

Even though the United States and the Soviet Union were nominally allied against the Fascists, anti-Communist zeal continued to creep back into American society. For example, the FBI was actively tracking alleged Communists and other leftists working for the federal government, and Congress was moving to grant the renamed House Un-American Activities Committee (HUAC) permanent status. In 1944, having been frightened by his experience at the War Department in Washington and seeking to protect his young family in an increasingly oppressive political climate, Kramer moved to Twenty-eighth Avenue in Astoria, Queens, a neighborhood that had become a safe haven for New York leftists. On December 5, he joined the Astoria Club of the CPUSA, holding card number 36288. Kramer's FBI file opens with a photograph of that card. At about this time, because of his fear of exposure, Kramer went to the main branch of the New York Public Library and secretly removed the catalog cards listing his first book, *Another Fountain,* and its subvention by the International Workers Order and the Young Communist League of Bensonhurst, even though he still occasionally published in *Worker* and *New Masses.*

All the while, Kramer continued to write unabated as his conscience led him to respond to the central issues of the day. His poetry appeared in *New Masses, New Currents, The Span,* and *Jewish Life,* among other periodicals. In 1944, his work was included in the anthology *Seven Poets in Search of an Answer* (Bernard Ackerman) along with contributions by Maxwell Bodenheim, Joy Davidman, Langston Hughes, Alfred Kreymborg, Martha Millet, and Norman Rosten, and edited by Thomas Yoseloff. The introduction by Shaemas O'Sheel, the New York poet and champion of the Irish renaissance, begins by posing the question "Poets: are they delicate creatures dealing with sweet sentiments and mystic fancies, but not with stern social and political issues?" and answers at its conclusion, "This very book is more than an ordinary anthology. It is a kind of cooperative assault upon the fascist horror darkening the world." A quotation from Kramer's "United Nations' Cantata" closes the introduction.

The Bernard Ackerman imprint is actually one of the many house names used by Thomas Yoseloff, who would become Kramer's longtime publisher. Yoseloff, founder of Associated University Presses, would also publish under his own name as well as under A. S. Barnes and Cornwall Books. In the anthology, "Natchez," "García Lorca," and "Barcelona Celebrates Three Years of Franco" are reprinted from *'Til the Grass Is Ripe for Dancing.* "Guernica," "Berlin Air Raid," "The Pogrom in Detroit," "Stalingrad," and "United Nations Cantata" appear for the first time and are reprinted in later volumes. In 1945, Kramer privately printed *Thru Our Guns,* which contains "Guernica" and "Sunrise in Paris" as part 4 of "Liberation Song."

By this time, HUAC had become a permanent congressional committee with the intimidating power to cite uncooperative witnesses for contempt of Congress, although its notorious first chairman, the virulent anti-Communist Martin Dies of Texas, had resigned. With renewed vigor, HUAC now began to pursue trade unions, New Deal agencies, alleged Communists, and other people or organizations accused or suspected of being subversive. The Kramers still lived in fear of exposure and of the subsequent loss of their jobs. Kitty was also pregnant with their second child, and in 1946 their daughter Laura was born in Manhattan and brought home to Astoria.

Kramer's caution was not baseless. American society really had become more dangerous. A single word, misused, could expose a person to censorship or condemnation. For example, the composer Charles Wakefield Cadman (1881–1946) set Kramer's "Marching Song" to music in 1945. Tragically, the composition would turn out to be his last work. Yet when he sent it to his publishers, they refused to print the song despite Cadman's international fame because they believed his lyricist, Kramer, wrote for "subversive" publications and because the word "comrade" appeared in one line: "I will climb the stairs and enter: a comrade, unafraid; / and wherever dreams are defended, I'll build a barricade." Finally in late 1945, Leeds Music, not Cadman's original publisher, would release the song, retitled "The Road I Have Chosen" and dedicated to Wendell Willkie (1892–1944), the liberal Republican who ran for president against Franklin Roosevelt in 1940.[5]

Kramer decided to stop publishing in *New Masses* due to infighting between pro- and anti-Stalinist writers and editors. Furthermore, because Charles Humboldt and Thomas McGrath, both of whom favored Modernist poetry over Kramer's style, were literary editors of the new CPUSA literary journal *Mainstream,* Kramer was unable to publish in it. He would not again submit poetry to the magazine until 1954, when it had become *Masses and Mainstream* and was not under Humboldt's and McGrath's control. At this time, in 1946, Bernard Ackerman published *The Glass Mountain,* which includes "Victory Comes to the Unbombed Cities" and the antiracist "To Festus Coleman in Prison" in a back-to-back hardcover volume with Don Gordon's *Civilian Poems.*

On February 6, 1947, Hyman Kramer died at fifty-three. The early death of Hyman haunted Aaron throughout his life, in part because he felt that he had been too young to develop an appropriately adult relationship with his father. Aaron inherited his father's wedding band and watch but never wore either. Late in his life, Hyman Kramer had strongly encouraged his son to revive an interest in his Jewish cultural heritage and to study Yiddish again. After his father's death, Kramer fulfilled that wish. He recommitted himself to Yiddish, which he had first studied at eleven under the tutelage of Yuri Suhl, an immigrant from Galicia, one of the left-wing, working-class, Proletpen poets and later a World War II U.S. Army veteran. With Suhl as his friend and mentor, Kramer began his lifelong avocation of recovering and translating the work of Yiddish poets.

During 1947–48, at the request of the writer and Romantic-era scholar Frederic Ewen, Kramer, balancing his typewriter on his lap in the Astoria apartment, worked furiously at the first of his large translation projects, the rendering into English of 110 poems by Heinrich Heine, who along with John Keats was his favorite poet. By early 1948, he had completed the translations including the 508 quatrains of *Germany: A Winter's Tale* (*Im traurigen Monat November wars*). Later that year, Citadel Press published *The Poetry and Prose of Heinrich Heine,* edited by Ewen, with additional translations by Louis Untermeyer and Emma Lazarus, among others. Kramer's translations have been reprinted continually in biographies of Heine, collections of Heine's verse, and the *Norton Anthology of World Literature.* Kramer also published the first of his many Yiddish translations, the much-anthologized "Partisan Song" by Hirsh Glick, in *Jewish Life* in April 1947. He would soon follow in the late 1940s and early 1950s with major selections from the Yiddish working-class sweatshop poets: Morris Winchevsky, Morris Rosenfeld, David Edelshtat, and Joseph Bovshover.

In 1948, International, the Communist party–controlled New York publishing house, issued Kramer's fifth collection of poetry, *The Thunder of the Grass.* Significant poems in this volume include "Isaac Woodard," which demonstrates Kramer's continuing outrage over the violent racism of American society, while "See America First," "Switch to Calvert," and "Encyclopedia" provide a satirical take on postwar consumer culture. The lyric "Prothalamium," in the "Astoria" sequence, was later set to music by Michael Sahl and recorded by Judy Collins on *Whales and Nightingales* in 1970 and used as the epigraph of Barbara Kingsolver's novel *Prodigal Summer* (2001). During his lifetime, more than one hundred of Kramer's poems would be set to music by Pete Seeger, Donald Swann, Irwin Heilner, Waldemar Hille, Serge Hovey, Lukas Foss, and Eugene Glickman, among others.

In 1949, Kramer became the only white member at that time of the Harlem Writer's Club and was appointed to the editorial board of the new journal *Harlem Quarterly.* Fellow board members included Langston Hughes and W. E. B. DuBois. The same year International published his

The Golden Trumpet, which includes beautiful love lyrics to Kitty in "Serenade," as well as strongly political statements like "The Golden Trumpet," "Ballad of Washington Heights," and "Neruda in Hiding." Additionally, e. e. cummings, then secretary of the Poetry Society of America, contacted Kramer on behalf of society officers and invited him to join. Kramer remained in the society for the next decade, serving as chair on various committees, and only resigned "after the mean politics of the organization became unbearable."[6]

A major sharpening of Kramer's political activity and its expression in his poetry occurred because of his and Kitty's attending Paul Robeson's Peekskill, New York, concert on September 4, 1949. They both endured a vicious post-concert attack by vigilantes and veterans' groups that injured more than two hundred concertgoers, sending 145 to hospitals. The *Peekskill Evening Star,* the Peekskill Chamber of Commerce, local veterans' groups, and even the assistant district attorney had called for action against the approximately twenty thousand concertgoers, portraying them as anti-American subversives. Kramer recalled writing parodies of nursery rhymes on paper scraps in order to try to stay calm while he, Kitty, and some of their fellow concertgoers lay on the floor of their bus as it ran the gauntlet of hurled rocks and debris along Route 100 outside Peekskill. On September 6, the *Peekskill Evening Star* compared the rioters to patriots at the Boston Tea Party. In 1950, Kramer was among the witnesses who testified before a grand jury in Westchester County examining the Peekskill riot. The grand jury would ultimately exonerate and praise the nearly nine hundred state troopers and local police who did nothing to stop the riot and who had actually participated in it.

Kramer's next book, *Thru Every Window!* published in 1950 by William-Frederick, contains "Peekskill," first printed in the winter 1949/50 *Harlem Quarterly,* in which he responds to the riot in verse, defiantly predicting that "though our song be stoned and burned and barred and banned / it will yet go thru every window of this land!"

The following years marked the continued rise of cold war hysteria and more virulent anti-Communism, including President Harry Truman's loyalty boards of the late 1940s that hounded thousands of federal employees accused of disloyalty; HUAC's continuing investigation of Hollywood screenwriters, directors, and actors; and the McCarthy hearings of 1952–54. Each event signaled a further turning to the right of American culture and the fear-driven silencing of many voices on the left. Even when family members and friends agreed about politics, which was not often the case in the extended Kramer family, they now stopped asking or even talking about personal politics, especially if someone had a previously safe, but now vulnerable, job. The fear of being called in and forced to testify drove people into silence. The less one knew about the politics of others, even if they were family members, the safer one would be in front of a loyalty committee. Beginning in May 1950 and unknown to Kramer at the time, the New York field office of the Federal Bureau of Investigation placed him under surveillance and opened a security index file concerning him. The Kramer family's caution about revealing its politics, however innocently, was well justified.

After their neighbors who owned a television set moved, the Kramers purchased their own television so that they and their friends could continue to watch the close of the Army-McCarthy hearings as well as their favorite program, *Your Show of Shows* starring Sid Caesar and Imogene Coca. All the while, they were deeply fearful of the possible exposure of their political involvements. For example, *Roll the Forbidden Drums!* of 1954 still lists among Kramer's publications his first volume, *The Alarm Clock* (1938). However, after 1954 and for the rest of his life he would never again list or publicly acknowledge *The Alarm Clock* except for a single mention in the liner notes of his 1957 Folkways recording *Serenade*.[7] He and Kitty had their family and their jobs to protect. Self-defense through silence developed into a necessity. Their past would become even more deeply hidden.

Still working as a bookkeeper, but driven by his intellectual curiosity and love of scholarship, Kramer returned to Brooklyn College at night and by 1951 earned a master's degree in English, reviving his dream of teaching. His master's thesis was titled "Emma Lazarus: Her Life and Work," excerpts of which appear as "The Poetic Career of Emma Lazarus" in *Neglected Aspects of American Poetry* (Dowling College Press, 1997).

In 1952, Kramer privately printed *Denmark Vesey and Other Poems*. This slim volume contains the twenty-six-part "Denmark Vesey," which details the 1822 slave uprising in South Carolina, and "October in 'Freedom' Land," one of his earliest anti-McCarthy resistance poems. For the first time, Kramer also included his translations of other poets, in this case the Yiddish sweatshop poets Morris Winchevsky, Morris Rosenfeld, David Edelshtat, and Joseph Bovshover. "Denmark Vesey" received much attention and, within a year of its publication, Waldemar Hille (1908–95)—Paul Robeson's accompanist, sometime collaborator with Pete Seeger, and the composer whose setting of "We Shall Overcome" became the anthem of the modern civil rights movement—set the poem to music as *Denmark Vesey: An Oratorio*. The oratorio was performed across the nation and first recorded by Electrovox in 1954. Kramer remembered meeting the white Southerner and human rights activist Emma Gilders Sterne one sunny afternoon on the steps of the New York Public Library on Forty-second Street and, at her request, reading "Denmark Vesey" aloud to her.

The catalyst for Kramer's final break with the CPUSA began on August 12, 1952, when Stalin, in an anti-Jewish purge, secretly ordered the execution of Yiddish writers and other members of the Jewish Antifascist Committee, including Leyb Kvitko, Peretz Markish, Itzik Feffer, most of whom had been imprisoned since 1948. Kramer had had an ambivalent relationship with the party since the Hitler-Stalin Pact of 1939. His disenchantment with Stalin deepened as Stalin's ferocious anti-Semitism, epitomized by the so-called anticosmopolitan campaign of 1947–48 against urban Soviet Jews and the Doctors' Plot against Jewish doctors publicly launched in January 1953, became more widely known in the United States. By 1955, rumors of the disappearance and probable execution of a number of Yiddish writers also began circulating in the West. In March 1956, the rumors were confirmed in the New York Yiddish newspaper *Forverts*. Kramer's response was immediate. His memorial poem "For Peretz Markish and Itzik Feffer" appeared in an obscure corner of the November 1956 *Jewish Life*. It was the first admission by the journal that the Soviet Yiddish poets had been murdered, a fact subsequently ignored by its editors for years. As a result, Kramer terminated his connection with the journal for almost twenty-five years. He was infuriated that so few of his fellow poets and writers admitted to, let alone condemned, the mass murders of the Soviet Jews, some of whom had been partisan fighters or decorated members of the Red Army during the war and all of whom had been loyal Soviet subjects.[8] His break with the party was also precipitated by his becoming, in his own words, "increasingly disgusted with the narrowness of the cultural Left in the United States, and with the blatant double standard that demanded civil rights here while denying or even defending the deprival of rights in the 'socialist' world."[9]

In 1953, the Kramers moved to a railroad flat on Tenth Street across from Tompkins Square Park in Manhattan. During this period, Kramer severed his relationship with the CPUSA and with many of his associates in the party by dropping his membership. His decision must have been remarkably painful to him because he made no public announcement of the break until several years later and then only in an elliptical manner in two sonnets published in the *New York Times*. Furthermore, the continual fear of exposure as a member or former member of the CPUSA, of subpoenas, of the intimidation to name names, and of the loss of employment all weighed heavily on Kitty and him.

He was also experiencing professional difficulties as a result of getting fewer (and less-favorable) reviews. In the 1940s, he had been reviewed in the *New York Times* and the *Saturday Review*, but by the mid-1950s he was receiving attention only in less prestigious, lower circulation periodicals like

Masses and Mainstream, Jewish Life, People's World, and *The Chicago Jewish Forum.* His rhymed lyric poetry had now long been unfashionable in academia.

Meanwhile, the FBI's investigation of Aaron Kramer intensified until June 16, 1954. That morning, two special agents placed the family apartment on East Tenth Street under "discreet surveillance" and followed Kramer as he left for work at 7:45 A.M. The agents stopped Kramer as he was walking uptown on Avenue A, identified themselves, and, as recorded in their field report, "advised the subject that it had come to the attention of the FBI that he had knowledge of Communist activities and they would like to discuss this with him on a confidential basis." Kramer told the agents that he was not in a position to furnish information and that even if he were, "I would never give information that would hurt anyone. . . . I might be called an idealist for I am firm in my beliefs." Kramer repeated that he would never provide information that would hurt anyone. He also honestly denied being a current CPUSA member and refused to comment on his past membership or activities. The two agents finished their street interrogation by asking Kramer if "in the event he received information concerning espionage or sabotage, would he furnish such information to the FBI?" Kramer told them that he would provide such information but no other information and continued on his way to work. The agents' report closes with the recommendation: "Inasmuch as the subject refused to furnish information to the FBI . . . it is felt that further contact with him would be unproductive. The subject's name should be retained on the Security index."

Nevertheless, FBI surveillance continued. On September 3, 1954, while her parents were at work, the Kramer's younger daughter, Laura, answered a knock at the door. The men standing outside on the stoop identified themselves as agents from the FBI. She told them her parents were not home. The agents were making a "pretext call" to verify Kramer's residence as they would make a similar call at his place of employment later in the day. Laura remembers that her father became furious when she told him about the visit. The continued attention of the FBI could have only aggravated Kramer's real fear of exposure although Laura does not recall if the FBI ever made a return visit.

Even so, Kramer continued to speak out vigorously in poetry about the political climate of the McCarthy era. That same year, Angus Cameron's new imprint, Cameron and Kahn, published Kramer's *Roll the Forbidden Drums!* which the liberal William-Frederick Press had already set up in type but at the last moment decided was too great a risk to print. Cameron, who was Little, Brown's editor for J. D. Salinger, Lillian Hellman, and Evelyn Waugh, had recently been blacklisted and fired by the publisher. Now, he was the only one willing to chance publishing Kramer. The slim volume contains some of Kramer's most aggressively anti-McCarthy poetry, such as "Patriotism," "Halloween," and "The Crucifixion." The widening focus of his poetic material is also evident in the semiautobiographical sequence "The Minotaur: A Poem in Twenty-Four Hours," which describes a worker's day at home and on the job.

The year 1955 was emotionally harrowing for Kramer because, as he wrote in an unpublished memoir some thirty years later, he finished "disentwining myself, fibre by fibre [*sic*], from associations with which I no longer sympathized. As long as the McCarthy assault, however, persisted, I held my battle-post." Now that the Senate had censured McCarthy in late 1954, Kramer was ready to make public his final severing with the CPUSA. He recorded this time of sharp personal pain and "deep spiritual darkness which flooded places formerly brightened by belief"[10] in two poems later

Kramer in 1955.

published in the *New York Times*, "Threnody" (July 21, 1956) and "The Widower" (October 8, 1958). Both sonnets are collected in *Rumshinsky's Hat* (1964). They describe the poet's exhausted and depressed state of mind. "The Widower" begins "I woke one morning: lifeless at my side / after much agony, lay my belief." The appropriately titled "Threnody" closes with a harrowing lament for what has died:

> no stone's been cut, no stone to mark what vanished—
> only the dream by which I lived is dead . . .
> And I, that bellowed so, must learn to be
> silent—except for this one threnody.

His youthful idealism and subsequent decades-long loyalty to the sociocultural objectives of the CPUSA ended with what Kramer would later describe as his "publicly acknowledged embarrassment and contrition."[11] Ironically, on July 29, 1955, the New York FBI field office had received instructions to close the security index file on Aaron Kramer because "there is no specific information regarding subject's activities" that warranted the bureau's further attention.

However, Kramer's reason for leaving the party may have been more complexly motivated than is indicated by his memoir fragment. The decades-long aesthetic struggle to defend his poetic style of employing, for the most part, rhymed lyrics against such champions of the more opaque, modernist poetry as Charles Humboldt and Thomas McGrath had also worn him down. Kramer had enjoyed the early support of a CPUSA cultural authority, V. J. Jerome, who was jailed between 1955 and 1957, having been convicted under the Smith Act of "conspiracy to teach and advocate the overthrow of the U.S. government."[12] Now in 1956, with Jerome in jail and with Humboldt the newly appointed managing editor of *Masses and Mainstream*, Kramer would never again publish in the journal. His apparent decision to give up the aesthetic fight coincided with his decision to leave his "battle-post" in the CPUSA.

During this personally traumatic period, Kramer was still employed as a bookkeeper; however, at the invitation of groups that would give him some comfort, he began a new direction in his life. At the Golden Agers at Bronx House, the Hillside Hospital in Queens, and the New York Guild for the Jewish Blind, he gave readings, organized poetry workshops, and befriended many clients, patients, and employees. From 1955 until 1959, he functioned as part-time lecturer and dramatics director for the New York Guild for the Jewish Blind. He would later recount that this new activity saved him from falling completely into despair over the failure of American progressive political action and would lead to his lifelong commitment to exploring the therapeutic uses of poetry.[13]

Two volumes of his work appeared in 1955. The privately printed *A Ballad of August Bondi,* commissioned by the Jewish Young Folksingers, describes an incident in the life of Bondi, who fought with John Brown against proslavery forces in Kansas. The poem was later set to music by Serge Hovey (1920–89), a screen and stage composer who had studied with Arnold Schoenberg. It was first performed at the Brooklyn Academy of Music with Pete Seeger singing the role of Balladeer. *The Teardrop Millionaire,* published by the Manhattan Emma Lazarus Clubs, collects Kramer's translations from the Yiddish of Morris Rosenfeld, the most well known of the sweatshop poets.

That same year, driven by the fear of having been blacklisted and, therefore, of losing publishers and what little income they provided, Kramer briefly branched out in a new direction, writing a school textbook, *Day of Glory: The Guns of Lexington and Concord* (New York: Scholastic Book Services, 1955, 1962). Given the political climate at the time, he decided, unsurprisingly, to publish it under the pseudonym Philip Spencer. When *Day of Glory* found a publisher in 1955 and met with success and large nationwide sales, he went on to write another Philip Spencer textbook, *3 Against Slavery: Denmark Vesey, William Lloyd Garrison, Frederick Douglass* (New York: Scholastic Book Services, 1972). The second volume, however, did not sell well, so Kramer abandoned this new career.

The Kramers moved from Tenth Street to a three-bedroom apartment on Riverside Drive in 1956. Their daughters were growing up, and the family needed more room. Although Kramer was still writing poetry and translating Yiddish and German poets, periodical publication of his work almost stopped and would not begin again until the early 1960s.

In 1958, Thomas Yoseloff printed what is probably Kramer's most beautifully designed volume, *The Tune of the Calliope.* The large-format hardcover includes eighty poems celebrating Kramer's love of New York City, more than half of which had been published earlier. Facing the poems are forty-eight full-page black-and-white drawings by twelve New York artists including Alice Neel, Saul Lishinsky, and Hilde Weingarten. The drawings match their facing poems in subject: for example, Alice Neel's *Old Man and Boy* faces "Death Street," a brief elegy for Hyman Kramer; Hilde Weingarten's *Woman at the Window* faces "Serenade," a love lyric to Kitty; and Edward Strickland's *Workman* faces "Work Day" and "Unemployed." Kramer and each of the artists signed a numbered subscriber's edition of five hundred copies. He reserved number 444 for himself because that was the street number of the building on Williams Avenue in Brooklyn where he was

Carol, Aaron, Kitty, and Laura Kramer, about 1955.

born. The entire edition of *The Tune of the Calliope* quickly sold out, but Yoseloff never ran a second printing.

The Tune of the Calliope was anticipated by *Serenade*, a 1957 Folkways recording of Kramer's reading to the blind, probably at the New York Guild for the Jewish Blind in Manhattan. Along with poetry by Alexander F. Bergman, Maxwell Bodenheim, and Morris Rosenfeld, *Serenade* includes fifteen Kramer poems that would later appear in *The Tune of the Calliope*, and the liner notes, written by Kramer, are accompanied by a number of the drawings that would also appear in that volume.

The late 1950s witnessed the gradual waning of McCarthy-era virulence and with it the loosening of requirements for employees to sign loyalty oaths and to answer preemployment questions about their current or past political affiliations. Having worked as a bookkeeper for almost twenty years, Kramer decided it was time to pursue his original dream of becoming a teacher, and fortuitously there was a teacher shortage in New York City. He applied to Erasmus High School in Manhattan and was accepted for a student teaching position in English during the fall of 1958. That following fall, having received his provisional license, he began teaching full-time at Bogota High School in Bogota, New Jersey, where he would stay until 1961. However, the habits of concealment due to the risks of being associated with the Left during the McCarthy era were still a reality for Kramer, so it was only natural that he was alarmed when in 1960 his elder daughter enthusiastically and publicly joined the Young Socialist League in her high school.

In 1961, the Kramers moved once more, this time farther uptown to Inwood. That fall Kramer had accepted a full-time instructorship in English at Adelphi Suffolk, a small liberal arts college in Oakdale, Long Island. Adelphi Suffolk was then a branch of Adelphi University in Garden City, Long Island. In 1969, the college, renamed Dowling College, became independent of Adelphi University. Kramer would be one of the team of faculty and administrators who would lead the movement to become an autonomous college. He would also continue to conceal his past political associations in fear of their discovery and of his thereby being denied tenure. Kramer made sure his lifelong habit of suppression and denial would endure even after his death. For example, the late 1997 biographical sketch introducing the bibliography of the Kramer archive at the University of Michigan contains the following misleading statement: "Although never affiliated with a party or ideology, Kramer pursued progressive political themes in his poetry." Since Kramer began sending material to the archive as early as 1994, he most likely provided this "information" himself.

Kramer's teaching areas included both English and American literatures. Although he proudly considered himself a nonspecialist, he preferred teaching poetry-intensive courses on Chaucer, Shakespeare, the English Romantics, Whitman, African American literature, and modern British and American literature. His teaching duties gave him a more flexible work schedule enabling him to begin his doctoral studies at New York University.

Moses (O'Hare, 1962) was Kramer's first book publication since 1958. The slim volume includes translations of sweatshop poets as well as of World

War II–era poets like Dora Teitelboim and Hirsch Glick. *Moses* also includes work poems such as those from the *Santa Fe Night* sequence and the dramatic ballad *Moses*, set to music by Richard Neumann and first performed at Wagner College, Staten Island, New York. The following year *Songs and Ballads: Goethe, Schiller, Heine*, which includes thirteen new Heine translations, would also come from O'Hare. But not until 1964 and the publication of *Rumshinsky's Hat and House of Buttons* would Kramer return to publishing the activist and powerfully personal poetry he had mostly abandoned in the middle 1950s following his break with the CPUSA at the close of the McCarthy era. When he did return, it was as if the still raw but suppressed emotions from that era instilled his poetry with renewed strength and commitment.

Rumshinsky's Hat and House of Buttons is actually two separate books providing an instructive window through which to view the tension that had driven Kramer's writing since his teenage years at Brooklyn College. Kramer was acutely aware of contemporary academic fashion that scorned rhymed, lyrical poetry and encouraged the anti-Romantic Modernist conception of poetry as unrhymed, not lyrical, and text-centered rather than author-centered. He was convinced that it was as much the style of his poetry—still rhymed, still lyric—as its political content that lost him reviewers in the late 1940s and 1950s, along with (as he always suspected) publication in poetry magazines. He decided to experiment by writing in the Modernist style. *Rumshinsky's Hat and House of Buttons* contains two invocations; the first, in *Rumshinsky's Hat,* unapologetically proclaims that he is "Obliged to none, / and laureate to none" but then (seemingly paradoxically) follows with forty-six mostly unrhymed poems, often in free verse. The second invocation, in *House of Buttons,* more plaintively observes, "I could've sworn there was a lyric / still crouched within the shadows of my spirit" and follows with sixty-seven rhymed poems. Political subjects, as in "Tidings from Spain," mix with the intensely personal in "Letter to My Sister" and "Dogs," and with the intensely painful in "Threnody" and "The Widower." His experiment succeeded in that Kramer produced a small body of verse observing the Modernist conventions, but he was never comfortable with the style and from then on returned to his lyric impulses. *Rumshinsky's Hat and House of Buttons* received two reviews, one in the *Kansas City Star* and the other in a newsletter from Adelphi Suffolk College. Kramer despaired of ever again receiving the critical attention he had attracted during the 1940s.

However, the attention Kramer was receiving in other venues ameliorated somewhat his dismay at the critical silence his publications received. In 1961, he had begun occasionally hosting a radio program on WBAI, the

Pacifica Foundation radio station in New York City. The next year he also began acting as guest host on the *Spoken Words* program of WNYC, the city's public radio station. He devoted shows to lectures and readings of his own work as well as that of Heine, Robert Browning, Thoreau, Melville, and Dickinson. He also dedicated programs to contemporaries like Kenneth Fearing and Nicolás Guillén or to reading anti-McCarthy poetry. He continued these broadcasts well into the 1980s. Furthermore, he was giving frequent public readings in places like the Donnell Library in Manhattan and in neighborhood branch libraries throughout New York City, to large audiences, and usually to great accolades. A poster announcing an Aaron Kramer reading would regularly draw a crowd to the event, and afterward Kramer would do what so many unreviewed poets did: from a display table at the side of the room, he would sell and inscribe his books to his fans. The experience of reading to hundreds of people at a time, many of them returning again and again to hear him, was deeply satisfying to Kramer and gave him a sense of his poetry's contact with people that belied the lack of critical attention his books received. In "After the Poetry Reading," written years later in 1975, he celebrates as well as gently mocks himself and his gypsy life traveling from reading to reading.

Kramer earned his Ph.D. in English and American literature from New York University in 1966, but there was a point just before his hooding when departmental officials threatened to withhold a diploma from him. The war in Vietnam had begun, and the commencement speaker was Robert McNamara, secretary of defense, who was at NYU to receive an honorary doctorate. Kramer explained that when McNamara began to speak, he (Kramer) and a number of doctoral candidates would publicly walk out of the graduation in protest. Officials countered that if Kramer and his fellow candidates walked out, they would receive no diplomas. As McNamara began the commencement address, Kramer and the others stood up, walked out, and joined a picket line that included his family. After a few weeks, he received his diploma in the mail. Two years later, Fairleigh Dickinson University Press would publish his revised dissertation as *The Prophetic Tradition in American Poetry, 1835–1900*.

The widening war in Vietnam and the continuing civil rights movement caused Kramer to reassert the strong political voice he had largely abandoned by the late 1950s. His conscience drove him to respond in poetry. Kramer had recently been publishing antiwar and antiracist poems in *Freedomways*, the *Adelphi Quarterly*, and *Lyrismos* when the Folklore Center in New York City approached him to collect and publish them in 1968 as *Henry at the Grating: Poems of Nausea*. Among the poems in this volume are "Blues for Medgar Evers," "Calvary: Philadelphia, Mississippi," "Loyalty

March," "Considering My Country," and "Henry at the Grating," his cry of solidarity with a fellow war resister from an earlier generation, Henry David Thoreau. Interestingly, the FBI turned its attention to Kramer once again by reopening his file in late 1959 and placing him on its reserve index until 1968. Apparently his association with the civil rights movement and with the African American journal *Freedomways* was sufficient to rekindle its surveillance.

The late 1960s and early 1970s saw major changes in the Kramers' lives. Their daughters had both married in 1967. In 1971, Aaron and Kitty left New York City for the suburbs and moved to a small house in Oakdale, Long Island, within walking distance of Dowling College. They also began to travel in Europe as early as 1956 and would return for regular visits between 1968 and 1977. True to their lifelong ideals, the Kramers visited neither Greece until after the fall of the military junta in 1974 nor Spain until after the death of Franco in 1975 (political events Kramer would later commemorate in

Kramer in the 1970s.

poetry). Travel throughout Europe and visits to sites associated with European Jewry and the Holocaust widened the scope of Kramer's poetry. His privately printed *Ghosts* of 1970 contains three deeply moving poems devoted to those places: "Night at the Concertgebouw," where empty seats are filled by "Amsterdam's evaporated Jews"; "Tour," to a wall in Prague engraved with names of "seventy thousand Czechoslovak Jews, / their dates of birth and deportation"; and "Zudioska," to the street of vanished Jews in Dubrovnik. Aaron and Kitty also toured Mexico in 1974 but, saddened and upset by widespread poverty and the great disparity of wealth in the nation, they never returned as they did to Europe.

Kramer also continued his avocation of translating Yiddish poets. Dowling College published *Poems by Abraham Reisen* in 1971, and translations of Reisen, as well as of Isaac E. Ronch, Abraham Sutzkever, Rajzel Zychlinska, and Dora Teitelboim, among others, appeared in such journals as *Bitterroot, Outlook,* and *Midstream.* It was during this period that Kramer conceived of what would become a more than decade-long project: to translate a wide range of Yiddish poets, from pre–twentieth century to the contemporary era, to represent their traditional rhymed verse and not cater "to the current bias against rhyme and pattern" (as he would later write in the introduction to the anthology), and to acknowledge that many of the poets were socialists, Labor Zionists, or Communists.

His academic publishing also continued with *Melville's Poetry: Toward the Enlarged Heart* (Fairleigh Dickinson University Press), a thematic study of three of Melville's lesser-known poems, "Bridegroom Dick," "The Scout toward Aldie," and "Marquis de Grandvin" in 1972. That same year Macmillan published *On Freedom's Side: An Anthology of American Poems of Protest,* in which Kramer, as editor, grouped poems dealing with native Americans, African Americans, war, justice, dangers of mob rule, and the poor. He included his own "Newscast" and "Peekskill."

The next collection of Kramer's own verse was *On the Way to Palermo,* published by A. S. Barnes in 1973. The volume represents the approximate thematic form that Kramer's collections would take for the rest of his life, being evenly divided among personal and family matters, travel, and political observations. Family is embodied by the poignant "Homecoming," a sonnet for his daughters, travel by the title poem, and the political, fueled by Kramer's opposition to the Vietnam war, by "Considering My Country," "Newscast," and "Dirge," among others.

O Golden Land! followed in 1976, published by Dowling College Press. Kramer had originally shelved the project, an edited version of a 3,500-line travelogue written in 1963 to record a cross-country trip he and Kitty made from New York to California, as too "monstrous" to publish. Moreover, its "playful bitterness" seemed inappropriate in the face of the assassinations of the Kennedys and Martin Luther King Jr. and the war in Vietnam. Kramer published a few sections such as "Des Moines and Council Bluffs" as stand-alone poems in journals. However, the looming bicentennial caused him to revisit his poem. In the foreword he writes, "Whatever their rate as verse, I am proud of the anger coursing through these pages. Because it is an anger that should not have gone out of fashion so readily." Kramer's "personal bicentennial gesture" reminds readers that to love one's nation requires one to speak out when necessary against its arrogance.

In 1977, Dowling College's new president let the faculty union's contract expire. With no swift resolution in sight, the faculty voted to strike at the beginning of the fall semester. A picket line, on which Kramer walked every day, closed the college until a contract was signed in early October. At the victory meeting, Kramer read his uncollected "The Well," describing the strike. The poem was included as an addendum to the minutes of that union meeting and later published in *riverrun*, the college's literary journal.

Two significant events in Kramer's life in 1980 were the publication of *Carousel Parkway and Other Poems* from A. S. Barnes and Kitty's growing struggle with rheumatoid arthritis. *Carousel Parkway* contains many spirited poems from his and Kitty's 1975 travels in Greece, like "Herakleion: The Hidden Beach" and "Thessaloniki: Three Sleeps"; from their 1973 England tour in "Grandparents in London" and "At Westminster Synagogue"; and, in a celebratory group from their 1976 tour of post-Franco Spain, "Madrid: Coming Home" and "Granada: The Rose." The 1974 trip to Mexico resulted in the remarkably angry "Dogs of San Miguel," one of a group of five poems Kramer would always refer to as "My Mexico Is Not Your Mexico." What is most striking about the collection, however, is his inward turning toward a mature, deeply personal examination of his family's life. The Kramers had become grandparents of Laura's daughters, Nora in 1973 and Joanna in 1978, and Kramer was himself beginning to acknowledge his own mortality. Poems such as "Granddaughter on Beach," "Now, Before Shaving," "Phone Call," and the title poem compassionately reflect on time and the generations. Unfortunately, *Carousel Parkway* would receive only seven reviews in journals like *Visions, People's World, New England Review,* and the *Brooklyn College Alumni Literary Review.* At this point in his career, Kramer had given up hoping he would ever again receive major critical attention.

Thomas Yoseloff, who had been Kramer's publisher on and off since the mid-1940s, approached him in 1981 with a proposal to print a selected edition of Kramer's work in chronological order. Kramer was flattered and immediately agreed, but, ever cautious about his political past, he insisted that the collection begin in 1940 thereby hiding *The Alarm Clock* as well as his other 1930s publications in CPUSA newspapers and magazines. The project took two years to complete with the finished collection appearing in 1983. *The Burning Bush: Poems and Other Writings (1940–1980)*, from Yoseloff's Cornwall Books, is dedicated to Kramer's granddaughters. Many of its 108 poems, divided into seven thematic sections, are revised, re-grouped, and retitled from his earlier volumes. The collection includes a revised and expanded "Carousel Parkway"; "The Dance," which had been printed as a chapbook in 1978; and a number of personal poems written over the decades using Kramer's persona, Mr. Glücklich (sometimes appearing in earlier and later poems as Mr. Lucky or as Fortunato). In 1983, Kramer also published a group of new poems in the chapbook *In Wicked Times* (Arlington, Va.: Black Buzzard), which includes "The Chair: Notes for an Elegy" for his old acquaintance Muriel Rukeyser, the prophetic "Fourth of July Dialog," and the antinuclear "All-Star Neutron Day: Aug. 9, 1981."

During the 1980s, Kramer continued to publish poetry and translations regularly in periodicals including *Antigonish Review, Icarus, Kenyon Review, Modern Poetry Studies*, and *Outlook*, averaging more than twenty publications annually, with a high of forty-four in 1987. His public readings continued, but he stopped broadcasting on WBAI and WNYC. In 1986, he published another chapbook, *In the Suburbs* (Winterville, Ga.: Ali Baba), which includes the haunting "The Death of a Friend" and "After the Hospital," the latter expressing his growing concern about Kitty's declining health. In 1984, Kitty had spent eleven weeks in the hospital recovering from cryptococchal meningitis, during which time she endured temporarily blindness from the disease. She was now forced to leave work on permanent disability.

A Century of Yiddish Poetry (Cornwall), the project Kramer conceived in the early 1970s, was finished and published in 1989. Dedicated to his mother and father, the book represents many years of translation and re-search. The text includes selected poems from more than 130 Yiddish po-ets, starting with the late-nineteenth-century poets of the First Golden Age and concluding with poets of the Holocaust. Kramer provides a biographi-cal sketch of each writer, establishing his or her political position.

Because the pace of Kramer's activities—teaching, writing, public per-formances, and at-home responsibilities—was beginning to wear him down, after thirty years he decided to retire from full-time teaching at the end of the spring 1990 semester. As an incentive, Dowling was offering a full year's salary following retirement, and Kitty had been pressing for years for the freedom to travel to warmer climates during the winter, the cold being especially painful to her. However, he was never able to cut himself off com-pletely from the classroom and his students and continued to teach as an adjunct until 1996. He was also able to devote more time to assisting Kitty,

AUTUMNAL   Aaron Kramer

Imagine so much
so easily
taken care of in one fall!
You won't have to
answer Miriam's
three-year-old letter after all,
nor make the phone call
Cousin Will
so loyally awaited,
nor ~~visit~~ smile for
Aunt Harriet
in the nursing home whose smell you hated.
Putting a line
through their names should also
be easy -- there isn't a crime
awaiting confession;
then why are they waiting?
and why do you still mark time?

in one fall

AUTUMNAL   Aaron Kramer

Imagine so much so easily taken care of in one fall!
You won't have to answer Miriam's three-year-old letter after all,
nor make the phone call Cousin Will so loyally awaited,
nor ~~visit~~ smile for Aunt Harriet in the nursing home whose smell you hated.
Putting a line through their names should also be easy -- there
                              isn't a crime
awaiting confession; then why are they waiting? and why do you
                              still mark time?

Kramer's experiments with line breaks (ca. 1984).

who required multiple joint and spinal surgeries due to the advanced rheu-
matoid arthritis and osteoporosis from which she suffered.

In 1991, Cornwall published *Indigo*, which brings together Kramer's
poetry of the late 1980s and early 1990s including from his two chapbooks.
The 108 poems in the collection demonstrate that Kramer had lost neither
his poetic power nor his social passion. *Indigo* includes politically provoca-
tive poems like "Bhopal" and "Bitburg," both part of the sequence "In the
Fortieth [Reagan] Presidency." Travel poems from Greece and Kramer's

beloved Spain include "Mycenae: On Brushing One's Shoes in Athens," "Madrid: July 1978," and "Granada: First Showing." His most poignant poetry, however, focuses on what had become the central concerns of his life: Kitty's health and his own nascent feelings of mortality. He examines Kitty's anguish and his own fears for her, as well as their small victories together, in "Going In," "Homecoming," "Postoperative Care," and "Anniversary." Mortality is examined in "Reunion," "Night Thoughts," and quite forcefully in the sonnet "On the Death of Someone Else's Grandchild."

Kramer continued to feel wounded by his lack of critical attention. He had spent more than fifty years writing poetry, reading, and teaching. In 1996, even the publication of *Border Incident* (St. Petersburg, Russ.: Journal Neva), a selection of his poems translated into Russian, and of *Majestic Room* (Sofia, Bulg.: PAN) a selection of his poems translated into Bulgarian, did little to ease his growing fears that he would be forgotten after his death and his life's work vanish.

By late September 1996, Kramer had become so exhausted that he canceled almost all his remaining public commitments to lecture or to read. His doctors diagnosed him as having leukemia. That winter he underwent two blood transfusions, surgery to remove his spleen, and chemotherapy. Despite his seriously weakened state, he continued to work on proofreading galleys of the three works that would become his posthumous publications.

Neglected Aspects of American Poetry (Dowling College Press, 1997) collects a number of critical essays that range widely from Joel Barlow, Whitman, and Melville to Kramer's elder contemporaries, Langston Hughes, Sol Funaroff, and Alexander Bergman. The collection also includes elegiac memoirs of Muriel Rukeyser and Owen Dodson. Of special interest because it offers an insight into Kramer's own difficult relationship with modern poetic style is "John Hall Wheelock: 'Grave Music . . . to Capture You in Language'" in which Kramer honors Wheelock's decision to resist "the over-intellectualized trend that has prevailed in 20th century American poetry and poetry criticism, contrasting its pompous juicelessness with the affirming music of the universe."[14] It is as if Kramer were describing and defending his own fifty-year struggle with poets and critics.

The Last Lullaby: Poetry from the Holocaust (Syracuse University Press, 1998) contains translations from the Yiddish of both poems and lullabies by Holocaust victims and survivors. The longest translation is of Viktor Ullmann and Peter Kien's 1944 opera *The Emperor of Atlantis* (*Der Kaiser von Atlantis*) that had remarkably survived destruction at the Terezin concentration camp although Ullmann and Kein died in Auschwitz. Unfortunately, Matthew Paris's well-intentioned homage "Aaron Kramer: A Tribute," with which the book concludes, contains significant biographical misinformation regarding Aaron and Kitty.

In *Regrouping* (Birnham Wood, 1997), his last collection of poetry, Kramer demonstrates that he has remained true to the ideals and interests of his youth, for example, the plight of African Americans in "Judgment," the condition of workers in "Elegy for a Carpet Boy," and the Spanish Civil War in "Madrid: the Ghosts of Its Defenders." At the same time, he continues to struggle with the tension between the personal and the political, the introspective and the social, that had concerned him all his life. The most powerful and poignant poems in the collection focus on his family and his heightened sense of time's passing, as in "Home," "Regrouping," and in the valedictory final poem of his final collection, a loving celebration of his and Kitty's fifty-fourth "Anniversary."

On January 8, 1997, Kramer's mother, Mary, died in Los Angeles not long after her one-hundredth-birthday celebration on December 25, 1996, which Kramer was too ill to attend.

During the early morning hours of April 7, 1997, Aaron Kramer died quietly at seventy-five years in his home, having fought a battle with leukemia. Kramer was survived by Kitty, his daughters, his granddaughters, and his sister. Kitty would die three years later, on June 9, 2000.

Because he and Kitty loved the seashore of Long Island, where in his last years he enjoyed eating the forbidden seafood to which he had long been allergic, his ashes were scattered in the Great South Bay of Long Island.

NOTES

We would like to thank Edward Brunner, Karen Ford, Marsha Bryant, Alan Filreis, William Maxwell, and Alan Wald for their suggestions in response to drafts of this essay. And we offer our heartfelt thanks to the Kramer family for their continuing support of this project.

The first epigraph for this essay is from Aaron Kramer's "To the White Minority of South Africa"; the second is from his poem "The Swan."

1. See Nelson, *The Wound and the Dream.*

2. Kramer's February 4, 1994, letter is excerpted on pages 155–56 and 160–61 of Wald, *Writing from the Left.* Wald kindly provided Cary Nelson with a copy of the whole letter.

3. Aaron Kramer, "Miss Bynoe," *Renaissance Faire* 3.1 (Fall 1973): 5. "Miss Bynoe" is a section from Kramer's unpublished autobiographical novel *It Hurt till I Laughed: Memories of Boyhood.*

4. Kramer, "'A Short Memoir.'"

5. Kramer, "Interview with John Hudson Jones."

6. See Kramer's "Long Footnotes" for more details about his stormy relationship with the Poetry Society of America.

7. Thanks to Edward Brunner for bringing to our attention the listing of *The Alarm Clock* in *Serenade*'s liner notes.

8. An accurate chronology of Soviet persecution of Jewish Antifascist Committee members is now available in Rubenstein and Naumov, *Stalin's Secret Pogrom*. For details about the Doctors' Plot consult Brent and Naumov, *Stalin's Last Crime*.

9. Kramer, "Long Footnotes," 83–84.

10. Kramer, "1985 marks the 30th anniversary."

11. Kramer, "Long Footnotes," 85.

12. For a full description of V. J. Jerome's influence, see Alan Wald's *Exiles from a Future Time: The Forging of the Mid-Twentieth-Century Literary Left* (Chapel Hill: University of North Carolina Press, 2002).

13. In "1985 Marks the 30th Anniversary," Kramer seems to reveal unconsciously how his turning to public readings and poetry workshops worked as poetry therapy for him as well as for patients and clients.

14. "John Hall Wheelock: 'Grave Music . . . to Capture You in Language,'" *Neglected Aspects of American Poetry* (Oakdale, N.Y.: Dowling College Press, 1997), 318.

BIBLIOGRAPHY

Bernstein, Carl. *Loyalties: A Son's Memoir.* New York: Simon and Schuster, 1989.

Brent, Jonathan, and Vladimir P. Naumov. *Stalin's Last Crime: The Plot against the Jewish Doctors, 1948–1953.* New York: HarperCollins, 2003.

Caretta, Mario. *The Peekskill Story (Parts 1 and 2).* May 6, 2001. *History in Song.* <http://www.fortunecity.com/tinpan/parton/2/peekskill.html> (accessed March 28, 2002).

Click, Phillip. Personal interview with Donald Gilzinger Jr., January 25, 2002.

Elie, Marilyn. *The Robeson Concerts: Peekskill, New York, 1949.* July 9, 1998. *Voices of History Video Project.* <http://www.highlands.com/Robeson/Default.html> (accessed March 28, 2002).

Fast, Howard. *Being Red: A Memoir.* Boston: Houghton Mifflin, 1990.

Kramer, Aaron. Interview with John Hudson Jones. *Daily Worker,* January 14, 1949, 13.

———. "Long Footnotes to Brief References: A Memoir." *Spring* 3 (October 1994): 80–86.

———. *Neglected Aspects of American Poetry: The Greek Independence War and Other Studies.* Oakdale, N.Y.: Dowling College Press, 1997.

———. "1985 marks the 30th anniversary." Unpublished essay [ca. 1985] in Donald Gilzinger Jr.'s possession.

———. "'A Short Memoir'—About the *Observer* Mostly." *Brooklyn College Alumni Literary Review* 1.1–2 (Spring–Summer 1981): 51–52.

Kramer, Carol. Personal interviews with Donald Gilzinger Jr. December 27, 2001, August 9, 2002.

Kramer, Laura. Personal interview with Donald Gilzinger Jr. December 27, 2001.

Mishler, Paul C. *Raising Reds: The Young Pioneers, Radical Summer Camps, and Communist Political Culture in the United States.* New York: Columbia University Press, 1999.

Nelson, Cary, ed. *The Wound and the Dream: Sixty Years of American Poems about the Spanish Civil War.* Urbana: University of Illinois Press, 2002.

Rubenstein, Joshua, and Vladimir P. Naumov, eds. *Stalin's Secret Pogrom: The Post-war Inquisition of the Jewish Anti-Fascist Committee.* Translated by Laura Esther Wolfson. New Haven, Conn.: Yale University Press, 2001.

United States. Department of Justice. Federal Bureau of Investigation. Freedom of Information / Privacy Acts Release. *Subject: Aaron Kramer.* Washington, D.C.: FBI, 2002.

Wald, Alan. "Radical Poetry, 1930s-1960s." In *Encyclopedia of the American Left,* edited by Mari Jo Buhle, Paul Buhle, and Dan Georgakas. 2d ed. New York: Oxford University Press, 1998.

———. "Re: Aaron Kramer." E-mail to Donald Gilzinger Jr. February 7, 1998.

———. *Writing from the Left: New Essays on Radical Culture and Politics.* New York: Verso, 1994.

Yoseloff, Thomas, ed. *Seven Poets in Search of an Answer: A Poetic Symposium.* Introduction by S. O'Sheel. New York: Bernard Ackerman, 1944.

PART 1
A Consumer Culture

See America First!

Tourist—why seek other shores
on which to focus your lorgnette?
Here, behind these bashful doors,
are scenes you never would forget.

Ghosts of ancient violence
still grapple in each faded home,
and the frightened air is dense
with promises of worse to come.

Why be off on tiring trips
to cities half the size of this?
Would you hear from Old World lips
a more exotic bitterness?

Would you find the Old World's fear
concealed behind a merrier mask?
Tourist—we're improving here:
our paupers, too, are picturesque.

Switch to Calvert

In this bottle lives a Magi
eager for his liberty.
He will offer grateful service
to the one who sets him free.

If you'd rather your apartment
were the state room of Versailles,
he can furnish all the brilliance
in the twinkling of an eye.

Birds will burst their throats above you,
jesters tumble at your feet,
while, to win your wink of favor,
France's fairest belles compete.

3

Other kings, when all is emptied,
must give up their royal state;
but the man who buys our bottle
never needs to abdicate.

Encyclopedia

Twenty volumes, one dollar each,
to share a shelf in your home:
facts about farming, the Gettysburg speech,
a list of the rulers of Rome,

pictures of ballplayers, paradise birds,
Beethoven's love affair,
the meanings of seventeen-syllable words,
games to distract you from care.

For twenty dollars we can't explain
life's meaning, nor give you a reason
for falsehood, oppression, payment in pain,
the triumph of hatred and treason.

Some customers never can have enough:
they'd rather frown at the walls,
or jeer as though it were childish stuff:
Grand Canyon, Niagara Falls!

—Remember that beautiful season of wonder
before you worked for a wage?
Here are the laws of lightning and thunder,
and less than a penny a page.

Treatment

Fix our firm in the back of your brain.
None of our customers ever complain.

We promise a treatment truly aesthetic,
fair and considerate, almost poetic.

Washing, trimming, waving your hair,
filing your nails, cleaning with care

the skin that has taken more soot than sun—
you'll seem like a movie star when we've done,

and all your neighbors at last may see
the wonderful person you wanted to be.

Fix our firm in the back of your brain.
We'll ride you away from the roar of the train

and find you a place on a pleasant acre.
What more can you ask of an undertaker?

Prayer

Neat and sweet is the death I've prayed for:
every cavity filled and paid for;
lights in the auto working fine;
no legal documents left to sign.

Having acknowledged the gifts I've gotten,
cleared the window of leaves gone rotten,
told no fewer truths than lies—
I might be willing to shut my eyes.

Progress

In the Borneo supermarket
men are now packaged in parts:
sixty a pound for buttocks,
seventy-nine for hearts,
ten off for noses with warts.

It's a blessing for the consumer
—spares her the screams and the blood;
but those who are starved for excitement
shop in a wistful mood:
it used to be more than just food.

PART 2

New York, New York

Esmeralda

The lady Esmeralda waits:
an oracle of wax;
and in her hand the cards of Fate
reveal their tempting backs.
>   Oh you who cannot sleep at night,
>   insert a penny here.
>   She'll read the cards from left to right,
>   and make your future clear.
She'll promise you a pretty wife,
two daughters and a son,
a salary, a quiet life;
and then her reading's done.
>   But if you aren't satisfied,
>   don't shake the old machine;
>   the penny will not drop outside,
>   the cards will never lean.
Just shrug your shoulders like a sport,
and laugh at what she lacks,
and, after all, who ever thought
a lady . . . made of wax . . .

April on Avenue C

> *How shall the Spring be known*
> *when it appears*
> *where nothing green has grown*
> *a hundred years?*
> *How, how shall the news be broken—*
> *by what token?*
You will know; the signs are clear.
Trumpeters will find your ear.

A sparrow on some fire-escape recites the proclamation.
Look east across the river! Look east at Brooklyn's sky!
At last the sun strides forward: it is a coronation!
The clouds, that were so lordly, crawl out of sight and die.

"Amnesty! Amnesty!" chants the exultant sparrow;
"you snarling winds, be silent! Too long we feared your sound.
You frost, that chained our pinions—you night, that
      frowned like Pharaoh—
find caves to hide your hate in—the enemy is crowned!"

     King of a million amnesties:
     what pardon shall be granted
     here, where no frost-bedeviled trees
     beg to be disenchanted?
     To these gray houses: humbled and haunted,
     marking each other's catastrophes—
     what pardon can possibly be granted,
     what pardon for these?

They have endured so much, so much!
so fiercely craved the crowning of the sun!
Now February's convicts, one by one,
receive the liberating touch.
And lo! half-crazed at going free,
they rise up to their full primeval height—
and lo! transformed by Spring's all-powerful light,
become what they were meant to be.

We find our friend, the vest-maker, at home
in Stamboul, under Saint Sofia's dome.
Three garbage cans away, sits Milkman John
between the pillars of the Parthenon,
and winks at Mrs. Berg, who waters flowers
across the street, in one of Babel's towers.

What if a wind once ripped away the stone
that crowned the great cathedral of Cologne?
What if the rains rubbed off each Phidian shape
at which the eyes of Athens used to gape?
They all stand side by side now, all agree,
and that is miracle enough for me.

     But how is John to understand
     he's Jupiter's high priest—
     the cup of coffee in his hand

a lush Olympian feast?
And how is Mrs. Berg to know
the milkman hopes to kiss
not her, behind the portico,
but Queen Semiramis?

Open a window
and lean outside!
The sun embraces you
like a bride.
See! and you thought
his love had died. . . .
Wrinkled? gray?
He does not care.
To him your forehead
still is fair.
He still can start
fires in your hair. . . .
Show him the plants,
the princes you wean!
One touch from their father—
how they will green!
One touch, Mrs. Berg,
and you are queen . . .

How shall the Spring be known
when it appears
where nothing green has grown
a hundred years?
How, how shall the news be broken—
by what token?
You will know; the signs are clear.
Trumpeters will find your ear.

Carousel Parkway

I

1. Bridgeward

It was a simple route.
We had made it often enough before:
eighty-seven and a half miles, door to door.
We were coming to salute
our Jersey daughter on her birthday, big with child—
the traffic reasonable, the weather mild.

Because this unborn would be someone I wanted to live to see,
I kept my eyes on the road
though Brooklyn's waters beckoned me,
my old beloved bays, that glowed
in pre-noon sun, and ultimately the Bridge,
built long past my time, but fixed as if endlessly there,
or, poised as a rested fire-drake—inspired—about to cleave the air
on its own Sunday pilgrimage.

2. The Hat

What with the lilt of Von Suppé's
Boccaccio duets I'd never heard till then;
what with the rays
that ricochet from needles only when
a grandmother crochets
a unisex green hat;
what with our chat
on grandsires' proper conduct and much else
in the same vein, I scarcely noticed that
we'd left the Island parkway and were now
wheeling around the one that belts
Brooklyn and Queens. Oh yes, somehow
out of the corner of my eye
I saw familiar entrances and exit signs rush by
swift as a lifetime in the mind
of one about to die;
but soon they fell behind;
two rivers and a state line lay between

my vague past and the future toward whose readying room
my wife's lap, a humming loom,
hurried her half-done hat of green.

3. *Home*

Later, on those eighty-seven and a half
homecoming miles, full of our daughter's birthday meal,
full of the new flesh I could almost feel
now that I knew what name it soon would have,
I noticed neither the entrance avenue that had been mine
lulled by the Canarsie Line
nor my father's exit sign
where bones and epitaph
slowly soften in the rains.

And, lying down that night, why should I hear the Brownsville
         trains
that long had rockabied me?
Why should the February of my father's death
once more heap the snows inside me?
—Full of the blood beginning in my grandchild's veins,
full of the breath
about to fill its lung,
full of the melody soon to roll off its tongue,
I fell asleep with *my* new song:
Andrew . . . Nora Elizabeth. . . .

4. *Mixed Dream*

Past the top landing and out the roof door,
through the next roofway and past the top floor,
gingerly bearing as often before
something of magic;

hushed in the hallway, a hand on the knob,
while from within comes a song or a sob:
"Sleep and grow hardy; someday, Little Bob,
you'll be important!"

lovingly noticed and called by my name,
proffering proudly, when asked why I came,

marvelous samplings, the prize in their game:
sister to sister . . .

time for my cousins: first she from whose wall
Harlow seductively leers down at all,
then my boy cousin, gray-headed and tall,
buying me ice-cream;

silly tongue-twisting with her, and with him
talk about Franco—prophetic and grim;
then with my uncle: moustachioed, trim,
dunking for apples;

finally past the top landing and out,
bearing home magic, but bumbling about,
seeking my roof door, unable to shout:
"Which is my building?"

lost with the magic so tenderly stewed:
sister to sister embraced through their food . . .
Which is my building??—in panicky mood,
trembling I waken.

5. *The Dream Untangled*

Trembling I waken—not on a tenement roof
in grassless Brownsville, lost amid ghastly shirts
and sheets and the haggard shrilling of mothers, but safe
beside the balanced breathing of my wife
in my own house: lien-free and termite-free,
as can be proved in notarized reports
filed with the county at the usual fee.

Nor do I clutch a jar of stew; that jar
was rinsed, refilled, and roofward sent—I guess
some forty-seven years ago or more.
And not till three years later did I hear
the lullaby, crooned unaware of me
to that new-hatched, already blighted face
in her benighted room, on her doomed knee,

on some gray street whose name I never allowed
myself to remember, Death Street to my aunt.
And later still the hair of Harlow glowed
in an altogether new, green neighborhood
where one robbed cousin joined my family
while the other, no matter how he felt, was sent
to some mill town where a half-room happened to be.

Of course he wasn't gray-haired then (perhaps
gray-hearted), nor especially tall, although
to me he seemed so; many years, many trips
later, he treated me to one of those cups
of two-cent ices . . . pineapple . . . and we
did talk of Spain, still later—for by now
I went to college and talked knowingly.

The apple-dunking—how did that get in?
Seymour—that uncle—belongs in another dream:
moustachioed, trim . . . such a high-voltage man!
He strung an apple once at Halloween
which sent our jaws on a lunging, biteless spree . . .
At thirty-one, after a handball game,
his heart cracked—no doctor would come—and he

went unflamboyantly into the ground.
As for the building whose roof door I tried
so desperately in my dream to find,
within whose walls so many waltzed and moaned,
not one brick's left of it; I shall not see
either its shape or shade; a sick green sod
is there now; broken jars; rats running free.

6. *The Two Uncles*

What a mixup of streets, of years, of uncles!
The one who'd have been right for this particular dream
wasn't even home
when in fact I came
with the jar;
he's still alive, sporting eighty-year wrinkles
—not a moustache;
even now his eye Europeanly twinkles:

15

he's no spender . . . probably hides cash;
never got the hang of a cigar;
never set foot in a bar;
never drove a car—
unlike Uncle Seymour, who one day
during the Depression
—when trainride nickels were rare
and beat-up shoes in fashion—
stopped his brand-new Chevrolet
before our stoop,
causing the neighborhood to gape
in open shock
as haughtily we whizzed away
around the block.

7. Setting Out Alone

I sit up sharply; hand under chin,
I struggle out of sleep.
What has aroused my spectral kin
to most
incongruous motion? But of course! it was our noontime trip
past Pennsylvania Avenue, Bay Parkway and the rest,
precious enclaves populous with ghost . . .
Of course! This is how ghosts reply
deep in the night, when one has galloped by
at pre-noon, scarcely noticing the past
out of the corner of his eye.

Wide awake,
determined not to be tracked down
by phantoms I myself should seek—
a Verrazzano, an inspired Drake
in search of all that I've begun, outgrown and done,
I set out, quaking and alone
although beside me, bone to anklebone,
just as she sat
by day,
hushes my wife, too deep within her dream of a green hat
to guess that I have slipped away.

II

1. Back on the Road

I'm back on the road—this time without traffic,
without *Boccaccio,* without green-sparking needles.
Into the corner of my eye, the unborn
grandchild occasionally rises, with the
blurred but important look of someone waiting
beside a carousel's rotations, as I
ride full force round a dream-wild diorama
swifter than can be told of it—first passing
my father patient in the place we gave him
twenty-six Februaries ago (the snowfall
had stopped, a bloody sun leaned out as witness);
now off the Island parkway, vaulted onto
the Belt—merry-go-round without music or stallions—
passing the all-night lamp of two who skoaled us
when last year's phone rang pregnant (she wept, somewhat
for joy at our joy, somewhat for being childless;
he, swollen with a more than nine months' creature)

—that night, awake at the same hour as this, supporting
the same cheek with the same fist, before my
reviewing stand, like an emperor, surveying
widowers, widows, expectant and delivered,
that night I made foolish, most unfair demands on
an embryo without fingernails, with scarcely
a heartbeat. . . .

2. Carousel Riders

It takes no time, no time to round them all,
all my old settlements
so separate then . . . light years apart . . .
now clustering points
on a music-box diorama.
And I strain to remember at which of those points
one night, writhing with time,
I saw an oval platform, innocuously churning,
its cavalry forever charging, never advancing,
with only so many bridles
and a line at the ticket booth:

—after that day, perhaps,
when the palsied beldame of invented lips
and the fresh-breasted bank clerk who patronized her
leaned as one toward the window-grating?
when a boy, trying manhood on, brought grandpa by
and lifted him, lowered him into a barber-chair?
when November exposed
three grandmotherly trees
broken amid their straight-backed sprouts?
—or maybe when parents of friends began dying,
when my own father died
soon after his granddaughter's birth . . .

And suddenly I behold *her* unborn child
not as my solace, a delicious elbow
replacing vanished friends,
but as my replacement
on the coldly rising and sinking stallion
I have come after fifty-one years
to consider mine.

3. *Bay Parkway*

What I would like now
is to go not one yard further on this road.
What I would like
is for a helicopter to lift me
or a ferry to take me on
and over to Jersey,
or a way to zigzag through strange inland streets
till I reach the Verrazzano's, the fire-drake's ramp.

And it is not so much
because one can almost see from the highway
the bedroom on Bay 29th
where my father, through his oxygen tent,
introduced me and the doctor to each other
with one last joke: "Poet and Doctor . . ."
—a take-off on the overture of Von Suppé.

It is more
because one can almost see the windows

of the basement on Bay 32nd
where, stuffed with caresses and cake, I beheld
the *kazatske* weddings of my six big cousins
(now all widowed or dead).

It is mostly
because one can almost see the stoop
near the corner on Bay 34th
where on a game night in May
I assured the "Milkman" that I'd
"found thirty-six dancing spiders in my milk"—
and for ten whole minutes held to my words without laughing,
no matter what he asked,
until he made me answer that my mother
was thirty-six dancing spiders.

But no ferry, no helicopter
comes to the rescue;
nor is there time to sneak off the parkway.
In less than a second
my ancient nest of games and welcomes
approaches, passes, not even noticed by the other riders.

And since it would be not just unseemly, unmanly,
but downright dangerous
to turn one's face, even for that second,
and stretch forth one's arms—
firmly I move toward the Bridge,
the by now really rested fire-drake
impatient to take me on his back and fly.

III

1. Soubise

Because the recipe called for at least three cups
of onion thinly sliced,
I sat myself down (an arm's length from the grapes)
and, getting the hang of it after a while, released
from the past
dozens of phantom dinners we'd prepared, to which our friends

had come,
dozens we'd come to, which our friends prepared,
the menus blended now, the occasions blurred,
the company, cluster by cluster,
like browning bunches of grapes, name after name,
body by body, heading for disaster,
blighted in unpredictable fashion,
in irresistible sequence of attrition.

And because it was onion I sliced, alone at the table,
I let myself weep without control or shame
for faces long grown undistinguishable
and those about to come,
about to hush some of their hungers
and ours with handclasp, and soubise, and jest:
he with the throat condition not to be discussed,
she with the missing marvelous breast;
and for my wife, too crippled in her fingers
especially before rain
to slice an onion thin.

2. *Phone Call*

I don't believe this dinner or its faces
will be blended
with the rest.
Some time before it ended
—in fact, just as I passed
the casserole and Dave cried, "The soubise is
out of this world!" the telephone
rang out its tidings like a new year's bell:
our daughter's toil was done—
nine yammering pounds had joined us in the noontide sun—
full-faced, full-fingered, and female.

Nora Elizabeth! *her* graduations!
her first daughter!
—From this night
I'll drink less wine, more water,
cross only at the light,
go off on longer, frequenter vacations,
do twenty push-ups twice a day,

seize the slick reins of my uncaring roan
and make the beast obey
for one more up and down before he's done with me
and takes my great-granddaughter on.

Indeed, I'll be back on the Belt tomorrow,
pass my old
entrances,
old exit signs, behold
through a new pair of eyes
new birds, new baseball diamonds, a new borough,
the um-pa-pa of Von Suppé
outshouted as I pass my father's aisle
with hurrying hurray
away via fire-drake across the Lower Bay
perhaps to answer her first smile.

PART 3
The Poetry of Work

Ballad of Tom Mooney

In a dungeon of San Quentin, where the
      bars are strong as stone;
They have dragged a daring labor-man,
      and locked him there alone.
It is dark for him who struggled that his
      brother-slaves might see,
And it chains a heart of courage, that
      would set his comrades free.

Tom Mooney, imprisoned now these
      twenty years and one;
We'll tear the old bars apart and let
      you greet the sun!

He had come among the workers—he had
      witnessed all their pain . . .
and he saw them lose their liberty, and
      saw the bosses gain.
He had seen their meek obedience and
      showed that it was wrong.
And he told them they could fight for
      joy—together they were strong.

But to those who reaped the gains of all
      their wage-slaves' work and sweat,
Young Tom Mooney was a criminal—his
      challenge must be met.
Young Tom Mooney was a danger to their
      prosperous machine,
And his message must be silenced—his
      solution lie unseen.

On a day the world remembers, when the
      San Francisco streets
Were resounding to the shouting, and the
      drums' excited beats
Out of nowhere, bombs came falling on
      the marching thousands there,

And the scores of scattered dead replied
      in silent rage: "From where?"

Our Tom Mooney then was taken, and
      to him was put blame . . .
And a choking blotch of blood was used
      to mar his magic name.
They have tried to murder Mooney; he's
      been tortured all this time;
But we know and shout that love for us
      has been his only crime.

In a dungeon of San Quentin, where the
      bars are strong as stone,
They have dragged a daring labor-man,
      and locked him there alone.
But our hearts have lived with Mooney,
      and his strength has been our guide,
And his body will march with us, when
      we force his way outside!

Tom Mooney, imprisoned now these twenty
      years and one;
We'll tear the old bars apart, and let
      you greet the sun!

Thought on a Train

They that live in dark and pain
Fixed this light that never fails.
They that built this mighty train
Walk, heads bowed, beside the rails.

The Shoe-Shine Boy

One long-past day, while riding on the train,
I saw a sight whose memory will remain.
I saw a ragged child, whose thin, starved face
Seemed like a little angel's out of place.
And there he was, although the hour was late,
Tied there as though it was his woeful fate
That while most children slept, in large, soft beds,
He should stay out, his childhood torn to shreds.
And from that day I could not understand
Why this is called a great and noble land. . . .

For once I saw a child whose shoes looked old,
Shining another's, till they shone like gold.

Work Day

I've been working arms and back all day
where sunbeams lie in scraps upon the floor,
until I'm caught in a machine-like sway
that rocks asleep whatever lived before.

I watch the clock, as though my looking there
might egg its finger to the touch of five,
when, stumbling through the crowds to Union Square,
I'll pick the sunniest bench, and grow alive.

Unemployed Song

Last month I worked in a hell-hole shop
with just enough light to see the machine,
where the motors yell and the hammers drop
and the boss marks time till you leave the latrine
and your favorite dream is a bench on the Square
feeding pigeons and swallowing air.

I've sat here now through a stream of hours
where the waterfall sounds a familiar sob,
and I envy the simple routines of flowers,
the pigeons that never seem out of a job,
and my favorite dream is the motor's yell
high up in that shop, in that hole of hell.

Help Wanted!

For wrecking and upraising
a temple in this land,
men and women are wanted
who're tough, both heart and hand.

Men and women are wanted
who won't begin to complain
whenever the sun beats strongly,
or when they must work in the rain.

Hours will be long and tiring,
vacations far between—
no time for idle chatter,
no time to loaf and dream.

Bruises and mocking laughter
will be the wage they earn,
with signs that warn of danger
posted at every turn.

Wanted are men and women
to toil against great odds,
to raise in this land a temple
where they shall be the gods.

from "The Minotaur"

EIGHT O'CLOCK WHISTLE

Now begins the dread carnivorous roar.
Now each factory, each monster-bull
cries for the most quick, most beautiful;
and I see them swallowed through the door.

It reminds me of the Minotaur
(whom I learned of long ago in school)
waiting in his subterranean pool
every April fourteen morsels more.

Every year they'd come, the loveliest ones,
past the hill whose peak they'd often climbed,
past the tree upon whose bark they'd rhymed,
past the moons forever and the suns,
past believing, past all hopes and fears,
past the taste of one another's tears.

ALL HAIL!

"Oh storm-wracked ship of state, uncaptained at the helm,
take heart, take heart and quicken at the word I bear:
your king is ready to deliver safe his realm—
send forth a chariot! He's on the barber's chair."

It happens: Number One vacates the sacred seat
and hides his tabloid; Number Two, the charioteer,
flies to the barber; Number Three stalks down the street
in search of a mistake at which to scold and sneer;

while Numbers Four and Five, the princelings of the Court,
rehearse their parts, try on a range of frowns and smiles.
Determined to present a royal-sized report,
they rummage feverishly through ten years of files.

Outside a horn honks twice: "All hail! It is the king!"
Umbrellas rush to shield him from the cheering clouds

that hurl confetti, while the winds in chorus sing
hosanna. Modestly he waves to them, and bows.

Inside the hat-racks quarrel: WHICH WILL HOLD HIS CROWN?
Six hands take off the coat, and every hanger begs.
Impatiently he shoos away the smile, the frown,
drops wearily upon his throne, and *"Oh, my legs!"*

Five ministers surround him—with a grunt toward each
he settles back, puffs hard at a cigar, and wails:
"Last Year, by this time, I was sunning on the beach—
now look! Three hours my back is turned: HOW MANY SALES?

"Not one? So what? *You're* paid on Friday just the same.
The worry's on *my* head—all night I turn and toss. . . .
And *that* damned bunch outside—they're either blind or lame. . . .
Look! Three: I'll bet they're cracking jokes against the boss!

"Next thing they'll start a union, tell *me* what to do!
I'll teach them all a lesson soon. . . ." The cat struts in.
"Come *here!*" he croons, "come *here!* I brought some *fish* for you."
Croons: "Pussycat! hey pussycat! where have you been?"

A TRICK ON NICK

All the king's men, since eight o'clock,
have had three rounds of coffee and buns.
They've bought and they've sold the leading stock;
inducted everyone else's sons,
equipped them and shipped them overseas,
and brought the whole universe to its knees.

Till lunch is delivered, they've nothing to do
but suck at cigars and twiddle their thumbs
and look out the window, cursing the crew.
—Then wearily up through the snowstorm comes
bowlegged, hunchbacked, one-eyed Nick.
"Hey!" cry the king's men, "let's play a trick!"

His time-card's switched to the topmost row,
and another man's card is hooked in its place.

—The door creaks open; surrounded by snow,
cascades of melting snow on his face,
snow-streams finding the holes in his suit,
snow-pools formed by his torn left boot,

Nick stumbles in, and clutches the knob. . . .
Then he takes the card from the same bottom hook
he's had for thirty-two years on the job,
and punches his time without stopping to look.
But the king's men halt him halfway to the door:
"Don't you punch your own card no more?

"Whatsamatter? Forgot your name?
Sleeps all morning, and wakes up for lunch!
Don't think you fool us! We're wise to your game—
we're sick of you and the whole goddam bunch!
Can't walk, can't bend, can't see your card!
You one-eyed old bastard: *get out of the yard!*"

He smiles; but back in the storm that smile
turns into a curse as he stumbles off.
They mimic his walk and his talk for a while;
then Harry comes in, with the shakes and the cough;
and I know they've something special planned
that'll scare the time-card out of his hand.

The king sits laughing, stroking the cat.
Before he discovers the look on my face,
quickly I put on my coat and hat,
and get myself far from the smell of the place,
and hold out my hands, so monstrously warm,
and let them be frozen, freed by the storm.

IN THE LUNCH WAGON

There is no cafeteria in Hell
more clangorous, more foul of sight or smell.
Yet at the stroke of clemency, we race
from every labyrinth to that one place.

Past whirling dishes, waitresses, and steam,
I see the clock (that killed my nightly dream)
still smiling, and my own smile cannot live
—as though I'm a discovered fugitive.

In threes and fours, some use the hour of food
to make a fiery anvil of their mood.
The whispers leap like flame. They forge a sword.
In secret armories it will be stored. . . .

Some steal to freedom, or pretend they do,
by eating in the rear, away from view.
They drop their nickels in the music box;
and hear a song that overcomes the clock's.

And while they chew, the passion of the tune
returns them to a face, a tree, a moon. . . .
Once more they're clung to, all their worth is seen:
not mocked and ground to dust by a machine!

The flesh revives, the eyes renew their flame;
for three sweet minutes they are not the same—
until a record's over. At the shock
they look up, and behold the smiling clock.

THE TRAP-DOOR SHUTS

The Minotaur has grown polite
since Theseus slew him with a spear:
he nods Hello to still our fear;
he does not finish us—not quite.

It's true, the place could stand more light,
but there's enough to make things clear;
and actually the exit's near—
we *could*, at least we have the *right*

to slip away; and through the pane
we *are* allowed a piece of sky
in which our thoughts might almost fly;
occasionally there's a train,

and on the tracks of its refrain
we *might* escape—but it roars by
too thunderous to hear a sigh,
too quick to notice someone slain.

FIVE O'CLOCK WHISTLE

The glutted factories one by one announce
that they have had enough for the time being.
Again their gates swing open—like a yawn—
and out into the sunset, hardly seeing,

the pale ones tumble, stumble toward the train. . . .
Where I work, too, the slaughter is suspended:
bent creatures drag themselves upstairs, punch out,
and turn to go—but since their day is ended

they have the right to linger at the door
for one last silent look, one smile at Sadie
who's winked them back to manhood all year long;
and she—kind-hearted girl, though not a lady—

winks from the calendar as they go past.
This gives them courage; now their step is faster;
they wash their faces, comb the thinning hair;
and march, heads lifted, from the day's disaster.

Song No. 1 from Santa Fe Night (a hobo fantasy)

I come from a land
where there ain't no snow,
where every hand
says: HI! HELLO!

where wine rolls down
like waterfalls
to a chocolate town
with lemon pie walls;

33

where you turn to the south
and say one word
and into your mouth
flies a roasted bird;

where you turn to the east
and make one wish
and a holiday feast
is on your dish;

where melodies drop
from the sun and moon,
and the mountain-top
takes every tune;

where a brotherly breeze
is heard to say:
AT EASE! AT EASE!
NO WORK TODAY.

Nick

At night, in a blizzard,
for the first time in twenty-one years
the face of a yard-worker comes back
—round, grimy, one tooth gone—
and his first name, Nick, and his husky laugh,
and that long, tough family name
I lettered on his envelope each Friday:
GEROLIMATOS...
Nick, youngest of the crew.

When he took sick (having worked outside
through a blizzard, thinking his hulk would protect him),
what a surprise, bringing him his pay,
to discover two grown children
—the boy a math whiz, wilting under his praise,
the girl coaxable to the piano—
both blonde and goggled as their mother

who kept them and her apartment as immaculate
as he was smudged with grease, but not that day.
How clean he lay, laughing in bed!
how clean, one month later, when we put him in the ground.

Elegy for a Carpet Boy

> Nobody loves a genius child.
> Kill him—and let his soul run wild!
> —Langston Hughes

By the time you were ten, Iqbal,
you had lived a very long while,
each day (as one says) a year.
But it was not of old age
you died, just two years later—
struck down on the streets of Lahore
by a carpet factory's bullet
(whatever the government says).

Your father ought to have warned you
what a tongue on fire would cost,
but it was he who had sold you
at four into Carpet Hall
to spare him the cost of your hunger.

Now nothing remains but a high
boy-voice, or rather a bird-voice,
echoing over the planet,
nesting safe in my soul.

Foolhardy bird, who escaped
(perhaps on a magic carpet)—
why was it not enough
to rejoice at last in your wings?
What nudged you to rage instead
for those still caged amid looms?

In your city of ambush, Iqbal,
are friends I would like to embrace,
and for me (as one says) they surely
would roll out the red carpet.
But the red of Pakistan carpets
is suddenly not to my taste.

If I ever set foot in Lahore,
it will be, Iqbal, to bring you
a rose, whose red is not suspect.

PART 4

African American History and Struggle

Paul Robeson

Tonight Paul Robeson sings.
His feet are enough of a stage.
His voice is a hammer that rings.
His voice is a bull in rage.
Tonight Paul Robeson sings.
His eyes are enough of light.
His smiles are eagle wings.
A tree of steel is his height.
Come out of your room, your cage!
Come out to the Concert Hall!
Here is your waiting's wage.
Here is your chance to grow tall.

He'll sing of trees, remind you
that some of the earth is green.
He'll sing of the hopes behind you
for a porch, a limousine.
He'll sing of the steel that rose
like a jail around your choice;
like a jail that would even close
its bars on your timid voice.
He'll sing until your throat
is Robeson; 'til you hear
your pain in every note,
your wild and lonely fear.

Then suddenly he'll sing
in a strange, volcano tone
with great arms welcoming
you who have sobbed alone.
He'll welcome you who have grown
the trees of steel so tall,
you who only own
the strength to raise a wall.
He'll sing of the sap that must rise
to make its tree abloom,
of the roots that must grope their eyes
for sun-food deep in the gloom.

He'll sing until your veins
are swollen with sap of steel,
'til your eyes are hurricanes
from which the shadows reel.
He'll sing until your hand
is Robeson; 'til his feet
are the stage on which you stand
an eagle over your street.

Natchez

THE BALLAD

There's a town in Mississippi too small for its fame;
town in Mississippi, Natchez by name.
Once it had a dance-hall no bigger than a barn,
with only one doorway and the paint all gone.
But whenever it came evening of a hardwork day
the Negro gals and fellas couldn't keep away.
On a night like all the others they started to jive
'til the jazz-band was beating like a heart alive.
They forgot the sun that pounded 'til their backs were numb;
they only remembered the sax and the drum.
Like a gang let out of prison they hopped and they clung,
as though at any moment they'd be chained and hung.

Suddenly a fire grew on the floor,
but the band was sizzling music and nobody saw.
It grew along the woodwork 'til it touched their feet.
Someone hollered "Fire!" and ran for the street.
It grew like a windy cornfield in a storm of smoke.
The drummer jumped screaming; the sax-player choked.
The children shoved and jostled but the door was small;
the fire ran after and climbed a wall.
"Help!" yelled the children. "Save us, God!"
They beat the walls, 'til their fingers were faucets of blood.
The fire ran after and climbed their clothes.
Smoke crawled through fingers into eyes and nose.

They screamed, "Oh Lordy, save us!" But the door was small.
The fire tore coffins out of the wall.

Town in Mississippi, Natchez by name.
A hundred tabloid writers ran to the flame.
When the bodies of still children were dragged from the door,
the tabloid writers counted 'til there were no more.
When the bodies of still children were dragged to the street,
the mothers watched their fingers and their quiet feet.

PRAYER

Listen, Lord, to the prayer of the people of Natchez,
who mourn this day the ashen limbs of their children.
We speak for their souls: oh grant them Heaven, Lord!
They are the souls of children; grant them your cooling grass.
Hour and hour went, yet we wept from body to body,
two hundred and fifty bodies, and not one foot that moved.
What was their sin, that you planted Hell 'round their laughter?
What was their sin, that you chain their feet forever?
Listen, Lord, to the prayer of the people of Natchez.
We have been meek in our prayers; even now we are meek.
We have not asked for jewels and silk, for castles,
for sprawling lands, for lordship over the river.
We've brought you thanks for labor without the whip,
for Sundays without rain, for clean and beautiful children.
We have been meek, but Lord, hear our confession:
some nights our souls beat at their walls, and shriek.
How long, oh Lord, how long shall our anguish prosper?
Again, again your children are crucified.
How long must we wait 'til the grass is ripe for dancing,
and walls no longer stand guard against our sky?
Forgive us, Lord, we speak for the souls of our children.
Oh let them dance forever; we know they are clean.

Isaac Woodard

Because the color of my skin
is dark, and yours is light,
the jury counted it no sin
to rob me of my sight.

And thus it is that you go free,
Patrolman Lynwood Shull;
and thus, while night envelops me,
your world is beautiful.

But though the sun will never rise
and never set again,
my blindness lets me see what eyes
have seldom shown to men.

I see a midnight on the lands,
parched lives and prospering flowers;
I see black deeds upon white hands,
black hearts in gleaming towers.

All this, and stranger things beside,
I see now, thanks to you:
I see great Justice turn and hide—
you've gouged *her* eyes out, too.

The Seamstress

> (a true incident from slavery times, recorded in
> B. A. Botkin's collection of ex-slave interviews,
> *Lay My burden Down*)

In the spinning cabin two wheels would run and run:
always there was plenty of sewing to be done.

Master went on business to Baton Rouge one day;
there he found a seamstress and wheedled her away.

She was young and yellow, fine-fingered and fine-dressed.
Master built her cabin a distance from the rest.

Under "Missy's" window was where the dollhouse stood.
"Missy's" children played there, and no one else's could.

Once, while they were playing, the "seamster's" kids came in.
"Get away—this dollhouse is not for colored skin!"

"Don't you talk so haughty—our dad's the same as yours.
Many nights he wakes us with trinkets from the stores.

"Daddy's what we call him—our mamma calls him dear."
Mistress at the window, she couldn't help but hear.

"Evening!" said the Master, but Mistress held her breath.
"Honey, what's the matter? You're looking pale as death."

"It's this yellow woman whose children look like mine."
"Honey, I just fetched her because she sews so fine."

"Back in Mississippi I'd have a place to stay . . ."
"Honey, don't you listen to what some gossips say."

Master bought her horses next time he went to town—
strong, white surrey horses together with a gown.

She had no more babies; the seamstress bore a brood,
but they never ventured to where the dollhouse stood.

Denmark Vesey

THE KIDNAPPING

When the last Carolina brave lay still
by his beloved poplars, and his lawns
surrendered to the shadow of a stranger,
a new unholy Genesis began:
of acres rooted by uprooted hands. . . .

A voyager (whose name is not remembered)
showed in that time astounding business sense.
Sailing along the coast of Africa
he passed a hundred villages unknown
except to those who lived there; and one morning
or night he had a demon's inspiration:
why not seize quietly a stray child here,
a maiden bathing in the bay alone,
a strong-armed fellow dozing on the rocks—
and sell them to the planters overseas. . . .

That inspiration swiftly turned to gold.
The first shocked screams were muffled in the hold
of ships—and there in chains the kidnapped lay
while those who loved them wept, a world away.

What frantic thoughts stampeded through their brains
on that dark journey, while their hands and feet
lay numb and fevered in the grip of chains
among the rats there, in the stench and heat?

If sometimes a shrill cry upset the air
and reached the state-room, did the captain care,
or any of the crew, did they translate
their cargo's message of despair and hate?

Perhaps the free winds and the unbound waves
rendered the lamentation of the slaves
in language that the sky might understand:
"When will we see you, Sun—in what strange land?
For what vile purposes have we been torn

from all we knew and loved since we were born?"
But from the sky's red mouth no answer came.
—The port was reached; the cargo seemed quite tame. . . .

AUCTION BLOCK

Your lips are pale, your forehead's moist,
and your pulse is quick. . . .
>   *Not right, not right! a dreadful sight!*
>   *Please take me home—I'm sick.*

What sight? Was there some thing I missed?
Tell me what you mean!
The slaves were brought, and sold and bought,
It all went smooth and clean.

>   *A mother taken from her child!*
>   *Husbands from their wives!*
>   *—The sobs and moans cut through my bones*
>   *more cruelly than knives. . . .*

You like a rug in every room;
diamonds in your hair.
Without those blacks to bend their backs
your wrists would soon be bare.

>   *They glared so when you named your price:*
>   *glared as if to say*
>   A CLEVER TRADE! AND YET YOU'VE PAID
>   NOT HALF WHAT YOU SHALL PAY!

The whip will teach a sullen few;
chains will do for most;
and soon they'll come to call this "Home,"
forget their fathers' coast.

>   *It may be so—and yet tonight*
>   *I'll not sleep a wink . . .*
You'll sleep, my dear—and now, let's hear
no more of what you think!

PLANTATION SONG

How many days will it be,
oh how many days will it be?
I'll count them, Lord, I know how to count.
How many days will it be?

Master's alone with his gold,
old Master's alone with his gold.
He counts it, Lord, he knows how to count
more than his hands can hold.

Lady's gone shopping in town,
oh Lady's gone shopping in town.
She's counting, Lord, she knows how to count
jewels enough for a crown.

Overseer came with his whip,
mm, overseer came with his whip.
He counted, Lord, he knew how to count—
until my blood would drip.

How many days will it be,
oh how many days will it be?
I'll count them, Lord, I know how to count
until my hands go free.

REVOLT IN SANTO DOMINGO

The whip worked magic everywhere it fell;
the chains performed miraculously well;
the threat of starving cast a mighty spell.

But plundered veins swore to avenge their blood;
chained limbs at last their power understood;
a hunger grew more frantic than for food.

Santo Domingo was the first to learn
what comes to pass when feet may not return
to the beloved soil for which they yearn.

46

They crushed the whip that they'd been baptized with.
They broke the harness they had bent beneath,
and kicked it back into their masters' teeth.

And though the lords of Charleston raised a wall
to keep the news away, it was not tall
or thick enough—the news reached one and all.

SONG OF RETURNING SAILORS

We bring forbidden tidings
from harbors near and far:
of feet once bound together
that now unfettered are;

of joys like corpses buried
that rise up from their graves;
of slaves that now are masters,
of masters that are slaves.

We bring forbidden tidings
from harbors far and near—
and some will dance who hear it,
and some will die of fear.

THE PLANTERS' FRIGHT

Oh what a wringing of diamonded white hands!
Each year, each month new bells of ruin tolled.
The bedrock under Charleston seemed like sands—
the planters' voices all at once were old:

> It happened in Santo Domingo,
> then Mexico and Brazil:
> the weak have made themselves mighty
> and do whatever they will.
>
> They curse at all that was holy,
> make holy all that was cursed.
> The wise old judges are sentenced,
> the last-fed now eat first.

47

It happened in Venezuela,
then Cuba and Martinique:
the weak have made themselves mighty—
and the mighty—the mighty are weak!

REFUGEE RELIEF

Into the outstretched arms of New Orleans,
Richmond, and Charleston, ran the sobbing rich
spat out by nations that had outlawed chains. . . .
What tales they brought! what lessons they could teach
to those who still slept soundly!

                                    Charleston planned
a benefit to buy new wigs and gowns
for those heroic Lords Without a Land.
Invited were the cream of nearby towns;
the loudest orchestra they could assemble
would lash the night with waltz and minuet;
the oldest wines would help their hearts forget
that more than music caused the walls to tremble. . . .

The shops were emptied of their choicest food,
that all might eat as much as they were able;
and for this banquet, a gigantic table
was ordered—of the rarest, sturdiest wood;
and who else could be called upon to build
a piece so sumptuous, but the most skilled
of Charleston's carpenters: the order came
to Denmark Vesey.
                    Do you know the name?

THE DENMARK VESEY SONG

Who rocked the cradle of Denmark Vesey?
Who taught him the names of trees?
In what hidden lake did he learn of his beauty?
Who kissed him at night but the breeze?

Do you know the name? have you heard the story?
He was fourteen summers old—

cradled in a slave-ship, kissed by a slave-whip,
his beauty bought and sold.

Do you know the name? have you heard the story?
He bought his liberty back—
but even in freedom he couldn't feel free
while chains bound those who were black.

Do you know the name? have you heard the story?
He won the planters' trust:
they hired his hammer, but night after night
he hammered their chains into dust.

CHARLESTON NOCTURNE

When Charleston shuts her thousand eyes
and rocks asleep the clamor,
she listens to the lullabies
of Denmark Vesey's hammer.

On beds of down, white ladies smile
to hear the hammer beating:
"At a table of the newest style
tomorrow we'll be eating!"

But slaves imagine other words,
and in their sleep smile often:
"Beat, hammer, beat! Nail down the boards!
Make slavery a coffin!"

THE MINUET

Through Col. Prioleau's majestic shutters,
music like wine poured into evening's cup,
until it overflowed along the gutters
where greedy coachmen stooped to lap it up.

"Sweet Maestro Franceschini! play that number
you wrote for Washington so long ago—
when you and I and Charleston were much younger . . .
The minuet, at least, before you go!"

And desperately there, with half-shut eyes,
the minuetting dowagers imagined
a time when lanterns told no brilliant lies,
when laughter wore the crown at every pageant;

when Charleston's men—who'd helped to make a king go—
came home and were anointed in his stead;
before the doom of Haiti and Domingo
reached like a nightmare into every bed. . . .

But they were pale, for all the pirouetting;
haggard and hushed, for all the boasts and toasts.
Even the young: past grieving, past forgetting,
performed their fathers' graceful dance like ghosts.

VESEY'S NIGHTMARE

It took Vesey long to fall asleep that night.
Over and over he heard the minuet;
till—tossing and turning—he fell into a dream.
It was Col. Prioleau's banqueting-room.

There stood the Colonel, bursting through his coat,
flanked by half the legislature of the State
all busily sampling and praising the food.
Instead of an ordinary meal, they had
young Negro bodies, baked to the bone.
Their fountain of wine was a Negro vein.

The lovely brocade their ladies wore
had once been Negro grandmothers' hair.
The gems that blinked on their arms like stars
were bright Negro eyes that had lately shed tears.

The drummer was beating a broad Negro chest,
and, instead of on trumpets, the trumpeters placed
thin lips on the hole of a Negro throat
that made a lament of the minuet.

Now lightly, now heavily, dancers caroused
on black children's faces: moaning and bruised—

while one slave kept bending to mop up the blood,
for which he received many pats on the head.

The Colonel smiled proudly up at his lamps:
they were Negro souls, which he'd bought for worn pants.
Now they saw Vesey—they were pointing at *him!*
"Not I!" he shrieked, and fled from the dream.

SUNDAY OFFERTORY PRAYER

We bring you, Lord, a week of wounds and worry—
put forth your loving arms and take them in.
We wished to fill your cups of offertory,
but better coin than hurt we did not win.

Put forth your arms, and take us in, and tell us
that at the end it will be otherwise—
that we'll yet reach your everlasting palace,
and claim for all our agonies a prize.

Breathe to our souls again the sacred promise!
Remind us of the Hell that you prepare
for those who've torn the love and laughter from us—
for those who now like fiends of Satan are.

Our veins run dry between the rows of cotton;
our years run out beneath a whip of hate.
Put forth your arms—too long we are forgotten—
too long we wait, oh Lord, too long we wait!

VESEY SPEAKS TO THE CONGREGATION

My leg is weak from the chains you wear;
my shoulders break at the load you bear;
my back is marked by your masters' whips;
and from your wound my own blood drips. . . .

But when you bow, my beautiful sisters,
ah brothers, when you bow and beg,
my heart wears chains—for those who bought you
have shackled you both heart and leg.

You look for freedom in the sky?
Then chained you'll live, and chained you'll die!
You seek in heaven the promised land?
Then lost is the promise of your hand!

Israel whimpered once in bondage—
who listened?—and who saw her bow?
She cried aloud—and Pharaoh trembled!
She rose—and what is Pharaoh now?

Like Israel, brothers, let us be:
wait not for God to set you free!

Turn all your sobs to battle-cries:
cry freedom! freedom! and arise. . . .

THE LEGISLATORS VOTE

The hot word, Liberty, rushed through their limbs
and gave their eyes a strange illumination
that could not go unnoticed. When they bowed
a pause came first, an ominous hesitation.
And when at work they hummed their Bible-hymns,
even the faintest note seemed somehow loud.

It was a bad year for the buyers of men.
Their merchandise would not stay on the shelves.
Their cotton spoiled untended in the sun.
Their forests grew more fugitives than trees.
Their mansions all at once were fortresses
in which they quakingly besieged themselves.

Some sold their lands and fled; but those who stayed
whipped twice as hard, to prove they still had power.
And when their legislature was assembled,
they roared to show that they were unafraid—
and Col. Prioleau, for at least an hour,
proved that his voice still rang and scarcely trembled:

"... In closing I have this to say:
take heed of how the black men pray!

Discover every whispered word!
Let every sigh be overheard!
Be careful when you see them laugh:
the joke may be our epitaph.
And when they bow too low, beware!
It is our burial they prepare."

"A law! a law! let's pass one now!"
"A Santo Domingo we'll never allow!"
"Look out for whisperers!" "Fine them!" "Jail them!"
"Bind them!" "Starve them!" "Brand them!" "Flail them!"
"Who dares to challenge the might of the slaver?"
"A law!" "Yes, a law!" "All those in favor—
say aye!" "AYE!!" "AYE!!" "Not one opposed?
Unanimously carried! Session is closed. . . ."

A MEETING AT VESEY'S

Welcome, brothers, to my house
where lamps are not lit, where blinds are drawn,
where deeds instead of names will be known,
where friends greet friends with half a voice!

Beware of the informer moon!
Beware of trees that tell for a price!
Liberty now has no public place—
it is an outlaw in this town.

Brother Vesey, I am sent here by three hundred rebel slaves.
In your hands they rest their hope, and in your dream they place
    their lives.
Here are coins from harassed fingers—give them rifles in return!
Gabriel is what they call you—they are listening for the horn. . . .
Brother Vesey, I bring pennies, and a prayer from six plantations:
neither meat nor wine can fill us—we are hungry for munitions.
Do you need the angriest hundred? do you seek the most
    courageous?
Here's your list: my men are lions pacing back and forth in cages. . . .

Just like a wind with seeds to sow
whisper, whisper the word!

53

All through the cotton from row to row
whisper, whisper the word!
Wherever the whip has worked its woe
whisper, whisper the word!
Wherever no tears are left to flow
whisper, whisper the word!

Some will not answer though they're near you,
near enough to run and hide;
some, miles away, will hear you:
hear you and run to your side.
Some will rebuke and hound you,
hound you for the trouble you bring.
Some will put their arms around you
as though you are everything.

To all you know, wherever you go
whisper, whisper the word!
The trumpet of freedom is about to blow—
whisper, whisper the word!

TWO SLAVERS

There is a warning on the wind
that wakes me from my dreams at night:
"Your walls are doomed by angry eyes
that never shut—though yours be shut. . . .
In all your fields a frightful seed
has swelled, and burst, and taken root.
There'll be a harvest soon to reap
and underneath it you shall rot. . . ."

My slaves are secret as a great volcano
whose crater is too deep for eyes to know.
Alas for us who listen to such silence,
who watch for the first sign of wrath to show!
There'll be no sign, nor any sound of rumbling;
our doom will catch us dreaming in our beds.
The slaves will grow impatient of the secret
and pour their wrath like lava on our heads. . . .

PETER TELLS

"Why are there lights in all the rooms
and none of you asleep?"
"Peter has news to tell." "What news
so hot it cannot keep?"

"Take off your riding-boots, my dear,
and then come sit by me . . .
Now, Peter, let your master hear
the tale you told at tea!"

This morning, on my Sunday walk,
I passed along the Bay
and noticed much of busy talk
from which I kept away.

One whisperer went from crowd to crowd,
except where whites were by;
and when he came to where I stood
he looked me in the eye.

"You see that vessel, over there—
the one marked THIRTY-SIX?"
Then, leaning close against my ear,
he murmured: "All is fixed."

"What fixed?" I echoed. "Don't you know?
Haven't you heard the call?
The trumpet is about to blow—
next month our masters fall.

"Next month our limbs shake off the yoke—
come with us and be armed!"
"You wag an evil tongue," I spoke,
"to wish my master harmed."

I ran home quickly as I could,
and told my mistress all.
The devil strike that rascal dead
for wishing you to fall! . . .

"My dear, you're whiter than a ghost.
Here, take a bit of snuff!
Shall we allow a freedman's boast,
a word, to kill us off?"

"It is no boast—no idle word.
The state must hear this news.
Tomorrow, Peter, a reward—
my coat! no time to lose!"

IN THE WOODS

Vesey not here? *Not yet.*
He never was late before.
What message did you get?
The place and the time. No more.
Do you know what it's about?
Something about our Ned:
they say he's been found out.
Oh no! what dog betrayed?
They say a slaver's pet.
Such warning Vesey gave:
"Beware a bayonet
less than a petted slave!"
What now? *They'll make Ned speak.*
He'll blurt out Vesey's name.
If Vesey's wise he'll seek
in safer woods for game.
Maybe that's what he's done.
Maybe that's why he's late.
Better flee and live on
than stay, and die, and be great!
—Someone comes. *Who is he?*
Whose eye lights up the path?
It's Vesey. Denmark Vesey!
It is our Angel of Wrath.

BEFORE JULY!

Excuse me, brothers, for being late.
Patrolers blocked the city gate:
sniffing like hounds at every black
who tried to get out of Charleston or in.
If I had nothing to show but my skin
they'd have mocked me, too, and turned me back.

But I brought this box to hand the fools:
my good old box of carpenter's tools,
and a well-nailed fable to go with it:
you can thank a slaver's make-believe chair
for wheeling me through. . . . Oh brothers, take care!
The hounds are awake! the bonfires are lit!

The hounds are awake, that slept so sound;
they stretch their legs, and sniff at the ground. . . .
Believe me: if once they catch our scent
no fleetness of foot will be fleet enough—
the sharpest pike will not hold them off;
our moans will be their merriment.

Before the lips of the slaver part—
before he commands the hunt to start—
before the full-grown moon of July
gives us away—oh brothers, rise!
take hounds and hunters by surprise!
tear out their fangs, and let them die!

NED'S SILENCE

"'More time! more time!' You've *had* three days
and not a single name!
The days are running out for us
while you keep up your game.

"Last evening, and the night before,
you thought him weak enough."
—I've dealt with many stubborn men,
but never one so tough:

57

three hours we whipped him; but he bit
his lip, and made no sound.
We burnt his fingers till he writhed
in torment on the ground.

We held a lantern to his eyes;
we kicked him out of sleep;
we told him that his son would die,
and still he did not weep.

Now he sits hungry in the Hole,
with rats to call him brave—
soon he will pray, and soon he'll beg
like any other slave.

"Offer him liberty and gold
to give the plot away!
Don't let him die—we need the names!
I'll wait just one more day."

He sobbed this morning in his sleep. . . .
"An optimistic sign!"
I thank you for your confidence;
—tomorrow he'll be mine.

GOODBYE

There was a bend in the river
where weeping willows grew,
where the waves at night spoke softly,
and a wind from Africa blew
that only lovers knew.

"Why do you bring me, Denmark,
to our most holy place?
And why are my words, my kisses
not nimble enough to chase
the hardness from your face?

"This willow was my bridesmaid,
her shade our bridal bed;
the moon was our guest of honor
carousing overhead;
the waves declared us wed."

"Let these bear witness, darling,
these friends that know us well!
No matter how high the price is,
they'll not be coaxed to sell
the secret thing I tell:

"I lead a desperate legion
with doomsday in its hand.
Before the next moon blossoms
we who are branded will brand
this rotten-hearted land.

"Wait every night in the shadow,
as long as you can or care—
if I come at last to claim you
I'll bring you a crown to wear:
a crown fit for your hair.

"But if the next moon withers
without once showing my face
—go home; and when you hunger
for someone to embrace,
let Vengeance take my place. . . ."

There was a bend in the river
where weeping willows grew,
where the waves at night spoke softly,
and a wind from Africa blew
that only lovers knew.

THE NAME'S OUT

Upon the fourth night of his agony—
while Ned's tormentors hovered in amazement
over the last faint embers of his life—
they suddenly imagined that his lips
stirred for a moment.
                              "Stop the fire and ice!
He wants to speak."

                              Then, shutting all the windows
to keep away the noises of the night,
they put an ear close to his lips, and listened
until a sound crawled forth: his leader's name. . . .

That night the home of Vesey was surrounded
by a great noose of eyes—tighter and tighter—
while Vesey and his brothers, unaware,
worked busily inside.
                        A knock.
                              "Who is it?
Who beats so late against my door with fists?"
"OPEN!!"
                        "Oh brothers, I have feared such visit.
Smile and be silent while I burn the lists."

                    ❖   ❖   ❖

A guard stumbled into the State Troopers' House:
his helmet bashed in, and his tongue of no use.
They laid him out gently, and brought a wet cloth
to wash off the blood from his forehead and mouth.

"Who fixed you so prettily, lad?" asked the chief.
"Three killed . . . and two captured . . . I ran for my life . . .
they leaped from the shadow . . . by sixes, by twelves . . .
they howled for our blood with the hunger of wolves. . . .

"In one hand a gun, in the other a pike . . .
a hymn on their lips . . . as they rose up and struck. . . ."
"Who were they? who fixed you so prettily, lad?"
"The legions . . . of Vesey . . ." he murmured, and died.

❖ ❖ ❖

"Now listen to me," said the chief to the judge.
"You've acted your part like a star on the stage.
You've nodded politely, your smile has been fair.
Now take a low bow, and retire for the year!"

"I can't understand," said the judge to the chief.
"They said to go slowly—you told me yourself—
you hoped with more time to win over the list;
what names will you capture when Vesey's a ghost?"

"We hoped, yes, we hoped—but how foolish it was!
As foolish as hoping to hush him with laws. . . .
We ordered a river to turn into ice!
We ordered a rock to surrender its voice!

"We hoped, yes, we hoped—and we wasted our time:
from Vesey's own lips not a murmur will come.
His rifles—*they* speak to us—each has a tongue.
They call out the names and the list will be long."

The chief to the judge said, "Now listen to me:
I want Vesey hanged so a blind man can see.
Prepare the last speeches, and let them be brief!"
"I see what you mean," said the judge to the chief.

THE SENTENCE IS ANNOUNCED

The word of doom went through their bars
to spend the night beside them.
"My friends, if tears are in our eyes
we have no need to hide them.

"The warden's footstep fades away:
he cannot see us crying.
Alone we sit, with much to say
of living and of dying.

"As for myself, I call it mean
to hang in such bright weather;

61

but there are meaner ways to swing
than six true friends together.

"What does it matter if we be
remembered or forgotten . . .?
Ten thousand guns of liberty
we leave beneath the cotton.

"Ten thousand guns will sing our mass
when we no more can hear it—
and those who dread us in the flesh
may dread us more in spirit."

The word of doom went through their bars
to spend the night among them.
Get out, bleak word—you are not theirs!
Go haunt the ones who hang them!

THE WORD OF DOOM

Your banners, they dance so brightly!
Your bugles, they sound so pleased!
Has something happened to save you?
Was it The Wrath you seized?

Was it The Wrath of a People
you pushed at the point of a gun—
and sealed it up in a prison—
and doomed it to die with the sun?

If this is the prize you've taken,
make sure that the bars hold strong:
The Wrath of a People is restless,
it won't stay locked for long.

If this is the prize you've taken,
don't stop to celebrate!
Prepare great nooses and gallows
for The Wrath of a People is great.

But if the prize you've taken
is one man, only one,
watch out for The Wrath of a People:
it will come to claim its son.

THE HANGING

Many a lofty scaffold-work the carpenters had built,
but none in Charleston great enough for Denmark Vesey's guilt.

The city sent surveyors out, and finally they found
a hillock on the Lines that would be seen for miles around.

Here twenty men were set to work, the best that could be hired,
with twenty more to take their place as soon as they had tired.

They felled and trimmed gigantic trees to make the scaffold-frame;
they used great nails to keep it safe from any winds that came.

So loud a hammering at night! the children woke in wonder,
and mothers taught them that they heard no ordinary thunder.

At last the job was finished, and the carpenters were proud—
what scaffold ever had been high enough to hang a cloud?

The word flew everywhere, that on the second of July
whoever cared could come and see old Denmark Vesey die.

The crowd stood still when Vesey and his friends were marched
                outside—
then, somewhere, while the prayer was read, a Negro woman cried.

And when six silent upraised heads were circled by the noose,
through rows of mounted guards the people suddenly tore loose.

And when the sun made bright the eyes in Denmark Vesey's head,
the slavers could not easily believe that he was dead.

And when the sun was almost gone, the shadows of the dead
became so long, so dark and long, the slavers ran to bed.

And when the moon herself was hanged while rolling down the
     night,
the slavers locked their windows, and the doors they bolted tight.

And when through shutters they observed the silences in groups,
they sent a rider galloping to Washington for troops.

THE HAMMER AND THE LIGHT

Sometimes I've been too mournful
to fall asleep at night—
so tired and so mournful,
I couldn't sleep half the night—
then I'd sit by the window
and look out at Vesey's light.

His light was like a fire
getting ready to wake the town;
a sudden midnight fire
for the rotten streets of this town—
and my heart beat loud and angry
each time his hammer came down.

Last night I sat by the window,
patient as the stars in the sky—
I looked and I listened at the window
till the last star was gone from the sky.
This morning my sonny asked me:
"What happened to make you cry?

"You never would cry when they beat you,
though the whip cut through to the bone.
You just bit your lip when they beat you,
when you lay there, cut to the bone."
"I'm crying for a hammer that's quiet;
crying for a light that's gone.

"Without that light before me,
I can't seem to lift my feet.
Without that bright light before me,
the chains are back on my feet.

And without that angry hammer,
well, my heart doesn't want to beat."

My son said, "Buy me a hammer;
I'll beat all day and all night.
I'll make it the angriest hammer
that ever was heard in the night."
My son said, "Buy me a lantern—
I'll take good care of its light."

THE END

The Bell and the Light

based on incidents in Botkin's *Lay My Burden Down*

1

When a newborn baby begins to cry
his mother should sing him a lullaby;
but the words of my song are bitter and wild—
they would not bring sleep to you, my child.

Sorrow in the sky, sorrow on the ground,
sorrow in the jaws of the howling hound.
Oh I wonder if you'll ever be safe and sound. . . .

When a newborn baby begins to weep
his mother should rock him till he falls asleep;
but my arms belong to a cotton crop—
if I dared to rock you, the cotton would drop.

Sorrow in the sun, sorrow in the shade,
sorrow in the faces that slowly fade.
Oh I wonder if you'll ever be unafraid. . . .

65

When a newborn baby moans without rest
his mother should give him to suck of her breast—
here's bile, not milk; but drink if you can:
it will turn you into an angry man.

Sorrow on the wind, sorrow in the tide,
sorrow like a harvest on every side.
Oh I wonder if you ever will be my pride. . . .

2

Here and now, with my friends nearby,
there's something I want to promise my son.
You angels, listening in the sky,
copy my words down one by one.

I wish I could promise to keep him from harm,
to burn every whip in the world for his sake,
to hold back the fiery brand from his arm—
but this is no promise a slave can make. . . .

What shall I offer my son against storm?
Against back-break, heart-ache, what pledge can I take?
—He shall hear about Africa, and be warm;
about Africa—and his keepers shall quake!

Whenever he watches a free bird fly,
whenever he sees a wild brook run,
their song will ring out like a battle-cry,
a battle-cry to the ears of my son.

From this day till the day I die,
my work for the master will never be done.
From morning to night let his cotton pile high,
from night to morning his shroud will be spun.

Here and now
I make this vow.

3

As soon as my babies
became a year old
they were torn out of my arms
and sold.

Of six
only the last is free:
one night I gave her
to the root of a tree.

I used to ask
my missing five:
do you thank me or blame me
because you're alive?

Sons—do you have
your father's fist?
Daughters—
are you sometimes kissed?

Do you wonder
of every old woman you meet:
"Is it *her* milk I half-remember,
so sweet . . .?"

As I wonder
of every grown girl and lad:
"Is this
one of the five I had?"

You who sell babies
because they were born black:
hear how a mother
pays you back!

For each one sold
a hundred more
motherless children
come to my door.

My breasts are dry,
but they drink from my veins
a hatred that makes them
tug at their chains.

Be ready, be ready!
When your shutters fly off
my children will ask:
WERE YOU PAID ENOUGH?

4

There's a boat at the banks of Jordan
with its face toward freedom's shore.
Night after night it waits for the arm
that will lift its mighty oar.

> Is yours the arm? Is yours the arm?
> Are you ready to take the pledge?
> Is yours the arm? Is yours the arm?
> Will you be at the river's edge?

When the moon turns its back tomorrow
you can sail away from Hell;
sail till you see a far-away light,
till you hear a far-off bell.

They'll be waiting to bid you welcome,
they'll be there to show the way:
sweet as a bird the bell will chime—
and the light will glow like day.

There's a boat at the banks of Jordan
with its face toward freedom's shore.
Night after night it waits for the arm
that will lift its mighty oar.

5

Tell me something about that land!
    What would you like to hear?
Tell me something about that land!
    I said, what would you like to hear?
Will my sons have honey and milk there?
Will my daughters go dressed in silk there?
Will the Lord hold out his hand
when they appear?

Tell me something about that field!
    What would you like to know?
Tell me something about that field!
    I said, what would you like to know?
Will my sisters rest in the shade there?
Will my brothers be unafraid there?
Will the bruises all be healed
that hurt them so?

Tell me something about that shore!
    What would you like to learn?
Tell me something about that shore!
    I said, what would you like to learn?
Will I stand at the judgment seat there?
Will I wear no chains on my feet there?
Will I live forevermore
and never mourn?

6

I'm beginning to wonder, Lord, and
I'm praying that you'll let me know:
how wide is this river of Jordan?
how far do I have to go?

Oh I'm sick of the darkness, Lord, and
I'm longing for a glow of light.
How wide is this river of Jordan?
am I going wrong or right?

Oh I'm sick of the silence, Lord, and
I'm longing for a bell to chime.
How wide is this river of Jordan?
will I reach the shore some time?

7

My heart announced it to the hills,
and the hills passed it on to the breeze,
and the breeze went crying to my brothers:
will you rise up from your knees!

Will you rise up from your knees,
and roll the forbidden drums—
for your time in Egypt is over,
and the hour of judgment comes!

Blues for Emmett Till

I've got the blues, friend—
don't know how to keep still;
the Mississippi blues, friend,
won't let me keep still.
One name is moaned by every wind:
the name of Emmett Till.

Been hearing a blue story—
that's why I feel blue;
Emmett Till's story
makes me feel so blue,
can't breathe another day, friend,
'less I pass it on to you.

He went down South for the summer:
Chicago's a boiling slum.
Flew down like a bird for the summer,
but he should've stayed in the slum—
the South's no place for a Negro
to buy a stick of gum.

Foolish little bird!
His feathers were all brown . . .
They should've warned that bird,
if you happen to be brown
better not chirp
when Mrs. Bryant's around.

Poor young Emmett Till!
He will never get his wish.
I'm sorry for Emmett Till—
it was such a little wish . . .
He went down to the Tallahatchie,
but he didn't go down to fish.

Seems like in Mississippi
murder's doing all right;
in Money, Mississippi,
to kill a young bird's all right
if the young bird is brown
and the killer's white.

Jury knows who killed him—
knows the place and the time,
Jury knows just who killed him,
that terrible midnight-time.
But his face was crushed so bad,
it couldn't be called a crime.

Next time you pass a courthouse,
look at the marble word.
Slow down when you pass a courthouse
and laugh about that word—
laugh about "Justice," friend,
and cry for a young brown bird . . .

I've got the blues, friend—
don't know how to keep still;
the Mississippi blues, friend,
won't let me keep still.
One name is moaned by every wind:
the name of Emmett Till.

Blues for Medgar Evers

who died of an ambusher's bullets on the way to
a hospital

I should have been there when darkness
came around your neck like a noose;
—not night, but that other darkness
choking, tight as a noose,
till even you couldn't stand it
and you whispered "Turn me loose!"

I should have begged them to go faster,
but what would have been the use?
They drove till they couldn't drive faster,
but it wasn't any use.
Turning the corners of Jackson
is not the same as turning you loose.

We'd better watch out for triggers.
We'd better pray hard for a truce.
The hand that turned that trigger
turned more than a bullet loose.
My hand should have been on your forehead
when you whispered "Turn me loose!"

Calvary: Philadelphia, Mississippi

Last night I gazed on Jesus
pinned fast atop a hill:
the moonlight froze upon his brow;
his singing lips were still.

And though I knew his silence
was more than man could break,
I asked him questions seldom asked
by dreamers when they wake:

"Why could you not stay happy
with hammer and with nail—
die old and fat, beside a wife,
instead of lone and frail?

"Was there a need, my brother,
to prophesy so loud:
to wake a hope among the poor
and terrify the proud?

"Was there a need, my brother,
to tell the mailed police
how touched with beauty are their feet
who preach the word of peace?

"Was there a need, my brother,
to die so young, so thin,
with vinegar upon your tongue
and iron through your shin?

"And must you rise tomorrow?
And must you die again
upon some other hill and cross
reviled by other men?"

Last night I gazed on Jesus
pinned fast atop a hill:
the moonlight froze upon his brow;
his singing lips were still.

St. Nicholas Avenue Blues

Quiet along St. Nicholas—
nobody out in the rain;
quiet as sleep along St. Nicholas—
only the bus and the rain;
and the drops beat down on the windows
like a melancholy refrain.

St. Nicholas, this morning
you're quieter than you know.
Maybe you'd moan this morning
if only you knew what I know:
way up on A Hundred Forty First Street
the man who loved you lies low.

I've been in plenty of busses,
gone north on plenty of trips—
but never, in all those busses,
but never, on all those trips,
did I go to look at a singer
who couldn't get open his lips.

No harm will come to Langston—
his songs are all safe on the shelf.
When we come away from Langston
we can lift his songs from the shelf.
If anybody asks why I'm crying,
I suppose it's mostly for myself.

Quiet along St. Nicholas—
nobody singing the blues.
You're oh so quiet, poor St. Nicholas!
Now who's gonna sing your blues?
There was one man who knew how to sing it,
and his name was Langston Hughes.

Judgment

FOR ELINOR BUMPERS

Shooting her dead, the woman (old, poor, black),
although regrettable—the Judge decreed—
was lawful, being for a buddy's sake
(officers both young, white). So he was freed.
At once roared forth, head high, a thousand crack
motor-troops, he, proud deathsman, in the lead,

leaving arms wide, mouths wider, in their wake:
"Sweet God, if man stays silent, intercede!"

Silent we stayed, under deep layers of quilt;
but certain hundreds, late from play or work,
beheld above Connecticut, New York,
New Jersey, red as a life unrightly spilt,
some eerie object scream across the dark.
—Was it a meteor? a spaceship built
on Mars? or you, God, still incensed by guilt?

PART 5
Friends and Family

Mother

My mother's face is a weary child's
with a frame of loose black hair.
Her forehead loses half its lines
as she falls asleep in a chair.

The book has nestled into her lap
and her hands are resting, too.
Her hands are strained, and pink, and chapped,
and her feet are lined with blue.

The walls are scrubbed as clean as the sky,
and the shelves are sparkling gold;
the carpets and curtains are fresh and bright
although they are getting old.

My mother's face is a weary child's
and her hands are resting, it seems;
but the years she lost for her children's lives
have given her sinews and dreams.

The Rockabye Love

Rockabye love on the fire-escape;
each of your eyes is a shiny blue lake;
each of your breasts is a billow of cream;
softly now sing me a boat for my dream.

Let me hear nightingales all the night through;
see how the trees build a web on the blue;
let me go rocking from star to wild star
up to the lands where the elf-people are.

Rockabye love on the fire-escape;
tell me the tenement ogres are fake;
tell me the screech of an automobile,
the wail of a beggar, is never so real

as one little sunbeam, one little dove:
rockabye, rockabye, rockabye love.

Serenade No. 1

Home to your eyes
where moons arise
across the night I ride;
home to your breast
where storms would rest
I come, my magic bride,

my bride, my bloom
because of whom
the street lamps burn so well,
each factory-spire
is set afire
and seems a citadel.

Serenade No. 2

Though one and one make more than one,
sometimes they don't make two.
A strange new being was begun
my being one with you.

For winning you, I lost some thing
and won some thing you lost.
(It was a rapturous bargaining,
and worth whatever cost!)

We're more than one, now, each of us—
but two we'll never be,
though waters broad and perilous
dismember you from me.

Prothalamium

Come, all you who are not satisfied
as ruler in a lone, wallpapered room
full of mute birds, and flowers that falsely bloom,
and closets choked with dreams that long ago died!

Come, let us sweep the old streets—like a bride:
sweep out dead leaves with a relentless broom;
prepare for Spring, as though he were our groom
for whose light footstep eagerly we bide.

We'll sweep out shadows, where the rats long fed;
sweep out our shame—and in its place we'll make
a bower for love, a splendid marriage-bed
fragrant with flowers aquiver for the Spring.
And when he comes, our murdered dreams shall wake;
and when he comes, all the mute birds shall sing.

Winter Song

Under a willow
close by a brook
her lap for a pillow
her eyes for a book

she like a drummer
practiced her art
all spring and all summer—
the drum was my heart.

Hear how the willow sighs to the sun:
It is over and done with, over and done!
Hear the cold brook, that can hardly run:
It is over and done with, over and done!

Under what maple
close by what lake
will she lie next April?
Whose heart will she break?

Dogs

Looking foolish next to the tree in a one o'clock rain:
umbrella aloft, the leash in my other hand—
I wanted my late-coming neighbor to understand
that dogs are worth the expense, inconvenience, and pain;

their tails are truthful, no coiled rebellion beneath
a loving look; they are quick to kiss you, and quick
to fetch for you, and—should you raise a stick
threateningly—they are quick to show their teeth;

and better still (but this I never revealed),
when you bring downfall home, the death of a hope,
their nonchalant manner does more for you than a drink;
and best of all, when triumph's to be unsealed,
such lack of respect they show for the envelope,
—your fingers halt, the brain cools, and you think.

Uncles, No. 1

"Uncle Seymour," our father would frown,
"has the heart of a child and the looks of a clown:
bright straw hat with ribbon and feather,
a tie that guffaws, and howling shoe leather. . . ."

"Uncle Seymour!" our mother'd remark;
"to him the world's a Steeplechase Park:
stuffs his belly with hot dogs and cola,
while his brain rolls around like an empty victrola . . ."

When Uncle Seymour at Halloween
teased us with apples that danced on a string,
we forgot his indifference to politics and art,
the delinquent anapests of his heart.

When Uncle Seymour sent us reeling
round and around till we scraped the ceiling,
we forgave his naughty mustache and tie,
the off and on of his neon eye.

But even Uncle Seymour became thirty-one,
with a nine-year-old daughter, a two-year-old son;
even Uncle Seymour learned his lesson:
lost his job in the Great Depression.

Even Uncle Seymour sold his car;
had to think twice about buying a cigar;
and this was the reason (as few men know
in this kingdom by the sea) for his overthrow.

O Uncle Seymour, no longer twenty-nine:
in the Sunday sun, did your shoe leather shine?
Was your hair slick-parted, mustache slick-curled,
as you stepped outside to steeplechase the world?

O Uncle Seymour, was your heart the same—
young and jazzy—up to that seventh game?
Were the neighborhood fellows forced to admire
the way you could still set the handball afire?

O Uncle Seymour, when you trounced your foes
did you do it for them, or yourself, or Aunt Rose?
And when you sank back, green in the face,
did you suffer a heart attack, or disgrace?

"Uncle Seymour!" our folks would whisper,
to keep the facts from me and my sister:
"A doctor? On Sunday? Who'd take a chance
without a penny paid in advance . . .?"

For My Grandmother

who died on the road to Grodno in the winter of 1927

1. HEAVY WITH GHOST

Although it is of my grandmother
I tell, it is not at her prompting:
all her life she was silent, and her
lips till doomsday will be shut. Something
urges me, after nine and forty
years of carrying, to deliver
that soundless woman who brought forth
my mother, and so be quits with her.

2. THE DEATH OF A GRANDMOTHER

A child of six, amid his sunlit pals,
cawing, clawing, nevertheless can view
with half an eye the carrier man who crawls
from house to house up Williams Avenue.
One corner of his brain knows just about
what stoop the mail has reached; although the shriek
thrills no one else, his heart thrums at the note:
it is she, she who never has shown herself weak,
who has not so much as sobbed, till now. He drops
his sunray quietly, leaps the long street,
soars upstairs, at his own landing stops,
hears the mysterious voice of his aunt repeat
Hush, Mary, hush . . . , is discovered hunched at the door,
and is told to go play. There'll be many a Friday before
he figures out why Mother lights candles no more.

3. GHOST IN A SLAVIC LAND

By day the hunt for a room, a service station,
a Roman ruin, a cafe;
at night, on a road broken as these, in a kerchief
limp as these, surrounded
by such a rural deafness, dragged

84

in such a dying cart by such a beast
of skin and bone whipped on by such a scowling
husband—my grandmother, wracked with guilt
for her expensive fever, and with shame
for not having fixed the old man's supper,
and with aching for her children across the Atlantic,
and with the cough which, after a lifelong silence,
she allowed herself, since no one, not even
the doctor, was destined to hear it.

4. SOUVENIR

(In October 1942 the partisan poet Avrom Sutzkever,
returning to the Vilna ghetto, found no trace of his
mother but a shred of her dress)

At least he held the echo of her voice;
at least he found a bullet-riddled dress.
All that I have are glimpses of a face
in Hartford, on Aunt Rose's mantelpiece:

hair thinning, graying, eyes without a laugh;
—*that* day, at least, the horse had time enough
to get to Grodno . . . a good photograph . . .
the only one she posed for in her life.

The one I have a copy of is not
that fine: my grandfather, in peasant hat,
bearded, bespectacled, a heavy coat,
hands clasped, high-booted, on her burial plot,

prayer book under the arm, a pensive gaze,
proof to his furious children overseas
that here he comes, even on blustery days,
and sobs to her unblemished soul, and prays.

Oh yes . . . I have, on a cassette somewhere,
my mother's eighty-year-old wisps of her:
lugging great pails (the river wasn't near) . . .
feasts made of cabbage, chicken wings, and prayer.

I call my grandchild "Sweet Face," kiss her brow,
but never have considered why till now.
Had my grandmother reached me, this is how
I think she would have kissed me; and, although
my face was not sweet, she'd have called me so.

Homecoming

Having both daughters at home does not give me
a very merry Christmas. Tall in the hall
they brush past mythic photos of their small
selves in camping days. Though they do love me
(in some new way now), it would ill behoove me
to fold them in my arms: satirical
silences from their scholarly eyes would fall.
Even their songbursts, their fits of laughter, grieve me.

Outside my window through the wide sky swarm
clouds that seem to know more than they are saying.
No comfort this night, when hailstones lash, to hear
both daughters breathing safely: what of the storm
next week? what of the storm next month? next year?
how will they be dressed? where will they be staying?

Ghosts

1.

Because they are sponsorless and shy,
five years—even ten—go by
before some of my ghosts receive
mysterious privilege: reprieve.

2.

Aunts who enfolded me, baked for me, played with my name,
uncles who lifted me, questioned me, gave me pennies:

once I knew the smell and touch of your foyers;
once you starred in my dreams and expectations;
now, with an ache that awakes me, I greet your gliding
entrance, aunt with hairy mole on the chin,
uncle with flashy tie, upcurled moustache.

3.

Sometimes in the deep of night
I find myself in the bathroom
clutching my forehead.
But I don't need a pill.
It's not my blood pressure.
It's the bloodless pressure
of too many ghosts.
They seem to empty through my bladder.
After that I can sleep.
What will be in a year or two
I am afraid to think.
Maybe one night my skull will burst outright,
or become so loaded
I'll begin to double forward when I walk
like my old neighbors
on their way to the benches.
If I, with only fifty years of phantoms,
must fight to hold my head up,
imagine them at seventy-five!
In hours of bench-talk, I suppose,
a few ghosts float through their lips
out into the air.
This lightens them a little.
They manage to crawl home to dinner.

4.

It is not so much
because I have you at my mercy,
because you counted on me
and I let you down;
it is because
even the most respected ghosts

huddle like beasts in a stall
or slaves in the hold of a ship
unable even to beg for air;
and I see myself soon enough
among you
awaiting my moment
in the dream of a middle-aged daughter.

Quebec

By now it is really late.
Our backs face one another.
My left hand finds her right
for the gentle mutual pressure.

Suddenly I recall
that the bed in which we are lying
is a few minutes' walk from the wall
through which Montcalm came dying.

And only a few miles off
a landscape seemingly peaceful
still writhes at the drum and fife
proclaiming Wolfe successful.

On streets entranced by their truce,
whose dream we so admire,
there could be no excuse
to break our own cease-fire.

For my sake she denied
several bright windows;
for hers, I disobeyed
several gray windings.

Yet, like two locked foes,
we fought our fight as always:
poetry versus prose,
on hilltops, in hallways.

Twice on the battle-line
there came to me a question:
will I ever be back alone
to wrap myself in this bastion?

But between the pressure of hand
in hand and the fall into dreaming,
I am answered; I understand;
nothing will come of my scheming.

No, I will never be back
alone on the St. Lawrence
to wring from the stones of Quebec
whatever may be their substance.

In through the siege-proof wall
my death would seep to find me;
unto my death all
these ancient windings would wind me.

On my Plains of Abraham,
whether in room or alley,
like my brothers Wolfe and Montcalm
I would fell and be felled in the volley.

She sleeps. No need to tell
why I press her hand as tightly
as were she the Citadel
that guards this city nightly.

Granddaughter on Beach

1.

That apricot protuberance of belly and buttock
against the gnash of breaker, the blanch of shell,
is less nutritious than seditious—like those tomatoes
in Hitler Paris hurling the Internationale from Picasso's sill.

2.

The sea's big guns begin; its offensive reaches her toes;
I scoop her up; we escape over Maginot shellbits lining the sand
as, foetal-safe, under my arm she curls, and through three layers of
    clothes
fixes her gulf-cold imprint as surely as a great rancher's brand.

Words

Having said too much, they now say nothing.
It is a marvel that the living room walls
are smooth, the pictures all hang straight,
the lights work. At least one slingshot,
had her brow not stopped it, surely would
have gone through the window; and if not
for his receiving groin, a tomahawk
must have split the Steinway in two.

Having said too much, they now say nothing.
Corbies should be circling the chan-
delier: peering down, counting.
It is quiet as a field of battle
after loud carnage: the last two arrows
have found each other's eye; a red
gurgling from gullet, chest, and thigh
has won the interest of vermin.

Having said too much, they now say nothing.
Withdrawn behind magazines, they quiver
with words inflicted and taken, as if
destined to resonate until
the head on the coffee table opens
its lips, or the cactus prophesies,
or the oil burner—whose stable voice
they never craved before—goes on.

Thanksgiving Day

He was unready to get out of bed,
let alone give thanks.
Yesterday
the cup had jumped
out of his hand,
and he'd dumped
a lump of margarine
instead of its wrapper
into the garbage.
Yesterday his joints had ached,
and his back,
though not dramatically enough
to mention at breakfast.
Yesterday's sun had set
like one's life, slowly,
behind the vulnerable trees
that resembled his friends.

It was only when he remembered them
that thanks rose
poisoningly
into his skull.
He was thankful
not to be Florence
whose cancer (probably) was caught in time;
Jack, who would never again
meet Lily at museum doors;
Fred, pacing the deathways of San Francisco
for a glimpse of his daughter;
Victor, ebbing without witnesses
in a germproof room;
Harriet, head awry,
as if snapped by the paw
of a dinosaur, triumphant
over nothing but her scream.

Now, Before Shaving

The blanket loosens.
But if she comes in, I'll pretend to be sleeping.
I'd rather not make orange juice,
slice fruit into cereal,
seek out the darkest suit
and argue which tie goes best with it.
I'd rather not promise to fetch home as trophies
a hospital's name,
its autopsy chart.
I'd rather not have the mortuary pinpointed on a street map,
my scene with the widow coached.
I'd rather not hear from a metal box it will be sunny all day.

To have fallen asleep without five minutes of mourning!
Now, before shaving, I want to see us
at college, the cafeteria group;
our Washington reunion, the Mellon Gallery concert;
home from war, still in uniform at that crazy party;
weddings, housewarmings;
New Year's Eves in the finished basement,
his improvised deadpan dance, lifting a partner in air;
The Merchant of Venice at Stratford,
disputing Carnovsky in Shylock's dressing room
over Shakespeare's intentions,
driving home the excitement, keeping it up till four,
spilling it over through brunch the next day;
our first quarrel: Israel, the Arabs;
a misfired phone call, declined invitations,
rumors of a musician son, an architect daughter,
his name in the paper once,
an unmailed note.

Now, before shaving, is the time to feel.
Three friends buried in three months' time
and a feel not of heartache so much as cold feet.
The blanket's come loose, I lie at the edge of a sea,
the tide covers my toes, my ankles.

She comes in, fixes the blanket,
but there is no time.
A drowned face waits at the mirror.

Matilda

Behind, in rows, her cousins sat,
her husband, sons, a brother,
with dozens more whose murmured chat
and clustered nod gave notice that
each mourner knew the other.

All hushed, however, when I stood
before her at the coffin,
as if my gaze might change her mood—
so deep estranged—might wake the blood
and make the features soften.

And so I watched a painful while
her lips, but never made them
so much as simulate a smile.
Back through her kin I crawled. The aisle
was long. I had betrayed them.

Phone Call

Dry, remote
as the Long Island leaf
my granddaughter
this morning set afloat
from shallow water
toward the open seas,
I phone
Los Angeles
where, more than half my life,

Mother's
been heaped with singing
friends unknown
to me. It's ringing.
We rejoice
at the good health in one another's
voice.
What more? Talked out?
No; she reminds herself
to ask about
that sparkling elf
and thank me for the photograph
(it sits already on her shelf).
Then I report with what a victory laugh
the infant watched her leaf become a boat.
At this, across three thousand miles of wire, across
eighty-one years, without
the loss
of half a decibel, half
a hemidemisemiquaver note,
the absolutely identical laughter of my mother
leaps
at one parched hand,
while the other
frantically grips
the morning outcry of my grand-
daughter, who, amid heaps
of plastic friends
unknown to me, on a New Jersey pillow sleeps,
only a smile now nudging at those lips
as in a dream
she sends
her arboretum leaf once more downstream
toward the great ships.

On the Death of Someone Else's Grandchild

And so the phone call ended; there was time
for others on the list, but they could wait.
Coffee as well would have involved the crime
of opening one's mouth; best face the gate,
and when it opened, trudge inside the train
and through a sooty window watch the sky's
appropriate grayness drop appropriate rain
to reprimand the dryness of one's eyes.
This left an hour and a half or more
out of whose hush a requiem might be wrung
before one reached his depot, then his door,
with a bizarre contagion on the tongue.

Home

1. RECLAIMING THE CAR

Although the port we left was Death
and death's the cargo that we carry,
at least these strangers shared our path;
but now, seatbelts released, they hurry—

strangers again—to who knows where?
Our past was a metallic city,
our future's the metallic chair
I wheel her in, beyond the pity

of uncommitted fellowship
that cannot guess my wife has broken
more than an operable hip.
And the metallic doors slide open.

Without his well-wrought maps to scheme on,
without his well-earned burst of joy,
I track, unswervingly as Schliemann,
my Chevrolet, as he his Troy.

But, unlike him, I mark in wonder
my masterwork of curves and chrome
unhurt by Time, nor huddled under
three hard millennia of loam.

The cold lock fits; the colder cushion
fits too; but dare I hope to drive?
dares the cold key demand ignition?
Yes! It's alive! Yes! We're alive.

2. ENTERING THE HOUSE

Somehow I locate the switch, em-
barrassing in dishabille
what appears to be a kitchen
in the middle of a meal

and what seems (the space adjacent)
some sort of a living room
out of which its inmates hastened
one atrocious night or noon.

You could almost cut the panic
in these quarters with a knife,
yet the plants they left—botanic
marvels—still declare for life.

I feel close to them; I wonder:
did these persons get away,
or were they reduced to cinder
in the alleys of Pompeii?

3. ANSWERING THE PHONE

Hatted, coated,
door ajar,
bags half-toted
from the car . . .
"There you are!"
sneers the phone

prima-throated:
"Welcome home!"

My heart, creature of habit, can't help twisting;
but why? it isn't him—never again
will it be him, no, nor a chum suggesting
we'd better be on the next plane.

It's an acquaintance: "All week I've kept trying
to reach you." "Been in Florida." "Have fun?"
"Not much; my father-in-law was dying."
That ought to do her; but she isn't done,
this old acquaintance with her Ph.D.
"Florida's lovely in the fall," says she.

4. PREPARING FOR CLASS

Tomorrow's dance is now tomorrow's job.
The Shakespeare syllables no longer throb.
My hand, however, does more than its share
of throbbing, as the luggage grows aware.
After such miles, these poor eyedrop dispensers
deserve their shelf; but like two drunken dancers
they wobble from my fingers till one falls,
then both, flat as the Shakespeare syllable.

"Did you put in your drops?" He nodded yes.
One must ask something; how was I to guess
that question was the craziest one could ask
a person drowning in an oxygen mask—
our absolutely last communication
after fifty-two years of conversation—
drops!—as if he'd best renew those old
eyes for a new world shortly to unfold.

5. MAKING THE BED

Bedtime of the eleventh day.
At last I face the frozen disarray.
At last I face the phone-call ten days back

that made us wildly pack
and leave without a word our lawn,
our curtains wisely drawn
as if they knew it was a state of mind,
not a mere state we'd left behind.

Bedtime of the eleventh day.
Once more the hands command, the quilts obey.
Fresh-cased, the pillows know their place:
it's here we'll face each other's face,
and when, like an iambic line, the wind blows strong,
tonight we'll heed its song
and love that well which we must leave ere long.

PART 6
Elegies

Ernst Toller

Suicide May 1939

You should be wading through the ripening fields,
watching the moon-ploughed river from a hill.
You should be sucking in the swarming city
and turning every living thing to music;
splashing great sentences of truth across the world
like cool pouring rivers to lift the people's hope.

The door is opened, and everyone, dismayed,
steps back, like birds who come to drink at a fountain
and find the water stopped. You are dry and still
dangling alone in the paleness of a room
with dreams of a lost land frozen in your eyes.
We must make another fountain from ourselves.

Einstein

The falconer is gone to his great sleep.
Those eyes—those mighty huntsmen of the air—
shall quarry no more birds. He'll crown the steep
mountains of night no more with his bright hair.

The furrower is gone. I do not weep
because of harvests he shall never share:
much did those eyes, those mighty farmers, reap.
They furnished grain for many a village fair.

It is for my own sake, not his, I mourn;
my own sake, and the sake of all mankind.
While those eyes led the hunt, I was not blind;
while those eyes plowed, I had my wheat, my corn.
Shut are the nests, the silos of his mind;
the field laments, the falcon wheels forlorn.

The Consummation

Although to most the face of Death is grim,
he followed with the frenzy of a lover.
Frame no regrets: the hard pursuit is over—
she halts; she turns; she gives herself to him.

Rumshinsky's Hat

That gray hat moving slowly past our window
was not Rumshinsky's—and I should've known.
There'll be no sunlight on Rumshinsky's hat
today, and certainly it isn't moving;
unless a stranger picked it off the pavement
before they came and picked Rumshinsky up.

Our superintendent thinks it rather funny:
"Rumshinsky? You and I should be so lucky!
No work, no worry—stretched out like a king:
and, best of all, he don't remember nothing."
The wink, the laughter, tell me that my friend
knows very well which one of them is lucky.
In fact, he knows which wife is lucky, too—
shows off his sturdy hide to advertise it.

He claims, and others claim, the old man's mind
fell long before his body did. I wonder.
Some say they'd meet him at the oddest hours
wandering empty-eyed along the Drive;
or, on a Sunday morning, in the lobby:
mumbling at the directory, inspecting
his letterbox. They take such bits of moments
to mean the sun no longer set for him,
Sunday no longer was a special day,
no longer could he come to his own pillow
without the help of a directory.

All this may be, but when I'd meet Rumshinsky
along that Drive whose every budding tree
had bowed to him for thirty years—to me
it seemed the man himself was sunset, dragged
silently from the last blue hill of day.

Then, on a Sunday morning, in the lobby,
he'd walk like a slow ghost of his old self
following again and yet again
his spry invisible footsteps, to the nook
of tidings, to that sheen of letterboxes
where quite important news, addressed to him
in penmanship long past, had often come.

I never could be sure, when I would catch him
at the directory, whether it was
the name: RUMSHINSKY—lettered large as ever—
the old man studied, or the strange new names
above Rumshinsky, and below Rumshinsky,
all up and down the list, in place of those
who'd said: "Wie geht's?" and waited for his answer
in years when there were really things to answer.
For me he had one slogan: "Man muss gehen. . . ."
"How goes it?" "One must go."—It was his joke.

2-E is all at once a bleak dominion.
Where is its queen? Her one meek subject's gone.
Across Broadway he won his liberation
while she was cooking lentils; her old crown
splashed in the soup precisely at the moment
Rumshinsky's forehead and the sidewalk met.

There'll be a new name on the letterboxes
one of these days—in the directory, too—
and on the landlord's books a higher rent.
No violent change . . . I'm sure it won't be mentioned
in any tabloid, even the most local . . . ,
as minor as the falling of a leaf,
as silent as the setting of a sun.
—Why should I then be, why have I been haunted
for three days by Rumshinsky and his hat?

The Pigeons of Maspeth

FOR ARTHUR KEVESS

Behind me, past Manhattan, past Morphia Island,
the sun was dropping, without a struggle,
into the uncouth jaws of Hoboken and Weehawken.
Ahead of me Long Island held up a great gray banner
as well it might.

I was glad to be driving alone,
uncompelled to be civil, to blaspheme with small talk
the passing of Arthur.
Bad enough that my stomach leaned toward the coming meal,
that my nerves slashed back at the surge
of radio news and traffic.
I wanted to focus entirely on the wasted face and frame,
the forthright confession of envy that I could move freely
while he lay pinned to his fate, to his bones, to his bed,
with power only to raise his torso by pressing a button
and then in a restless rage to lower it.

Suddenly beyond the windshield
a fireworks blossom burst—and another, another—
till five recurrent clusters of sparkles
flung their statement against the gray.
Fireworks! What ghoul was on the prowl,
making a holiday of Arthur's passing?
But no. These were no fireworks. Five companies of pigeons,
reprieved from the roofs of Maspeth,
were doing their dance, their soundless song,
and at one certain instant during every gyration
the sunset wand transformed them
into five fireworks blossoms.

Perhaps they had flung themselves so
into other dusks, and would again—
perhaps each burst was of joy at being loose in the wind
or of panic at the sun their god's decline.
But not to me;

for all at once I was privileged
to be sitting again by the bed, a witness,
as Arthur, ever-gentle, and now altogether strengthless Arthur,
gathered unto himself—for one last act of defiance—
a power like Prometheus', pinned to his rock,
torn by the beaks of furies;
and I saw that every luminous turning of those wingèd things
was Arthur's spirit, unbroken in the broken body,
breaking loose from the ninth, the terminal floor:
clutching his forehead, complaining that I made him think,
then, for an hour, between seizures of agony and thirst,
punning, rhyming, explaining the nature of his condition,
responding to my "Well, dear friend, I must be getting on the
    highway,"
with a long handclasp, a wisp of grin,
and then, to help his children smile,
a "Both of us must go—you on the highway,
and I . . . soon . . . on the potty."

This was Arthur's final prose. The fireworks were his final poem.
Driving into dusk,
that day and from now on,
the pigeons of Maspeth stood and will stand for his spirit
turning its clean breast, its broad wingspan,
for yet one more reflection—or, better, one more contradiction—
of the sun that, without a struggle,
had almost dropped from sight.

Uncle

Something deserves to be said.
Yesterday morning he was alive,
by afternoon he was dead.
He *was* the last of five
to bid the Poland of our grandparents goodbye.
My features *do* resemble
his: broad nose, green eye.

His life
did crumble
year by year behind the crumbling store:
a deafmute son, a shrewish wife
against whom in each letter he would pour
his gall out, till she died
—then pined as if she'd been a three-hours bride.
He *was* an early reject from
the world of trade:
kenneled, grateful for whatever crumb
a daughter-in-law delivered to the shade
of his cold basement
where, coughing thanks, he froze and burned
by turns, and gradually learned
what having neither name nor face meant.

I believe
all this, repeat
all this, in order to begin to grieve.
Maybe by tomorrow tears will mingle with my meat.

Bella

They have weighed my suitcases, but I carry
something more into the plane.

Day after day, across two desks,
Bella faced me: entrenched
in her beauty, her politics, and her British accent.
Five years later the beauty was shot,
and with it her marriage
(though which was cause and which effect
I could never be sure).
Then out leaked the zeal
like fluid out of a battery.
What faced me, against its will, in the hospital
was a battered, unmanned shell,
not the flag-flying Bella of old
—nothing left but her doggedly East End speech.

She'd boarded her mangy trophies with our dentist,
who had room to spare in his basement,
and in his X-ray file the slowly rotting
history of her teeth.

At last the fact made ready: the coiled, patient fact.
Having learned I was in San Francisco,
it slithered to the party.
On an innocuous tray,
among anchovies and liver,
it let itself be carried straight across the room.

And until I have opened my mouth
in the dentist's office
wide, wider than he asks me to—
until I have set it free and cloven it,
half for him, half for me—
I shall stoop, though the blind admire my posture,
under the venomous pounds of Bella's suicide.

The Ides of March

(FOR ALLARD LOWENSTEIN)

She broke; she wept; three forecasts of the weather
paraded in one ear and out the other.
It outraged her that I should stop to care
how cold it was, which undershirt to wear.

I neither broke nor wept. The victim's picture—
not lugged off faceless on a flimsy stretcher,
but bright crusader eyes behind wide goggles—
filled me as in the first smiles of our struggles.

But emptied of his bullets, of his passions
a staring, nightmare visage—the assassin's—
entered me too. While on my tongue sat weather,

both faces, everlastingly together,
sat without ceremony in my brain:
my stare, my smile—the slayer and the slain.

Elegy for Muriel Rukeyser

1. MEETING HER TRAIN

He was afraid her train would be late,
afraid she would not be on it;
what he wasn't afraid of
was that
moving toward his upraised arms would be
not Hippolyta
with massive stride and head
but thin legs bayoneted,
thin hairs strafed.

Forgetting she is a touch poet,
he does not meet her mouth . . . mumbles instead
something about a toothache;
but her bag, deep armory of books, he takes.
Already they are touching,
though he is slow to feel it.
She, hesitant at the stairs,
talks of an eye operation
and thanks him for holding her elbow.
In fact, again and again,
as if he has touched her in places of craving,
she thanks him: for fetching coffee,
guiding her to the washroom,
cheering her battle plans.

But when she aims square in the face
that level voice: "What would you like?"
he recoils, as if from a touch,
and lies that he really wants for little . . .
compared to others, is doing much as he likes . . .
and turns from his scar tissue, from an interesting

shell that seems to have landed in his chest,
back to her battered walls, back to the list
of their mutual dead and dying:
a long, golden list
which they quietly keen.

2. TIDINGS

It had nothing to do with lack of breeding.
The barest lowering of his head.
Then he went on kneading, kneading.
The oven roared for bread.

Then dinner. Then required reading.
Then the Olympics—who was ahead?
Four years he'd waited for those speeding
demons of skate, ski, sled.

Day. The pangs of emptying, feeding.
A chill has boldly climbed into bed.
The radio woos him: warm, misleading.
Not now. Muriel's dead.

3. SHE MARCHES PAST

May placarded her eyes, bannered her hair;
the teeth in her smile sixteen abreast
from curb to curb; her fist
roaring into the Square
    FREE TOM MOONEY AND THE SCOTTSBORO BOYS

rank on rank
bloomed or haggard
straight or bent
they seized the city—
Dashiell Hammett, Lola Ridge, Arturo Giovannitti
    DOWN WITH THE BOOKBURNERS OF BERLIN
Alfred Kreymborg, Waldo Frank,
Langston Hughes, Genevieve Taggard,
Rockwell Kent

in the wake of the furriers ten thousand strong—
leftright   leftright
>HOLD THE FORT

behind them the dressmakers' fiery song
>REINFORCEMENTS NOW APPEARING
Maxwell Bodenheim, Scott Nearing,
Kenneth Fearing

leftright   leftright
never till nor ever since that day
such a mix
of age, voice, sex, race, politics—
the Robesons, Soyers,
Untermeyers
>COMING, COMING
John Dos Passos, Steve Benét,
Clifford Odets, Edna Millay,
Granville Hicks
>MANCHURIA   HOLD THE FORT
>ETHIOPIA   WE ARE COMING

and she, just grown herself,
smiled
at the wild
cheering of a child of twelve
who already knew
what her marching meant
>WORK   BREAD
who leant
forward, far forward, almost grew
feathers, almost flew
into her lyric tread,
dreamt
the Square would someday feel him too
fisting through. . . .

May will not meet the regiment
she led
this year
so early; no May crowd

will cheer;
May will not praise her lion head
under the shroud;
a surly cloud
placards her eyes—

and behind her they are coming, coming—
Robert Hayden, posture once so proud,
Melville Cane, at last struck witless with surprise,
Millen Brand,
who used to set the pace with his heart's drumming
—dead, four weeks, four poets dead—
nor will James Wright
wake this time to tell us of his dreaming;

once more leaning
forward, I already understand
the meaning
of the Square toward which they flow
left   right   left   right
five mouths, so variously bright,
to form so hushed a band—
no one on the sidewalks cheering
left   right
till they're out of hearing
out of sight—
forward, far forward leaning
        HOLD THE FORT, FOR
one inch further and I go

The Chair: Notes for an Elegy

(FOR MURIEL RUKEYSER)

1. Lugs himself—doubled over with deaths, including his own—
   upstairs.
2. Unfamiliar voice in kitchen refers to him: "What he wants most is
   a chair—a recliner, a rocker maybe."

3. What he wants most is to tear plug out of socket, smash radio—
   with its furniture-store cooing—against wall.
   "Chair!" Chair?? Sunset-time, autumn-time on porch?
   solitaire-time, crossword-time, jigsaw-time? the marching
   over?
4. 11:15—midway through news, recliner all the way back; has, in
   fact, for years been sitting nightly into and out of five-hour
   doze from hot coffee to hot blanket before a float of
   concocted situations, jigsaw bits from his own life in search
   of reconnection, newsbits interfloating with the rest, seams
   hardly showing.
5. Midway through news, flotilla of horrors. The city's, land's,
   planet's penniless once again shafted, empty-eyed, empty-
   bellied; the pocket-stuffed once again smirking, with good
   cause, their wheels of command whirring . . . And Muriel
   dead, and who now ablaze against horrors, to shrug off the
   specialists' warnings? who now to fly, heart ominously
   enlarged, fly scarcely needing a plane, to Vienna, Seoul, to
   stand daylong in rain at the gate, to side with the wife of the
   poet who festers windowless somewhere inside for the sake
   of the wings of his poems? Who? Not he, not for years now,
   despite no specialist's warning . . . And loneliness suddenly
   lowers the world's thermostat, seeps through his bathrobe
   wool. He ups the recliner, ferociously jolts himself upright.
6. O that day! expecting an earlier her on the platform, then
   buckled by her buckling legs; driving her into April, putting it
   green to her lips, then wondering as he left her alone with the
   rostrum (chair declined) how those half-shot eyes,
   varicosities, that frail frame, pulverized voice, would endure
   the hour . . . Book opened, glasses adjusted, then all at once
   full-tide! the smile, the cadence, flooding the hall beyond its
   far seats to where door-stragglers tested was she for them;
   book closed, glasses away, holding the rostrum, the clock,
   one hour more (chair not even considered), each answer a
   great, calm rose, surging forth from her soil—still twenty,
   holding the fort, still fisting at falsehood, affrighting the vile,
   still trampling despair, scattering silence; her eyes—after one
   operation, before another—still flooding the hall with sight;
   her heart, so enlarged, so ominously large, still ominous in its
   hammering, the cadence beginning a hundred new hearts,
   the hundred at last reluctantly turning, Muriel's march still
   flowing down and into their toes.

7. The news, flotilla of horrors, floats off. The jigsaw connects. In his heart Muriel hammers. In his veins Muriel flows. Muriel, Muriel, Muriel marching in his toes. Quickly, on the verge of the next concocted situation, his back tears loose from the chair.

The Death of a Friend

Two weeks have passed since the first call came;
how then can it be to blame?
Nor did it come from him to me,
but from wife to wife in secrecy:
no longer would he go to his job,
nor Fridays to his district club,
nor to the window for sun or moon,
nor open a paper, nor lift a spoon,
nor, when she spoke, admit he heard,
nor open his mouth to let out a word.

Ten days have passed since the worst call came;
how then can it be to blame?
Besides, no germs had been involved;
they'd had a problem—now it was solved.
It wasn't a case of conventional ills,
but merely a matter of seventeen pills.
Besides, it had nothing to do with me:
our date was for seven; he did it at three.

The box was closed by the time we came;
how then can it be to blame?
I did shake hands with each of his sons,
did kiss his wife and his daughter once;
—perhaps from their eyes I should have hid:
eyes that, before the glossy lid
was lowered, had looked their longest and last,
and into mine their look had passed.

A week ago last night we came
back from the wake. Is that to blame?
Is that why my thoughts are astir with contagion,
symptoms, period of incubation?
Early this morning I became
aware of something, something to blame.
It's not that I'm medically ill,
but merely a matter of lacking the will
to look at the window or even the wall,
to march my body the length of the hall,
to hear my wife, to lift my head,
to open my mouth for a bite of bread.

Alfred Kreymborg's Coat

We shared initials and a passion for reform.
High in his Charles Street flat I drank my first martinis
and floated home.
Soon he signed his letters "Uncle Alfred"
and at sixty-five declared me his inheritor.
Three times my age, he poured into me what was his:
where I now sat, Sandburg and Crane had sat.

At last, while loving him, I marked those pourings
as lessons of how not to be if by some miracle
I lived past sixty.
One night he phoned, announced "a storm of poems!"
To me, whose years were then all storm,
his exultation at the floodgift was as strange
as the long drought preceding it.

Later his wife described how every morning
he shuffled to the typewriter
and sat there
as if the old keys might revive
what had so many years commanded them,
then mournfully arose, the cold machine
once more betrayed by, traitor to, his fingers.

Afterward we drove to Stamford one last time.
A ritual was called for: Dorothy must give me
some part of my "uncle."
I would have settled gladly for a snapshot,
a manuscript, maybe a first edition.
But she'd determined otherwise: an overcoat,
well made, not often worn, was my inheritance.

How could my face show anything but gratitude?
The sleeves, I lied, would instantly be shortened.
I never put my arms through.
My son-in-law was just the size: it solved
his shiverings awhile, then probably descended
to one of his impoverished younger brothers
if not into thin air together with that marriage.

Sixty-five now, it's not his coat I walk in, but his shoes,
pouring into poets not one-third my age accounts of
the great ones in my life,
but not yet willing to sit through a morning
with fingers motionless over my typewriter,
not settling yet for the betrayal of its keys
as my inheritance.

PART 7

The Loyal Opposition

Have You Felt the Heart of America?

A Fantasy

I once leapt out of the city
And ran as far as I could
Away, across the meadows,
And stopped by the edge of a wood.
The trees touched the clouds' white softness;
Their tops looked down on me
And saw me: light as a bubble
That bursts when it is free.
I flew from mountain to mountain,
I touched each tiny bloom;
I tasted the foam of rivers
And breathed the air's perfume.

At last I came to a roadway
Where men were fixing the ground.
I knelt down behind a tree-stump
And watched without a sound.
The sun sat, resting on hill-tops;
Embracing the earth with its gaze.
The sun was a golden orange
And scattered its gold-dust rays.
The workingmen stood silent
And let their shovels stand;
They looked up on the glory
That watched and warmed the land.

> (I heard the crickets whisper;
> And sounds of hidden birds—
> But all besides was quiet:
> Breathing a "song without words.")

The sun slid over the hill-tops,
And, after it was gone,
The earth grew a full shade darker;
And the workingmen worked on.
At last they dropped their labour,

Their muscles glistening with sweat;
They trudged back home to their suppers
But I stayed a moment yet.
    I felt the forests sleeping
    (The night fell down from the sky)—
    I crept up close to the river
    And kissed the stream good-bye.

I slowly came back to the city,
And felt the night-air change.
Tall buildings rose to stop me;
The hard cement was strange,
I dreamt of the sun, till morning
Came, cruelly piercing my eyes—
But the sun was the moon's pale shadow;
For smoke polluted the skies,

I saw some children, playing
Upon a time-broken street
Where life is a word in lyrics
That long ago met defeat.
    I wanted to speak of the meadows;
    I wanted to let them know
    That life is still living somewhere,
    And trees have room to grow.

I came to the children, smiling,
And quietly started to tell
How once I leapt out of the city—
And later returned to hell.
They listened in curious silence,
And heard how I spent my day.
They listened until I ended,
And then they returned to play.

    I thought of the perfect stillness
    When the workers watched the sun
    And it beamed back in golden pleasure
    That their work was nearly done.

I stopped the children, inspired,
And asked: "**Before I depart,
Tell me; you love your country—
Have you ever felt her heart?**"
My voice was bitter and gentle:
I wanted to hear them speak.
Instead, they ran away frightened,
"HE'S CRAZY!" I heard them shriek.

❖　❖　❖

The city, the brick-souled monster,
Has taken the life we've grown
And planted it all for the wealthy,
And left our streets the stone.
But once I escaped to the country
And felt my land's heart beat,
And now I have learned my mission:
To bring it back on the street!

The Breeze

There's a report that even the smallest breeze
carries across broad waters and continents,
'til women and men stand silent, and feel it seize
their senses, making them glow, and grow immense.

"Brothers!" the breezes whisper upon the lands;
"somewhere the toilers blasted what bound them down,
and built a titanic monument with their hands,
and planted seed, and took the stars for a crown."

Over the steepest mountain the breezes spread,
entering every town where the people listen;
'til even the miners hear them sweep overhead,
and dream of the stars, and say: "For us they glisten!"

Chainers of men, that thunder your wild decrees,—
how can you build a barrier to the breeze?

May First 1940

We do not know, when every door is locked,
what pledge you sign, what bargain you have made;
but we that stood outside and softly knocked
shall not become the stock in any trade.

The memory of being voiceless clay
with strings to move the fingers and the mind;
the memory of dying before May
has made us promise never to be blind.

The busiest streets are paralyzed for us:
we have learned to hold a nation with our song.
Come to the window, you who still connive
a plan of death, to grow more prosperous!
—Our eyes have gained the calmness of the strong;
We are the voiceless clay become alive.

The Golden Trumpet

A fable thunders through me
that once my teachers told.
There stood a splendid castle
of silver and of gold.

A pair of giants lived here,
and wicked was their spell.
Alas for any creature
on whom their shadow fell!

Some bowed as beaten oxen,
and some were changed to birds.
Their eyes could shed no teardrops,
their lips could form no words.

One day a lad came riding
along this luring road;
far off the castle called him:
its every turret glowed.

But as he reached the gateway
that beckoningly swung,
he saw a golden trumpet
near which a sign was hung:

"Whoever shall this trumpet,
this golden trumpet blow,
his music shall accomplish
the giants' overthrow!"

The lad took down the trumpet
with laughter and with fear.
He held it in his left hand,
and in his right a spear.

He put its golden mouthpiece
against his lips, and blew—
and suddenly it sounded
so that the mountains knew.

Its notes were like the eagle
that flutters far and free—
oh giants, hear and tremble!
oh giants, gape and see!

It is no more a fable—
before your gates I stand:
a sign, a golden trumpet,
a spear in my right hand!

Ballad of Washington Heights

Did guns, like larks of freedom,
once warble on these heights?
Did blood go down this very slope
because of wrongs and rights?

Bring maps to me, and records!
Place bullet-holes on view,
that I may see how Death once stalked
this cozy avenue!

For I cannot imagine
these heights to be the same,
these heights where faded corner-signs
ring out the rebel name.

Now boys are at the ballpark
and girls are nibbling sweets—
there's not a hint of violence
along the well-paved streets.

Now ladies dream of furcoats
and gents no longer dream:
they let their radiators hum
a lullaby of steam.

They let new tyrants lord them,
betray them, sell them cheap—
they let themselves be robbed and gagged
so long as they can sleep.

Who'll rap at every window?
Who'll race from door to door?
Who'll fly with torches through the streets
and spread the news of war?

Who'll fill the air with trouble?
Who'll bleed for wrongs and rights?
Who'll make the larks of freedom sing
once more upon these heights?

Patriotism

My love for America
is not pinned to my lapel.
If I had a house,
with lawns around it,
my love would not flutter there.
If I owned a radio station,
my love would not be broadcast on the hour.

Lear had three daughters
—as Shakespeare tells.
Two pledged allegiance,
sang passionate hymns.
Two sucked him dry,
and devoured his kingdom.
But when the storms came,
and their gates showed no mercy,
the third one,
the outcast,
fought to the death for him.

As King Lear learned,
my country will learn
—when the storms come,
when her retinue's vanished—
who among her children truly love her.

Monticello

A JEFFERSON CANTATA

I would not bother the bones of the dead,
but once a voice rang out in my head:

Go down to Monticello
where Jefferson is sleeping;
go down to Monticello
and wake him with your weeping!

Say that his tree of freedom
is stripped of every leaf;
tell him the birds grow silent—
silent with fear and grief!

Say that the roots have withered,
say that the gardeners hide;
tell him that on the branches
his sons are crucified!

I don't know when it happened—in April or November;
perhaps it was at daybreak, perhaps at fall of night.
The months make little difference: all cold, as I remember—
the hours make little difference: all strangers to the light.

I went to Monticello, and told the tomb a story
of how machines are drumming a death-march in my ear,
of how the land once sunlit is midnight's territory;
I told the dead a legend that live ones hardly hear:

of plunderers applauded, of music held for treason,
of murder decked with medals, of love declared a crime,
of hearts afraid to open, of minds afraid to reason,
of hopes afraid to waken and win a better time.

I don't know when it happened—in April or November;
perhaps it was at daybreak, perhaps at fall of night:
Tom Jefferson awakened—and all that I remember
is how the darkness trembled to hear his words of light:

"What is the name of this woeful place
from which the sun should hide its face?
Who are the mourners on this street
without a handclasp when they meet?
What hell has my soul descended to
where tongues are on trial for being true . . .?"

It is America

"I think I have seen such hills before;
I think I have heard such a river roar;
I think I have seen such meadows sprawl;
I think I have heard such an eagle call.
But the roar of this river is not the same;
these hills have turned aboutface in shame;
over these meadows the weevils gloat;
a death-howl sounds from the eagle's throat . . ."

It is America

"You call it America? Give me proof!
My children never were blind or aloof:
some things they ended, some they began.
They begged no help from a dead old man.
They hung their hearts like flags on the roof.
You call this America? Give me proof!

"WHEN FURY BLOSSOMS ON EVERY BUSH,
WHEN FISTS REMEMBER HOW THEY CAN CRUSH,
WHEN HOPE NO MORE IS AFRAID TO LIVE,
WHEN TRUTH NO LONGER IS FUGITIVE,
WHEN LIPS THAT ARE MUMBLING LEARN TO COMMAND,
AMERICA WILL BE THIS LAND!"

The Crucifixion

Find out and tell me where the poets hide
who warble still of Christ upon a cross—
the painters, too, who still show Barabbas,
that murderer, triumphantly untied.

Find out and tell me, that I may be led
to where they dream in comfort and at peace:
raging against a tyrant whose police
two thousand years ago were safely dead.

Awaken and arise! I'll cry to them;
your sleep was long—Caesar no more is King.
A hundred Christs the judges now condemn.
A hundred crosses to the hill they bring,
No more the city is Jerusalem;
come see! the grave is dug at Ossining.

New Jersey—December 1776

Do not revere these dwellings, though their shutters
remind you of the time of Washington,
though from each roof now valorously flutters
our banner of revolt; nor be you won
by this proud tablet nailed upon a door:
"Here Passed The Rebel Band."
               For still some trees
are standing who bear witness of that war;
and every time December comes, a breeze
reminds them, and they whisper to each other:
"Do you remember how it was that year?
The shuttered windows, and the doors locked fast?
The frost-delirious fighters, wailing: BROTHER—
ONE CRUST OF BREAD! And then how strange to hear
the answer from these hearths: a rifle-blast!"

In Power

What was that? it seemed like a foot on the stair . . .
You've checked the palace-guard? All at their posts
and sober? (There *was* a king caught unaware
one midnight, after too much drinking of toasts.)

Who ever thought I'd be one to imagine ghosts,
to quake at breezes because of a name they bear,
to plant not palms, but cannon, along these coasts,
to read unwritten messages in the air?

I who (how many months ago?) like flame
found tinder in every heart, on every hill,
until the winds bore nothing but my hot name
over this very gate, this very sill,
to where—at the same chill hour, in the same
chair—*he* heard a footstep, and sat still.

A Man Is on the Hill Again

Are you astonished, man?
Did you expect
a different hill?

Before you opened your big, fool mouth
against one moneychanger,
somewhere, someone should've told you.

Sure he had you shadowed
(that's the only way)
bought hammer, nails, wood
(he's done it before, knows every shortcut)

By the time he's through with you, man,
nobody'll care how *his* fingers smell.

Wait till they hear
how you wrote left-handed
till the 7th grade—
slept on your left side,
winked with your left eye . . .

And you really thought it would work,
like the late-late show
on Channel 2:
big thief crawling back into his hole;
brave little guy carried out by the crowd;
lady, all smiles, waiting to hug him.

Well, now you see.
This ain't Channel 2.
The crowd's yelling "VIVA!" to its thief.
The smiling lady's no lady:
she's blind, and I hear she's a whore.
As for the brave little guy, man,
when they carry him out, he's out.

Des Moines and Council Bluffs

The old State Capitol is now
a fairly distinguished college.
The new one, in Des Moines, does not
aspire to higher knowledge.

Tall amid monuments and trees,
like a proud sovereign mounted,
it takes the salute of insurance firms:
fifty are there to be counted.

You might suppose it was for them
the old fort was erected—
but Sacs and Fox, two Indian tribes,
were originally "protected."

Such aim it declared in '43;
but less than ten years later
the lands around were up for sale
to any redskin-hater.

The guidebook hasn't a word to say
of the Indians' endurance,
of how many Sacs and how many Fox
are covered now by insurance.

Over an hour we lingered there
at the busiest intersection—
but not one grandchild did we see
of those in the fort's protection . . .

We hurried on to Council Bluffs
whose footbath is the Missouri.
All my life I'd longed to see
that river's famous fury.

A sluggish, slimy stream limped by
—ashamed that I beheld it.
How wasteful that above it such
a wide bridge had been welded!

Surely my wife could have stepped across,
her skirt not halfway lifted;
she wouldn't, though—from bank to bank
cargoes of sewage drifted.

I looked back once from Omaha
at the bluffs across the current:
sachem-ghosts were seated there,
but living sachems weren't.

Around the phantom fires they puffed
as in their time of splendor;
once more their drumheads told the night
of triumph or surrender.

Give up the wheel, and shut your eyes,
and soon the steady bounce'll
permit you, too, a vision of
the sachems at their council.

Lullaby

Hushabye, baby, no sense weeping:
if one more village burns while you're sleeping
next year will come, or the year after
Ladybird Johnson with speeches and laughter.

Into the grave that once was a country,
into hushed forests, with vultures for sentry,

past orphans' eyes, like an Angel of Mercy,
Ladybird Johnson will come with a curtsy.

Magic white fingers this lady possesses;
love of all landscape this lady professes.
She shall advance, while the cameras follow,
through the black fields, the cities bombed hollow.

Ladybird Johnson, with wand like a witch's,
soon will make whole the wounds of our hutches,
soon will make green the woods and the meadows
under which lie the loves of our widows.

Hushabye, baby, no sense weeping:
if one more village burns while you're sleeping
next year will come, or the year after
Ladybird Johnson with speeches and laughter.

Henry at the Grating

I was not free at Walden Pond
although no man for miles around
was there to mock my somersault
or catch me running like a colt
or misconceive my evening song.
About my neck a burden hung;
no leap, no race, no chant for me:
at Walden Pond I was not free.

A burden hung about my neck:
the proud lads of Chapultepec
seemed to have emptied every vein
to keep the grounds at Walden green . . .
Is it not sickening, that blood
should quench the thirst of Walden Wood?

Is it not sickening that men
of Concord town, at Concord Inn
should clink their glasses and gulp down
a blood more manly than their own
and of these folk not one refuse
the beverage brewed at Vera Cruz?

In Concord town my burden swelled;
the stomach in my ribs rebelled;
from fresh-baked loaves I turned away:
was not their compost Monterrey?
Sick at the smiles of wine and bread,
by nothing but my nausea fed,
I found at last a public place
and vomited in Concord's face.

Loyalty March

You should have heard them holler KILL! You should
have seen them lunge by dozens from the line
of march, and fall upon a lad who stood
among the crowd, and kick his skull, his spine
because he said that killing wasn't good.
You should have heard them ram "*Die Wacht Am Rhein*"
down the world's throat. You should have seen how blood
can make the eyes of those who drink it shine.

Had you been here, you would not long have frowned
at their too martial step, too rowdy manners.
Out of your lips their anthem soon would sound,
and soon enough your hands would hold their banners,
and soon enough you'd help pin down some lad
among the crowd, whose traitor face is sad.

The Bloodied Young: August, 1968

Hope, foolhardy
in front of triggers
one day in Chicago
one day in Prague,

aims hair wildly
at sill, at sewer—
eyes roaring gold
at pane, at pavement.

Skullwood, laurel
bilingually swirl
about its forehead:
PATRIOT!!   TRAITOR!!

How can we know?
asks someone simple.
Clown! it depends on
who's at the trigger!

Considering My Country

Considering my country in my time
where Truth is flogged and flowers are strewn on Crime
sons of a future century may wonder
what happened to the rhythm of our pulse:
did men rush forth into the square, and thunder
"The land grows fiendish, her insignia false"?

I set down this, a witness's report:
when neighbors met, they talked of rain, of sport;
alone, they plunged into a dream-like story
and were not waked but by the cries of clocks;
their faces did not show them to be sorry,
nor did their graphs register violent shocks.

But this is not to say that unconcerned
they saw the fragile spires our champions burned;
perhaps, like me, they felt within their stomachs
a welling nausea, in their hearts hot shame;
perhaps, while lullabied in August hammocks,
they begged the sky for Sodom's hail and flame.

Perhaps, like me, at every fresh disgrace
they vowed to seek some less polluted place
where, in the furious currents of a river,
they might rub loose the foulness from their lives;
perhaps, while spreading blue cheese or chopped liver,
they thundered prophecy at yawning wives.

Fourth of July Dialog

Here comes that migraine, otherwise known as the Muse
of Politics, whose Greek name I have forgotten.
More and more forced, more and more unpleasant
her entry, and always with the reminder that once
I summoned her, opened a window for her
to tear the tongue from my throat and replace it with fire.

"Yes, and instead of falling asleep at the fire,
tonight of all nights, you need me," mutters the Muse.
"America's having her birthday—look at her
pulling out of the closet all her forgotten
costumes of freedom and kindness that suited once
when serfs adored her and despots found her unpleasant!

"Who if not you," she cries, "will proclaim unpleasant
tidings? The hearts of your countrymen are on fire
with hate for the poorest, which they themselves were once;
abroad, leagued with murderer kings, they amuse
their mother goose skulls with imperial games;—forgotten,
America's pangs, when empire pounded *her!*"

Two aspirins give me courage; I answer her:
"Old Muse—old friend—if what I say is unpleasant,
forgive me. It's touching, not to have been forgotten
by *you,* at least. The veins I set afire
long since ran cold, and mine await a Muse
of milder aspect than they welcomed once.

"Somehow the tidings that could rouse me once
from a young wife, the waiting lips of her,
no longer turn me. Soberly I muse
on shames as deep, days no less unpleasant:
Garrison mobbed, the Pequod tents on fire
—wickedness heaped on wickedness, forgotten.

"Find someone new; you cannot have forgotten
the way it happens: he'll welcome you at once;
his window gapes; already he's half fire;
his wife calls gently, but he sidetracks her;
and if she's jealous, things will grow unpleasant;
small wonder, being jilted for a Muse!

"Go tell him, Muse, America's forgotten
glories! Let his unpleasant rhymes that once
roared through my jaws, set her again afire!"

Seven Days

The first morning, we trudged (forget buses, taxis!)
in amazement to Raúl Martínez, a handclasp from New York.
For two hours he quenched us, down to the dregs of our questions.
The phone lashed: had he forgotten his luncheon date?
I praised his book designs; he gave me four. I asked
the price of a laughing silk-screen print. "For you it is free."

Next day, in old Havana, we saw it for fifty dollars.
There, pressing my nose to the glass of a library store-front,
I found, amid books on the other side, the librarian's nose.
She beckoned me in—Francisca—expounded the role of each nook,

led me to Lorca's very shelf, his rarest book,
saw that I lifted it like a rose, and said it was mine.

The third night, on the twenty-fifth floor, where Hilton once
surveyed his necklace-harbor and Morro Castle beyond,
we stood at the pianist's side: she was straight, she was black,
          she was Nora;
her round face, long hair swayed as she played, and we swayed too;
her fingers took our tunes, twined them into magic;
her eyes, wide as Havana harbor, took our eyes.

Next, at ten in the morning, brushing aside the bustle
of his beloved island's birthday preparations,
Nicolás Guillén bartered with me hug for hug,
jest for jest, laud for laud, book for book,
and at last a glimpse at his glowing archives, a tour of his
          trophies;
and later a fireworks handwave: "Next time send me a cable!"

Toward the end of the hospital visit, reaching the rows that pasted
heels onto sandals, I caught a murmur in English; she'd learned it
twenty-nine years ago, at fourteen, seldom had used it;
her name began with a Rosa and closed with a Casanova;
into the light she leaped for a snapshot grin with my wife,
then clutched my hand Good Luck as she turned to the heels and
          sandals.

After the final dinner, during the final folk-dance,
I was led to a private corner, a woman's solemn hand.
The gift was an envelope freshly postmarked, freshly engraved
with Cuba's tenderly issued faces of Ethel and Julius.
"Everywhere in Latin America we remember
what we were doing, whom we were with on the night of the
          burning."

Noon. The seventh noon. We'd lugged our bags and gnat-bitten
salt-swollen limbs to the final frenzy of weigh-ins, customs.
Estella, denouncing her English, her errors in planning: "I
          promise—
next time you come, I'll be better . . ." and, spite of our seven
          days' whining,

hugged the length of the line; and, spite of my uncouth blast
at her hero, her Hemingway, reached me her lips at the last.

None of them asked why my country for twenty years of torment
had tried to drag their country into the dust. No one
pointed with a frown at their wretched store-displays,
trucks and buses and taxis stricken, sparkless, gasping
for parts. No—not one. Theirs was the bounty; in seven
days they had broken the blockade around my heart.

In Wicked Times

It *is,* after all, my planet.
My father trained me to care.
Night after night at eleven
I've somehow managed to bear
shipwrecks, planewrecks, dreamwrecks
—with ice at the roots of my hair.

Once or twice per decade,
for several months in a row,
the times were more wicked than even
a trained man cares to know.
Those nights I moved toward the dial
with footsteps cramped and slow.

For several weeks I've noticed,
just about half past ten,
a cramp in the pit of the stomach,
a craving to flee the den;
I crawl to the dial—no question:
the times are wicked again.

All-Star Neutron Day, 9 August 1981

(On the morning of the annual all-star baseball
game, the president announces full production of
neutron weapons. The Asian sonnet form was cho-
sen to commemorate the destruction of Nagasaki on
9 August 1945.)

The mouths of Auschwitz's unholy pillars
sent sacrificial incense toward the skies.
Now men ask: From the womb of Bachs and Schillers
how could there be a leaping forth of killers
without one gasp, one turning down of eyes?

At 7:30, just as we were drinking
our orange juice, the pillar of the land
that was the womb of Whitman and Abe Lincoln
sent from his mouth a smoke. Men will be thinking:
With gasp, with lowered eyes, did no one stand?

Here's how it was: twelve hours went past; the smoke
had settled in all lungs; we settled too
and switched our tubes on; pandemonium broke
in Cleveland's ballpark—red and white and blue.

Grenada Symphony: First Movement

Early that morning we learned how, while we had slept,
the two hundred twenty millions of us had leapt
on a breadcrumb isle—a scheme top-secretly kept
and executed.

One should never refer to it as invasion, as war.
There were reasons, lofty of course, and there would be more.
We had saved, set free; a wickedness close to our door
had been uprooted.

Baskets of munchies would coax from the mouths of the poor
a welcoming smile, even cheers; but just to be sure
that none of our smilers preferred the disease to the cure,
we'd keep our sons there,

ferreting out of its hole each mutter, each frown,
shutting the unconvinced, insolent newspaper down,
till only Freedom and Decency dwelled in the town,
blessing our guns there.

Bitburg

Why suddenly astounded
does the planet gape
as if a new voice had sounded,
a new form taken shape?

Was he so much subtler
that you could be beguiled?
Long since in deep hell Hitler
guessed what he was and smiled.

Why should he not bring honors
for the brownshirt dead?
Look at his living gunners!
Listen to their tread!

Those killers, could he wake them
after forty years,
would leap wherever he'd take them
with bayonets and cheers.

Bhopal

There is a wailing in my skull.
Until I set it free,
my nation's poison ravaging Bhopal
will ravage me.

Each artery of mine, each vein
from forehead down to feet
is thronged with mourning, thunderstruck by pain
—a Bhopal street.

Two thousand ghosts in pantomime
beseech one word of blame.
Until I find a name to fit the crime,
it has my name.

PART 8

Against McCarthyism

The Soul of Martin Dies

1960 A.D.

Jehovah sits upon his throne
of icicle and ivory stone.
An angel, playing on a lyre,
accompanies the blessed choir.
But suddenly the marble hall
is shaken by a bugle-call.
An Entrance-Guard arrives and speaks:
"A mortal soul has tried for weeks
to crash the gate. I must confess
it seems to have the wrong address."
Jehovah says, "Well, send it in."
A spirit, with transparent skin,
is brought before the throne, in view
of mighty God. "And who are you?"
"I am the soul of Martin Dies."
Jehovah narrows both his eyes,
"I never heard of you." The soul
replies "My name is on the scroll
of Liberty. My hair turned grey
with worry for the U. S. A.
I pointed out how Moscow planned
to ravage all the virgin land,
how stealthily, by low intrigues
they made a dozen fronts and Leagues
to catch the working men, and fool
believing minds in home and school.
I heard a hundred-odd reports
of honest gentlemen, all sorts
of information—Lord, I tried
to rouse each town and country-side
against the plot that Moscow brewed."

The Lord said "Sorry to intrude,
but I have heard you long enough.
Some things, more urgent than your stuff,
are waiting for attention. Go

145

to Hell! This place, I'll have you know,
takes no subversive souls." And God
leapt up, and beat him with His rod,
and chased him to the Heaven's edge,
and hurled the spirit off a ledge.

A million miles poor Martin fell,
and crashed into the roof of Hell.
The scarlet Satan saw him drop
and helped the screaming soul to stop.
He spoke "Good evening; what's your name?"
"Dies . . . Martin Dies . . ." "I'm glad you came;
your colleague, William Randolph Hearst,
has told me why you should be cursed.
He spoke about the work you did
to murder the New Deal, and rid
the U. S. A. of anyone
who might refuse to take a gun.
Although your work did not succeed,
I laud your talent to mislead,
and know that every damned soul
bids welcome to the flaming hole!"
And now the Devil tried to pin
a medal on the spirit's skin.
But from the scarlet Satan turned
the soul of Dies, "I won't be burned
with reds!" he screamed and ran away.

Within a cloud of harmless grey
between the Devil and the Lord
the soul has taken room and board.
And you can always see him there
declaiming in the hot, hot air.

Peekskill

1.

Housewife of Peekskill,
what have I done to you
that you should shake your fist
as I ride by?

Neither my name
nor the street I live on,
neither my dreams
nor my loves do you know.

How I have spent my years,
how I have used my hands,
even the sound of
my voice is beyond you.

Only that I
have come past on a Sunday
to hear a man sing;
only this do you know of me . . .

Housewife of Peekskill,
what have I done to you
that you should shake your fist
as I ride by?

2.

Oh the grass was as green as green can be,
and the apples spread fire from tree to tree,
and the cups of the lilies yawned with sleep,
and the rocks were free, and the flags were cheap.

Oh the blue of the sky was deep, was deep,
and the corn was just about ready to reap,
and the lake was laughing immortally,
and the flags were cheap, and the rocks were free.

3.

Do you think, perhaps, if I went to Niagara
and stood there, listening, year after year,
that someday the sound of its waters cascading
might drown out the jibes and the curses I hear?

Do you think, if I traveled from ocean to ocean
and saw the tall wonders that tourists see,
perhaps someday they might throw a shadow
on the eyes of hate that are searing me?

Do you think, if I clung to the clasp of my sweetheart
and lay there, feasting, night after night,
that someday perhaps her peace and her passion
might put my Sunday of horror to flight?

4.

Thru every window of this land our song will go,
and not a single glass be shattered by the blow,
and not a single brow be bloody or in pain
when it is smitten by the rock of our refrain.

Though haughty towers may be toppled by our song,
and though each word is like a bullet on the tongue,
there need be no bewildered outcry of alarm—
because our melody will do your heart no harm.

But if among you some are driven by their fears
to build a barricade of hate around your ears,
then we will give our song the wings with which to fly,
and it will reach you—though your walls be mountain-high.

For it is fashioned of the river and the sun,
and of whatever flaming web the stars have spun;
and though our song be stoned and burned and barred and
     banned
it will yet go thru every window of this land!

Halloween

Forgive me, dear, if I did not gasp.
Being the father's no easy task.
Next time you show me your toothless friend,
I promise: my hair will stand on end!
He really deserves to see me afraid—
he's the best jack-o-lantern that ever was made.

Don't think I'm a stranger to Halloween:
I've known how to make old ladies scream;
they'd look out the window, and there I stood
moaning and groaning—in a white hood.
They'd open the door, and there I grinned—
my witch's hair blown wild by the wind.

At midnight, when all on the list had been shocked,
we beat a retreat to our fort in the rocks.
There we joined hands, and mumbled the word
that only seven had ever heard;
and while October flew off in a gale
we quaked in the dark at a ghostly tale.

I'd like to be able to quake and gasp
at a story of ghosts, at a Halloween mask;
I'd like us seven, turned women and men,
to huddle away from October again!
But Willie now is a ghost himself,
and Jean keeps hers on a secret shelf.

Philip's haunted—having grown rich;
and sweet, plump Ruth's being burned as a witch.
Mary and Bob have made friends with fear:
a black cat crosses their path each year.
—I, too, have been sometimes afraid to dream:
all year, one year, it was Halloween. . . .

Is This the City?

Is this the city where my time began?
Was it across these cobblestones my shadow ran?
The poplars I believe I know;
the clock, too, on that tower—
but now it strikes an unfamiliar hour:
an hour of woe;
and strangers are to me the trees
that bear no foliage but proclamations and decrees.

Are those the streets of childhood, that my brain
turned into meadows, where the laughter grew like grain?
A wreath of laughter decked my brow,
gathered from door to door.
Ghosts of the tenants who were there before
gape at me now;
and through the streets, as in a daze,
I go—it is a graveyard where the grim-beaked vultures graze.

City of gallows—city of mute men—
what wand is there to wave, to make you whole again?
Have I fantastic deeds to do,
a balm to fetch for cure,
or must I, too, grow silent and endure
the death of you?
City of wounds—city of tears—
whisper the secret of your agony into my ears.

October in "Freedom" Land

1.

Dragging a shroud of leaves across the land
October rides now in a hearse of wind.
The birds, that should be singing
a requiem, are gone.
The bells, that slowly should be clanging,
are silent, every one.

And I would like to ask the frantic trees
whose funeral it is.

The shades go down, and though no telltale wreath
hangs on the doors, it is a giant death.
And though I hear no wailing,
nor see a sorrowing face,
in all this land there stands no dwelling
exempted from the loss.
And I would like to ask the broken trees
whose burial it is.

2.

Those dreams that used to ravage me at night:
of uninvited boots upon the stairs,
of horsehooves reaching bodies that I love,
of friends becoming fiends with fiery claws;
—those dreams I dream no more. For in the bright
landscapes of my own city's favorite squares
all eyes can see what I was frightened of.
My nightmares now are published and called laws.

3.

Since dungeon-doors are opened
for men no worse than me,
and by tomorrow morning
who knows where I may be,

I kiss my wife more slowly
than those who've done no crime,
and clutch my children's laughter
as for the final time.

By day I pass my neighbors,
and wonder if they know
to what a dangerous fellow
they sometimes say hello.

By night I toss in slumber,
and suddenly awake:
perhaps my name's not listed
among the ones they'll take!

But since I love the meadows,
the mountains, and the streams,
and more than all together
I love my own free dreams,

then if the dungeons open
for men whose dreams are free,
how dare I not be listed?
how dare they not want me?

4.

Build high, build wide your prison wall!
that there be room enough for all
who hold you in contempt. Build wide!
that all the land be locked inside.

Though you have seized the valiant few
whose glory cast a shade on you,
how can you now go home with ease,
jangling your heavy dungeon keys?

The birds, who still insist on song,
the sunlit stream, still running strong,
the flowers, still blazing red and blue,
all, all are in contempt of you.

The parents, dreaming still of peace,
the playful children, the wild geese
who still must fly—the mountains, too,
like fists, are in contempt of you!

When you'll have seized both moon and sun
and jailed the poems one by one,
and trapped each trouble-making breeze—
then you can throw away your keys.

Visit

The stairs I used to rattle up
two and three at a time
are grown so pitilessly steep
this night, so long a climb,
it seems an hour at the top
before I find my breath
and gather power enough to creep
in through the door of death.

All the relations nod their heads
as though my face were known,
and chirp—like a branch of solemn birds.
Among them, yet alone,
the mother lifts her swollen lids
to see who moves a chair.
Both of us know—what need for words?—
I have no business here.

To the Silencers

Will that day never break, once and for all,
when I can rise forgetful of each scream
and fear no more the foaming ones that fall
on Orpheus, drop Hart Crane and his dream
sharkward, lop off the bright head of Chenier,
shut Raleigh's eyes—that precious pair of suns,
send Bruno's spirit blazing on its way,
drill Lorca with the spit of eighteen guns?

Must you still hound me, hack and fetter me?
still tear my fingers from the strings, the tongue
out of my mouth, and from my heart the beat?
Are you so blind, old foe, you cannot see
how—past these little deaths—the song is sung
when you lie rotting, nameless, at my feet?

Called In

We're called in; they've called us in.
Not the hailstones did us in.
Open the mailbox—out pops a crow:
"You're called in. They want you in."

What for? We rush about:
wake from their folders the stapled, the labeled;
shock from their shoebox the summed, the canceled.
Empty the closets! Empty the bureaus!
We're called in; they've called us in.

Breakfast of hemlock, dinner of stone,
night of wind accusing through teeth:
"Behind that wall, what were you up to?"

O stapled, o labeled, o dated and numbered,
o alphabetized, o crowded in,
innocence unto innocence,
like boxcar pilgrims headed for Auschwitz:
Astound the roads! make pale whatever
has called us in, whatever peeks
through blinds, whatever waits at checkpoints,
whatever picks from a desk without looking
one right rubber-stamp out of a hundred!
Let it see, not the dread that roars through our pupils
but a calendar year of innocence, stapled
in cartons, labeled in shopping bags!

We're called in; they've called us in.
What for? No asking now.
They'll do the asking, we the stammering.
But our innocence—what of that?
But the hailstones—what of that?
Who'll ever call us in for that?
hold out a hand, a trophy in it?
They call our name . . . they hold our year
like testicles in the palm of their hand.

PART 9
Judaica

To My People:

Not by tears will we be free, my people;
tears cannot quench a tyrant's flame.
Not by prayers will we be saved, my people;
there is no mercy without shame.

Only strength will freeze the axe, my people;
strength that can wither any foe;
only millions joined as one—: my people
dealing their chains a bursting blow.

The Thunder of the Grass

In Warsaw, in the ghetto of the Jew,
a schoolhouse stood, along whose ancient walls
tendrils of ivy reverently grew—
as though to guard the rare Hebraic scrolls
asleep within—and greenly blushed their pride
for Friday's candles blossoming inside.

Around this sacred building rose a fence
of silence, that had never yet been broken;
even the neighboring flowers seemed to sense
that in those rooms uncommon words were spoken.
Bold grass between the cobblestones grew high
to hush the blasphemous boots of passersby.

For brighter than the candles, and more rare
than all the scrolls, were they that walked within:
the ninety-three young scholars, unaware
of war's harsh noise, and the foul smell of sin,
who learned old anthems, proverbs of the wise,
glorious legends—with enkindled eyes.

Bold grass defended them—yet even they
could not be deaf forever to the thunder
of Hitler's drums: and on too soon a day

their eyes were at the windows, fixed in wonder
while tight-lipped soldiers tramped from street to street,
breaking tall fences with their booted feet.

But harmless days went by and mocked their fright:
no guest disturbed the lessons—that is, none
but Captain Hess—and he was so polite,
so full of friendly questions—when he'd gone
the girls began to murmur cheerily,
wondering just how bad such men could be.

He asked how many girls they were, how old,
and scribbled down their answers in a book.
He noted that the heating pipes were cold;
glanced at the dining hall and bathrooms; took
great interest in the bedrooms; gently moved
a chair, and pledged that things would be improved.

. . . March came, the month of rumor-laden winds—
and, though their rooms were warmer now than ever,
often the girls would move aside the blinds
and watch, on broken streets, the bare trees quiver,
and hear, as though from deep within the ground,
as though from the earth's soul, a moaning sound.

It was a gruesome tale the March winds told:
of Israel dragged along the streets in chains—
women and men, the lame, the young, the old
crowded like cattle onto endless trains
that moved mysteriously out of sight
and came back empty in the deep of night.

What guilt they felt for all their wealth of rest,
the unstopped candles of their lone oasis
taunting the parched eyes of a tribe laid waste!
With what hushed sobs, what horror-stricken faces
they heard the frantic legend of the breeze,
until their souls quaked with the quaking trees!

And then, one morning, Captain Hess returned.
Outside, the beaten snow had disappeared.
Across the garden, sunlight gently burned
on buds and grasstops; soon the sky had cleared
its clouds, like heaps of wintry filth, away,
and rolled out carpets for a holiday.

Even the school fell captive to that season:
subtly its wildness surged from room to room—
each girl would laugh, with scarcely any reason,
take up a scarf and dance; or, like a bloom,
sway in the windy grass, crimson with blushes
for dreamed-of bridegrooms poised behind the bushes.

And as the Captain strutted through the door
he heard the giddy singing of a cello;
along the walls, over the faded floor
the sun had smeared a bright new coat of yellow.
He found the teacher, and politely bowed:
"I bring you tidings that should make you proud.

"Tomorrow night, promptly at eight o'clock,
ninety-three visitors will climb your stairs—
they're officers—the finest Aryan stock—
whose lips will answer all your pupils' prayers—
and, Beautiful," he winked, "don't lock this door,
for you and I can make it ninety-four!

"I'll have my staff of seven quartered here
to supervise the event . . . and, when they speak,
remember: foolish words may cost you dear:
lashes, or spiked boots through your pretty cheek.
Salute them, offer drinks when they arrive;
show them how grateful you are to be alive!"

Without a stir, without the faintest sigh,
she stood behind her curtains, peeping down,
and watched the captain as he strutted by
bullying daylight with his deathly brown.
She saw that he was tall and straight and fair,
and that he mocked the sun with his blonde hair.

Although her landscape soon was rid of him
she stood a long time, letting the cool glass
relieve her brow—till all that had been dim
these many seasons: sunrays on the grass,
bits of white cloud, a gang of wheeling birds,
things that had shriveled into classroom words

suddenly took on color, stirred, and swelled. . . .
Then all her senses shook with a shameless hunger
to hold the Spring—to be hungered for and held!
until she remembered ninety-three who were younger,
and turned aside, and let the curtains fall,
and slowly stumbled out into the hall.

. . . The word went galloping from door to door,
gifted with sorrow's speed, and everywhere
it left a trail of ruin—someone tore
a garland of wild roses from her hair
and hurled it down into the street; another
crouched in the dark, and whimpered for her mother.

Swiftly they gathered, shuddering and sobbing;
and it was then that Esther, in her love,
forgot how her own coward pulse was throbbing.
Like Deborah of old she leaned above
her wailing sisters, and from her own breast
dragged out the magic words to give them rest.

"It is a dark and lone thing to be dead;
but such a darkness will torment me less
than lying in the black shame of my bed—
and I am sure that such a loneliness,
hard as it were, could never match the pain
of living all alone among our slain.

"How shall we greet the sweet bells of their doom
if we salute them in their triumph-hour?
Shall each of us come running from her room
waving the soul that lay beneath their power?
Or shall we, when the million martyrs rise,
send up our hallelujah to the skies?"

"What must we do?" sobbed one. "We must be ice
beneath their fingers, marble to their mouths,
our eyelids shut, our souls beyond all price,
our minds safe from their frenzied threats and oaths,
our flesh beyond their boots' idea of pain,
our lips: a smile to drive them out insane!"

Such words she spoke, till those who'd been afraid
sat gaping at her fist, and finished crying;
then, while the gloom of dusk seeped in, they weighed
several choices, and selected dying—
death being the sole weapon in their store
to cheat the foe of what he hungered for.

. . . There were no sleepers in the school that night:
all eyes were on the planets, and all ears
drank the night's noise with savage appetite—
the moments rumbled past them, big as years;
the roses burst into gigantic bloom,
mating their scent with death in every room.

And on those tongues, where picnics once were planned,
Death, like a strange name, had to be said over;
for they were desperate to understand
this thing that they had chosen for a lover
to lie with them tomorrow—this dark thing
whose kiss would banish their beloved spring.

And when at last the sun rose, ninety-three
pairs of wide eyes admired it on its climb;
the girls put on their best, and solemnly
marched down to breakfast, and in pantomime
greeted each other, and with bitter zeal
savored their bountiful Passover meal.

Then, arm in arm, without a word they came
into the sunlight, among opening flowers.
Their hair, rose-wreathed, seemed to be set aflame.
While overhead, through all the morning hours,
the seven Germans sneered to see them pass
like goddesses tiptoeing on the grass.

Were they not blind to sneer when through the garden
the girls went kneeling in a wordless prayer
—as prisoners, who've gained at last their pardon,
might bow, ecstatic, breathing the free air?
Touching the bloom-filled branches of young trees,
they dumbly swayed—like spellbound votaries.

Those seven fat old men, were they not blind?
Never did such a troop of celebrants
show at a festival—with hands entwined
the girls began a solemn, nameless dance
around the flower beds. . . . Did they not wonder?
Did no one tremble at the grass's thunder?

They meaningfully winked, and smiled, and vied
with one another in lascivious jests,
rubbing their soft hands hungrily, to hide
their impotence, and pointed out the breasts
that each of them pretended to desire
—those fat old men, with only words for fire!

And when their store of wit was gone, they told
the teacher she must call her students in.
For one long breath, the girls bent down to hold
roses against their hearts. "Let them begin
taking their baths!" the Germans yelled, "It's late!
Our men are officers—they mustn't wait!"

. . . Deep went Death's hush down all the hallways, went
his night from room to room—a single flame
lived on the wall where seven Germans bent
over their watches—till the moment came,
the stroke of eight, and suddenly a sound
of martial music made them swing around.

They crowded the window with their glowing eyes,
and soon, around the corner, fiercely singing,
the officers came marching toward their prize,
those valiant conquerors of cities, bringing
conqueror-blood, conqueror-lips and hands
in quest of girls to overwhelm like lands.

"Where are they?" With a lunge the heroes swept
their bowing, smiling ones aside, and swirled
into the halls where holy treasure slept,
and with their boots that had trampled half the world
trampled the silence of that sacred place—
and would have spat upon Jehovah's face.

But when each knob was turned, when each had sprung
into his chosen bed, the promised form
that lay beneath him: clean and soft and young,
took all his passion without growing warm;
and when his breath was answered by no breath
he slowly recognized that it was Death

who had the virgin in his arms, that here
lay something strangely calm, and safe from force;
bewildered he arose, a thing of fear,
and fled the room's gigantic intercourse
that made a mockery of his own lust
and turned his bright medallions into rust.

Back through the hall they swirled, those ninety-three,
with drawn white faces and hysterical eyes,
hiding each in his mind the mockery
that raced behind him, laughing down his size;
and when they found the seven old men, they swore
and kicked, and flung them cringing to the floor.

Then through the tomblike hall ran Captain Hess
up to the teacher's room, and found her there;
he called her name, and dared in bitterness
to strike at her and drag her from the chair;
but she was cold and still, and when she fell
smiling, he fled away with a wild yell.

"Ungrateful bitches! Listen, everyone!"
his voice went raging through the hall like fire—
"the world must have no word of what they've done!
I'll give you virgins to your heart's desire,
but not this night for you've a job to do;
this night you'll have your vengeance of the Jew.

"Take torches, some, and set each room aflame—
take axes, some, and batter down the walls;
and some, bare-handed, make yourselves a game
of ripping all their cursed books and scrolls!
And when tomorrow dawns, let not one stone
remain—nor one torn page, nor one charred bone,

"nor one crushed rose, nor one dead candlelight,
nor one limp blade of grass—nor any broken
piece of a bed! What happened here this night
must be destroyed without a single token,
so that no passerby may ever see
this building's ghost, or hear its history!"

All night they toiled, without a moment's pause:
battering, burning, ripping with bare hand
the yellow page that held the holy laws;
and when the morrow dawned, their chief's command
had been fulfilled—for nothing could be found
of stone or flower to hide the ruined ground.

. . . And yet the folk of Warsaw tell their story,
to all who'll listen, of a certain time
in mid-March, when the ancient dormitory
rises again, and round its windows climb
tendrils of ivy, that greenly blush their pride
for Friday's candles blossoming inside.

And, whispering, they'll lead you to the street
with bared, bowed heads, and ask you to believe
that on that certain morning you may meet
a troop of silent girls, who slowly weave
and whirl like goddesses; and, if you pass
quite close, you'll hear the thunder of the grass.

The Hour

My heart announced it to the hills,
and the hills passed it on to the breeze,
and the breeze went crying to my brothers:
will you rise up from your knees!

Will you rise up from your knees,
and roll the forbidden drums—
for your time in Egypt is over,
and the hour of judgment comes!

A Ballad of August Bondi

1. WESTWARD

NARRATOR:
>This happened a hundred years ago,
>when the States—that lately had been a child
>needing the milk of peace to grow—
>suddenly jumped from their cradle, and smiled
>a wicked smile, and pounced like a wild
>beast upon infant Mexico!
>
>That was a feast! When they'd had enough,
>they flexed their muscles, and roared at the sun:
>"Look at us now: we're big and rough.
>Even *you'll* look puny before we're done:
>more gold's in the rivers and hills we've won
>than you at your shiniest ever showed off. . . ."
>
>Rivers and hills: a luscious land
>eager for plowing, open to claim. . . .
>The brander of slaves flew west, to brand
>the bark of every tree with his name.
>But, just as swiftly, another came
>with seeds of freedom in his hand.

BALLADEER:

The streets of Saint Louis looked busy and bright;
but Bondi, young Bondi, his smile wasn't right.
A wind from the river hissed into his ear:
"Say, friend! Aint'cha glad to be here?
The day I first met you, six winters ago,
how different your face was! The smile said Hello.
Now, year after year, you escape from this town
as though it were tracking you down. . . ."
The streets of Saint Louis looked busy and bright;
but Bondi, young Bondi, his smile wasn't right.
—The river ice cracking was so much like whips:
the sound of it twisted his lips. . . .
One morning in March, while he sat at his work,
he opened a paper that came from New York:
"Young men—are you anxious for freedom to win?
Then Kansas will welcome you in!
The ones who want whips to be heard in the West
are trooping in thousands to win the great test.
If Kansas is shackled, the world will cry shame.
Young men—will you stake the first claim?" . . .
Next morning young Bondi marched down to the store,
bought two saddlebags, and they asked him what for.
Instead of an answer, he gave them a grin:
"Excuse me—I'd better begin!"
He stayed just a moment, to polish his gun,
then out he went, whistling, and winked at the sun:
"Be seeing you, pal, in a prettier sky!"
—Then bid Martha Bondi goodbye.

AUGUST BONDI:

There is a land of unbitten fruit,
brooks never waded across or raced,
sunlight and starlight going to waste,
soil without suckling, seedling or root.

It lies like a gift for the greedy to take.
At night the four winds carry its cry:
"What ever you plant here will not die;
my life and my law are for you to make!"

166

I am greedy, mother, for such a soil.
Long enough we wander and weep,
driven away before we can reap
the golden harvests of our toil.

The wandering time is over and done.
I yearn for that soil as it yearns for me.
What rises out of my husbandry
may make you happy to call me son.

Not so much the corn and the wheat,
the peach trees neither, nor the cows—
but freedom, the frame of every house;
freedom, the stones on every street.

CHORUS OF FEARFUL FRIENDS:

Kansas? Is he out of his head?
Twenty-two's a young age to be dead. . . .
Before he sows one kernel of wheat
they'll find his heart, and sow it with lead.

After one night without light, without heat,
after one week without milk, without meat,
after one month without roof, without bed,
he'll wish he never had left this street. . . .

MARTHA BONDI:

Because there's a rumbling when you listen to the ground,
a rumbling from out of the West—
am I to hold my son back, safe and sound,
while others lunge to the test?

I—who made Freedom a childhood refrain
till it rang like a bell on his tongue—
shall I now strike those syllables out of his brain
as a fairy-tale word for the young?

Safe be *your* sons: the smith and the scribe,
the cantor, the counter of coins!
Safe with my son is the dream of our tribe:
safe in his arms, in his loins. . . .

CHORUS OF FEARFUL FRIENDS:
CHORUS OF FEARFUL FRIENDS:
    Kansas! The brooks there are running red.
    Kansas! The grass there cries out to be fed.
    Kansas! The blood of young fools is sweet!
    August Bondi are you out of your head?

MARTHA BONDI: There'll be trouble.
AUGUST BONDI: I've a gun.
MARTHA BONDI: Go, then. Go with God, my son!

2. LETTERS FROM KANSAS

The slaveholders are all in great glee over their fake victory at the polls. For the time being, Kansas is in their hands. Near the border, at the place where we stopped for dinner, a cavalcade rode in. From them we had a fine account of their expedition to Kansas and of their doings there lately:

Let's hear about it! Tell us about it!
If we hadn't seen it all we surely would doubt it.

Well, there came a young Missouri man to Kansas in the fall,
found himself a pretty little claim, prettiest little claim of them all;
laid four poles on the ground, like this, just the size of a squatter
    shanty,
then the winds came around and tracked him down, chased him
    back to Jackson County.

Let's hear about it! Tell us about it!
If we hadn't seen it all we surely would doubt it.

Well, soon as the winds got sleepy, came a devil from Vermont,
with his devil wife and four devil brats, and they found the place
    they want,
and they built their devil shanty where the four poles lay—prettiest
    little claim in Kansas,
and if you want to smile, sit still awhile, there's only two more
    stanzas.

Let's hear about it! Tell us about it!
If we hadn't seen it all we surely would doubt it.

Well, us fifty come a-galloping—"Oh ain't it the devil of a shame!
You've built yourself a mighty snug nest—but Missouri's got this
    claim.
If you're still around next time we come, remember, Mr. Baker:
you'd better prepare a special prayer, 'cause you're going to meet
    your maker!"

Let's hear about it! Tell us about it!
If we hadn't seen it all we surely would doubt it.

Well, next time we come a-galloping, right at the door he stands.
Says brave Captain Pate: "You're the devil of a thief—snatching our
    slaves and our lands!"
Then we chopped his pretty chairs, and we broke his pretty beds,
    and whacked his pretty walls a-splinter,
and we whipped him at the tree, and if no one cuts him free, he'll
    be hanging there next winter!

Let's hear about it! Sing it and shout it!
We'll do the same on every Northern claim, don't anybody doubt it!

❖ ❖ ❖

Work has been so hard, mother, I'd truly lost track of the calendar.
But the day came, which I suddenly remembered must be different
from all other days of the year. Alone in the wilderness, with only
the stars as guests, I celebrated the Passover:

> Where are the silver candlesticks,
> the damask-covered table,
> a sacred bowl in which to mix
> the flour of Moses' fable?
>
> Dear watchful stars—you should not scoff
> that I've no damask cover:
> the matzoh's done—here, break some off
> and mark my passing over!
>
> The rite begins: *Come, eat with me,*
> *all ye who know of hunger!*
> *Last year my bread was slavery,*
> *but I'm a slave no longer.*

Now all at once the words resound:
No more shall fetters bind ye,
for ye have put the poison ground
of Egypt far behind ye!

Over the thorns ye stumble forth;
under the winds ye quiver—
yet shall ye stoop to kiss the earth
the day ye cross the river.

That day the sun thy wounds shall dress,
a cleansing wind pass through ye;
that day, that day the wilderness
shall hear thy Hallelujah!

Perhaps I should not fret you with such news, mother. But you are strong of heart, and have the right to know. What happened to me this morning, has happened to all here who will not deny their love for freedom. Twenty galloped up to the door of my cabin:

WHO'S THE OWNER OF THIS CLAIM?
I am.
        BONDI?
            That's the name.
THIS HERE AIN'T NO SOCIAL VISIT.
What's it all about? What is it?
WE'LL ASK QUESTIONS—YOU'LL GIVE
      ANSWERS!
TELL US STRAIGHT—NO FANCY TRICKS:
WHAT WIND BLEW YOU INTO KANSAS?
WHAT'S YOUR PARTY POLITICS?
I got weary—thought I'd stop
wandering, and raise a crop. . . .
—And I want my crop to be
suckled by a soil that's free. . . .
FOREIGN-ACCENT TROUBLEMAKER!
PACK YOUR BAG! THIS SOIL IS SLAVE!
YOU'LL RAISE NOTHING ON THIS ACRE
BUT A TABLET FOR YOUR GRAVE!

Mother, here's news you'll like better than the last. This afternoon some thirty head of Devon cattle strayed into our field, and, half an hour later came two men to drive them home. They were Jason and Owen Brown. They stopped about half an hour with us and told us they were Free State men. I said we might need some help, as the proslavery settlers would sooner or later try to drive us from the Territory. They cheered us and said: Any time you let us know, we will come to your assistance. We are four brothers, all well armed:

A lad came looking for liberty
when Boston was hardly a town.
He did not tremble much at the sea
that wanted him to drown.
John Brown was the name of that fool, and we—
we are the sons of John Brown.

A man grew mad from bending his knee
before King George's crown.
He promised his wife that the land would be free,
—no matter if he go down.
John Brown was the name of that fool, and we—
we are the sons of John Brown.

A soul cried out, "What's freedom to me,
till slavery's day is done?"
A gentle and loving soul was he,
but grim as a pointed gun.

John Brown is the name of that fool, and we
are each of us his son.
If you'd like to join our family,
there's always room for one.

This time, mother, I sign the letter not only as your devoted son, but also—as a son of John Brown.

3. THE BATTLE OF BLACK JACK

Early in October 1855, thousands of Missourians in-
vaded Kansas to stage another "election"—this time,
for a representative to Congress. The Free State settlers
boycotted the polls that day, but on the ninth they
conducted their own election despite threats of blood-
shed. August Bondi left a sickbed that frosty morning
and insisted his friends drive him to the polls.

BALLADEER:

> "Young man, you look bad; if you want to look worse
> we'll take you—but mind, you'll come home in a hearse!"
> Said Bondi, "Let's go! I'll be fine in this coat.
> We're here to vote free, and we'll vote!"
> A wagon caught up with them. "Howdy!" "Good day!"
> Six Browns and a Brown-in-law sat on the hay.
> And there, with his cavalry sword belted on—
> plush cap, and revolver—sat John.
> *(Bondi was introduced to John Brown; they shook hands.*
> *"What do you think of this land?" he asked.)*

JOHN BROWN:

> I met those at the border
> who love the crack of whips.
> Winds came from their lips:
> "Our guns are loaded with thunder.
> This year's storm arrives
> on the lightning of our knives!"
> > Be patient, I whispered
> > to the rifles under the hay.
> > You will have your say.

> I passed those on the highway
> who brought a hope from far.
> Pale and cold they are:
> "Bolt the doors and windows
> from friend as well as foe!
> Keep the lanterns low!"
> > Be patient, I whispered
> > to the rifles under the hay.
> > You will have your say.

I found those trembling
in their tents, who were my sons,
—too weak to load their guns.
Did they not come here
to plow in freedom's name?
Where, then, is the flame?
  The rifles are losing
  their patience under the hay.
  They must have their say!

BALLADEER:

His rifles said plenty. At blossoming time,
John Brown was an outlaw, accused of a crime.
His kin lay in hiding, God only knows where,
their cabins deserted and bare.
On May 26, looking weary and weak,
a lad stumbled into the camp by the creek.
"Come in, August Bondi!" called Brown to his guest,
"And hang up your gun with the rest!"
Another Jew, Weiner, and six of Brown's sons,
and Townsley, a neighbor, had come with their guns.
And though the few muskets looked foolish and worn,
a mighty allegiance was sworn.

(Soon a messenger from Prairie City brought word that a hundred
Missourians were lurking in the woods, perpetrating much and
threatening more. Brown's little band marched to the rescue, and set
up camp near Prairie City, waiting for the promised reinforcements.
But day after day Captain Shore, head of the Prairie City militia,
returned to Brown with the same tidings: "My men are just now very
unwilling to leave home." Brown refused to fight for the town unless
its own men joined him.)

BALLADEER:

On May 31, Captain Shore galloped back:
"The enemy's gone into camp near Black Jack.
They've raided Palmyra—our village is next.
At last every settler is vexed.
A prayer meeting's called for tomorrow at ten;
before the prayer's over, you'll have sixty men.

Bring all your guns loaded, and fit for attack.
There'll be a day's work at Black Jack."

MISSOURIANS:

What will we do with old John Brown, with his each and every
son?
We'll beard them to the branches of a blackjack tree, and toast
them one by one.
When old Brown's head is redder than red,
we'll shake it off and shrink it.
There's many a ma'am in Birmingham
would trade for such a trinket.
Ladies, be quiet! Don't start a riot!
We've got here the crown of old John Brown—who's the lucky
gal that'll buy it?

BALLADEER:

The first streak of dawn was a call to close ranks.
With Captain Shore's company guarding their flanks,
John Brown and his boys lunged ahead for the kill.
Like daybreak they crested the hill.
Below them, half-hidden by oak trees, they saw
the smirking battalions of order and law.
"Now follow me, soldiers!" cried old Captain Brown;
behind him they avalanched down.
Before they had gone more than half of the way
the guns of the enemy wished them good day.
Three volleys resounded, three volleys in vain:
they shook off the bullets like rain.

*(Pointing to a hill south of the Missourians, he announced what
seemed an impossible scheme: August Bondi, Theodore Weiner, and
two others would follow him up that exposed hill, leaving seven at
the Santa Fe road. If they could reach the top, the enemy would be
surrounded.)*

BALLADEER:

The grass of last summer still clung to that slope.
It gave them some shelter, but not what they hoped.

Growled Pate of Missouri: "I see through the glass
five rattlesnakes stirring the grass."
The bullets flew after them, gave them no rest.
"Nu, Weiner," called Bondi, "was meinen Sie jetzt?"
"Was soll ich denn meinen?" was Weiner's reply:*
"Sof odom muves."—All men die.
"Wir machen ihn broges!"—Before he gets mad,
we'd better catch up to the old one, my lad!
They laughed at the bullets still buzzing around,
and raced up the hill to John Brown.

(Pate's men were panic-stricken, imagining that a large force must
be supporting the five on the hill. "I'm going ahead alone," said
Brown. "If I wave my hat, you follow. I've told the others to join us at
the signal.")

BALLADEER:
He walked twenty paces, and lifted his hat.
The fighting Free Soilers flew forward at that.
Said Brown: "You'll surrender—no ifs, buts, or ands!"
The rifles slipped out of their hands.
First Pate handed over his sword and his gun,
then twenty-four followed his lead, one by one;
then out of the bushes popped "brave" Captain Shore
to carry the trophies of war.
Then Pate turned his frown on a bullet-holed tree:
"Don't anyone ever breathe Black Jack to me!"
Said Brown: "You may hear of it once in a while!"
and Bondi, young Bondi—he smiled.

NARRATOR:
At noon the shade they cast was small;
but before the sun of that day rolled down,
the oaks of Kansas arose so tall
their shadow reached into Birmingham town;
and from every branch the name of John Brown
rang through the world like a thunderbird's call.

---

*"Nu, Weiner," called Bondi, "what do you think now?"
"What should I think?" was Weiner's reply.

175

Some say (though proof would be hard to find)
the roots of two young blackjacks grew
quite fierce, and groped till they intertwined,
like John Brown's hand, and the hand of the Jew;
and, deep in free soil, those flaming two
are everlastingly enshrined.

THE END

A Word of Thanks

Half asleep in the ground at Babi Yar
we waited long; and when at last your tread
sounded above, we wondered who you are
that dares to stir the spirit of the dead.

You called to us by number, not by name;
and suddenly we knew—although not bone
of *our* bone, flesh of *our* flesh—why you came:
it was to make our loneliness your own.

Are we to rise, then, and in dreadful ranks
march everywhere with you, live on your lip?
Oh thank you, lad, for fetching us! Oh thanks
for giving us your great young fellowship!

—If only there were something *we* could give
other than what it meant to die . . . to live. . . .

The Rising in the Warsaw Ghetto

Till that April we defined
April in the classic way:
battle figures came to mind—
green triumphant over gray,

silence brilliantly outflanked,
coldness grumbling in retreat,
love and life, superbly ranked,
trumpeting from street to street.

If a word from Warsaw came,
unsurprised we took the news:
April's sun had set aflame
fifty thousand ashlike Jews.

How could it be otherwise
in the month of cosmic strife?
Let those legions show surprise
who'd belittled love and life!

—Nineteen Aprils have been seen
since the tidings reached our shore:
gray surrenders unto green
every spring: a prize of war;

every spring the coldness falls;
silence, too, is overthrown—
but behind his fresh green walls
mankind makes a wintry moan.

Through his skull the north winds howl;
on his heart the ice holds firm;
at his high noon hoots an owl;
in his bright bud nests a worm.

We define the fourth month now
not by anthem-shrilling bees
nor a banner-flaunting bough
—bloodless, punctual victories!

We define it now by those
who, from Warsaw's frozen ground,
like a great green field arose
in a burst of fatal sound.

Night at the Concertgebouw

Center seats, hall high baroque,
program promising—
I've managed, managed it again!

This morning, amid the bright canals,
camera poised for every gable of note,
suddenly I was taken by surprise.
In his usual drone,
that had mixed together a hundred wisecracks, names, and dates,
our guide made mention of her house
and every camera swerved.
But I managed,
managed to turn too late:
the building was drowned behind a bridge. . . .
And if my wife remembered the name of the street,
she did not say so.

After the boat ride there was more to see:
cyclists with streaming hair
among the trucks;
Rembrandt's house, of course;
an ooze of shoppers thick
along the Kalverstraat.
But we remembered to buy tickets for the night,
because at night . . . at night . . .

Gentlemen balding, ladies in elegant hats,
Amsterdam files in: mellow, untroubled,
not quite filling the hall.
Under Beethoven's probing
I begin to wonder
which of Amsterdam's evaporated Jews
might have bought the twenty-three remaining tickets.
At once they enter
—so easily do specters move by night, by music—
and take their places: gentlemen balding,
ladies in elegant hats.

The applause at the close of the first half
fails to dislodge them.
During the intermission they wait in line
at the refreshment bar, the toilets.

Afterward, with the slow movement of the final trio,
she too floats in,
despite all my years of managing,
managing never to read a single entry
in her diary,
nor see the stage play, the movie
(though I did, by accident, one night
glance at Millie Perkins on TV).
In she floats, huge
over the heads of the audience,
thin arms flailing in time to the adagio,
the eyes in her Millie Perkins face
shut—whether in death or ecstasy—
filling the hall with her lilting,
chilling the hall with the draft of her motion,
the terrible air from her nostrils. . . .
peering down at us, as if to say:
You are gray, you are fat, your teeth are in trouble;
I am fifteen until Judgment Day!

It ends; and she, at the first applause,
hurries out as if anxious
not to be jostled by the crowd.
Lustily I clap for the bowing, depleted players,
but cannot manage not to see her as well.
She mounts a bicycle,
rolls away, hair streaming,
disdaining the wild night traffic around her,
gradually indistinct
amid the dark canals.

Zudioska

Smug in her Adriatic noon, Dubrovnik beams.
Within her walls, unconquered and intact,
was much to save—with guns or cunning.
It is all on file in the Rector's Palace.

The streets, in conscious harmony,
flow down from her twin hills
to merge in the Placa, where tourists go
marveling, that after a thousand years
in this world of wounded columns, ravished mausoleums,
no stone is vexed.

Here stands Zudioska, street of the Spanish Jews.
(Dubrovnik took in their banished scrolls;
not often made them wear the yellow badge,
pay special fees, stand trial for ritual murder.)

Ask no question of the stones. Go past.
You will find nothing peculiar on Zudioska.
Women dry their wash.
Children throw their ball.
A cartload rumbles down the narrow steps.
No room is vacant.
There are customers enough in the cafe.

Across from the cafe a door is open.
At the first landing the rabbi awaits you.
On the second landing is the synagogue—
six hundred eighteen years old.
The worshippers await you, though one cannot see them.

Ask no question of the stones.
The Jews had names, but what's the difference?
had women, children, trades—but what's the difference?
It is all on file, no doubt, in the Rector's Palace.
The rabbi could tell you:
>   two hundred Jews dwelled on this street.
>   The Italians came, and put us on Rab.

The Germans came, and took us to Auschwitz.
Seventeen crawled home, and not one child.

We sweep the floor of the synagogue each day.
We hold our service without a *minyan*.
Soon the synagogue will be perfectly silent,
as silent as the perfect stones of the city,
a museum with a guard collecting fees.

God saved us from the quake of 1667.
Nobody saved us in 1943.
And you, if you were Dubrovnik, would you have cried
    Shame!
as they checked off each name and shoved us into the
    boat?

Zudioska drowns in shadow.
The Placa runs in light.
Shield your eyes when you come back into the light
or the beaming stones will burn them as if you are crying.

Gimpl

Bloodless, aching
after a day at the machine,
it was for Gimpl he gave his child the coin,
for Gimpl his child skipped to the newsstand
and fetched home *Warheit*,
for Gimpl Beinish, the busybody,
the bearded little matchmaker
with beady eyes,
rushing off to the beach, the park, the Catskills,
any likely place of mating,
for Gimpl Beinish, who in yesterday's cartoon
had miserably flopped,
but, self-propelled,
was surely on the trail again,
unleashed by his creator, "Z,"

burying his initial
in a corner of the comic strip.

Where now is "Z"?
Ashes on Long Island.
And where that immigrant,
coughing, guffawing over Gimpl
six flights down the East Side airshaft?
A name in a crowded row these thirty years.
His child, surviving still another winter,
crawls toward the sunrays of the benches.
His grandchildren, graying in the suburbs,
wonder what matches their boys and girls make
in far-off colleges.
And Gimpl, the busybody,
bursting with energy, with hope,
Gimpl waits
for the slightest signal
to tear loose from the microfilm of 1912
and range the globe, self-propelled
in search of prospects.

A Wedding in Los Angeles

On Sunday at 2 P.M. in the Temple Akiba
the hands of the organist strike; then down the aisle
exactly as at the rehearsal, but now in costume,
they march, eyes forward, aware of us twisting sideways
to witness the strewing of flowers, the grandmothers' stride,
the balance of bridesmaid and usher, aware as well
of the crouched photographer careful to catch their motion.

On Sunday at 2:15 in the Temple Akiba
before the rabbi, under the canopy, perches
a pair of tremulous doves, aware of us straining
to witness the Word he rains on their awe, the word
they'd written each other in contract, the word they scarcely
have breath to repeat when commanded, aware as well
of the crouched photographer careful to catch their moment.

On Sunday at 3 P.M. in the banqueting-hall
of the Temple Akiba a hundred and fifty guests,
boisterous now, having witnessed that which they witnessed,
move with a clasping of hands, an embracing, a praising,
first to their food, then to the *sher,* the *freilachs,*
the *hora,* treading all griefs underfoot, aware
of the crouched photographer careful to catch their joyance.

On Sunday at 4:25, outdoors for a draught
of air, one notices traffic thundering down
Sepulveda Boulevard, slowing not in the least
before the Temple Akiba, as if unaware
that the band is now playing a waltz, the bride now whirls
with her father, the groom with his mother, carefully caught
for all time by the crouched photographer.

View of Delft

Circling Vermeer's Delft, I asked
our sailor—an ingratiating, enterprising lad—
whether the neo-classic structure overhead
with Hebrew letters poorly masked
was once a synagogue. His smile grew faint,
then vanished altogether: "Yes,"
anticipating my next guess,
"the Germans." "Can a town permit one coat
of Nazi paint
to erase
five centuries of ghosts?" His face
grew honest. "You
have come to Europe and aboard my boat
to find what's old.
Our Delft is new; we're new;
we're tired of being told
ghost tales, no matter how tremendous or how true."
At this he turned his back
on my gray hairs and questions. An exotic doll

with eyes and tresses black
as any ever mirrored in a Dutch canal
engaged him; each had read the other's sign;
that night, if all went well,
he'd share at least her wine
while, like a coat of paint, a seeping in of gas,
            the dusk engulfed
—gable by gable—Vermeer's Delft.

Tour

In four languages, the guide
explains as she has twice a day for years,
that we are entering
one of the quaintest sections of the city,
formerly the Jewish quarter.
Inside the synagogue she points out oddities.
"Notice the walls!"
Perfectly arrayed, as if being marched,
are names—
seventy thousand Czechoslovak Jews,
their dates of birth and deportation.
The calligraphers worked slowly, she explains,
so as not to be sent to the front;
thus the building and its chronicle remain.
Aside from this interesting fact
the room is bare; the group goes quickly.

I too wish to burst loose
as if from a tomb before the lid drops;
yet, summoned by the names so expertly lettered,
slowly I move, or am moved,
toward my destiny.
For this, instead of safe Copenhagen,
we came to Prague!
For this I was granted sight, a tongue.
Whether anyone brings me lunch or not,
today or next year,

I must memorize, memorize,
then hurtle into the ancient square,
open jaws wide, and howl forth a cloud.

REIMANN, VIKTOR 1892, GISELA 1887, EVA 1926,
    JOSEF 1930   26 X 1942
        ZIGMUND 1864, OLGA 1869   19 X 1942
        ANNA 1884, EDIT 1907   18 V 1942

A touch on the shoulder:
"Must you always be the last one
back on the bus?"
Meekly I follow, betray the deafening names
one of which may be mine.
Behind us the honeymooners from Pittsburgh
agree this was "a poor choice" for a tour.
A look from my wife—I hold my peace,
but it is costly: the madness
rushes into my legs, which tremble so
that I beg for the motor to start,
to spare me from embarrassment.

In her passionless, knowledgeable staccato
the guide announces
in four languages
that Hradcany Castle is next.

Westminster Synagogue

Ears afire, I knock at Kent House door.
My hands could not protect them if I tried
except from the drone of Heathrow jets, the roar
of a bus marked "Kensington." Too deep inside,
the tick of an Irish bomb at Harrod's store,
the swords forever committing chivalricide
athwart Knightsbridge, the million-footed squall
from Victoria's trains to Exhibition Hall.

The door shuts out those ghosts storming the Park
across the way; the dignity and calm
of my friend Rabbi uncurtaining his Ark
halts the old swords, defuses the young bomb.
But smilingly he chooses to remark
that where the Torah blazes now, Madame
de St. Laurent enjoyed her fireplace,
herself enjoyed through long years by His Grace

the Duke of Kent. At once his royal groans
roll 'round the room, her murmured syllables
mock what the cantor loftily intones.
But now a door is opened; silence drills
my skull; it fills my rib-cage, chills my bones.
With dignity, with calm the Rabbi tells
that in this room heal fifteen hundred holy
scrolls a scribe has been repairing slowly,

and as each wraith-loved Torah is repaired,
some living congregation takes it in.
—Not for such future were these writings spared,
the Rabbi makes me understand: Berlin
had a museum in mind; these would be aired
as trophies of a tribe that once had been.
I ask: Might one be opened?—but at once
desist . . . No need! Madame de St. Laurent's

syllables, and the groans of her high lover,
are hammered into dust by the dear notes
that—scroll by scroll, rack under rack—recover
their Sabbath force. Seventy thousand throats
flame in my ears. The interview is over,
I'm at the bus stop; but around me floats
a choral fire from every synagogue
of Brno, Pilsen, Bratislava, Prague.

The Dance

They have herded us in, as cattle are,
herded for slaughter, car by car;
they have boxed out each comforting ray of a star
and sped us away, who knows how far;

nothing, nothing to eat or drink,
and sick of each other, the way we stink. . . .
So, Anna, are you still able to think
This too shall pass—or does your heart sink?

I hear the wheels: they are fierce and fast;
I feel that the hour is coming at last;
I remember how many times in the past
a madness kept me from being downcast,

a madness that made me refuse to bow;
and even here, and even now,
starless, airless, a freighted cow,
the madness has found me again somehow.

> She did not whimper, she scarcely spoke;
> freely she slept, refreshed she awoke
> and stepped from the boxcar straight as an oak
> into the city of human smoke.

> Others might huddle, others might pause;
> she moved in rags as in royal gauze;
> more delicious than flowers and applause
> was the gape of her guards with their idiot jaws.

> Even at the very door to the gas,
> even stripped of her rags, the lass
> moved as if she were teaching a class
> with limbs, not lips: *This too shall pass.*

> Her captor, startled by such grace,
> startled that one of fleshless face
> should dare to enter the slaughter place
> high of head and proud of pace,

mumbled a question. When he knew,
"You!" his Luger waved at her; "You!
Dancer! Give us a dance!" His crew
jested and jeered: "A dancing Jew!"

Her deathmates—naked, empty-eyed,
looking as if they already had died
and did not need to be sent inside—
drooped from the walls. "Begin!" he cried.

One more test—once more to rebel:
ignore him? spit on his features? yell:
"My dance is not for such as dwell
under the Devil's tail in Hell!"?

Good; but better to cast a spell:
once more make fall the hush that fell
the first night ever I danced Giselle. . . .
—"The Dying Swan," *that* would do well.

Not well enough! no; I have on
the trappings neither of girl nor swan.
"A dancing Jew!"—Bleak walls, begone!
I weep at the waters of Babylon.

> Those leering guards could not understand
> the lift of her foot, the lilt of her hand;
> but her deathmates straightened, as if at command:
> She was Deborah, waking the blood of her land,

> Miriam, blessing the Dead Sea strand,
> Samson in Gaza, outmocking the grand,
> Masada's crown: Bar Kochba's band,
> Judith, craving to plunge the brand,

> Judith, in Holofernes' den,
> working her charms on that monster of men;
> her lips and her hips and her arms again
> held him, circled him closer; then,

softly the ghosts of her fingers glanced
across his forehead and mouth; against
his medals they brushed; from his entranced
claw the Luger suddenly danced.

One shot! Holofernes falls at my feet.
What if this time there is no retreat?
It will pass, will pass. My career is complete.
Even the bullets that fill me are sweet.

My dance will not stay behind in this room
as wildly you whip my friends to their doom
not drooping now, but afire, abloom
to roar from your chimney a dark perfume.

May 4, 1986: Austria Acquits Herself

In dream what marvel cannot come to pass?
As if by some long-gathering act of will
unboxed, uprisen from his length of grass,
Bluebeard is on the stand—once more to chill
a jury of his peers. Will he this time
sob forth: "O bless you for a second trial!
if only those poor victims of my crime
could share the miracle!" But no: a smile
quickens his face, as in the double row
he recognizes who the jurors are—
truly his peers—twelve pairs of hands aglow
with blood, like his—twelve murderers at the Bar.
I tear myself awake, turn on the news:
once more Vienna votes: Death to the Jews!

1906

The luckiest day of my life
came long before my birth;
it was the day my father
at thirteen issued forth
brow pressed to the window
of a westbound train
as if he could see New York,
as if there were no Ukraine
despite its fertile heart
out of which thrust a wheat
famously high, but never
half as high as its hate.

Bath Beach

> Mein Kind, wir waren Kinder
>   —Heine

My child, we three were children
in times of hunger and dread.
Our mothers pleaded and plotted
to bring us yesterday's bread.

And worse, because we were Jewish
in times of smashing and flames,
our dreams were of burning bedrooms,
of splintering window-panes.

PART 10
A Century of Wars

A Song for Freedom

Oh we who were born in freedom
and grew with a silent pride—
with love for our mother country
and love for her men who died;

oh we who were fed with stories
that told of the tyrant's fall
and sang of the brave battalions
that blazed a free life for all;

we tore from our hearts a banner
and kept it before our eyes:
the symbol of bitter struggles—
the passion that never dies:
the freedom that was our prize.

But traitors again are stirring
and plotting to bind the earth;
and men who were born in freedom
in fetters despise their birth.

And even the mother country
that stood up so tall and proud,
is trembling before the terror,
is blind to the spreading cloud.

We tore from our hearts a banner:
the symbol of those who bled;
—oh let us be fresh battalions
to save our flag from the dead
and blaze a new freedom ahead!

The Ballad of Two Heroes

Igasuki led his Army
through the bloody silent street
with its row of huts bewildered
by the sound of foreign feet.

"Well, it looks as though the devils
didn't leave a soul behind.
Wait! You see that house, Asima?
Is there smoke or am I blind?"

The Major went and soon came running
with a Chinese by his side.
"Who are you?" barked Igasuki;
"speak; there's nothing you can hide."

"Tan Tchi is my name, your Highness,
I'm a peasant of Luchu."
"What's that smoke?" "My wife is cooking;
she can make delicious stew."

"Careful or I'll stew your liver;
—why did you decide to stay?"
"Does it matter who rules China?
I am hungry either way."

Soon the general grew thoughtful;
"Look! the sun is going down;
can your house find room for twenty?"
"It's the largest one in town."

In the best part of his dwelling
all the officers grew gay
and their noisy laughter echoed
through the quiet fading day.

Igasuki, drunk and happy,
shrieked "we'll teach these stupid swine,
—when we've taken all of China
we won't drink such rotten wine."

Holding in his hands a package
slowly entered poor Tan Tchi,
Now he broke their thirsty laughter
"I fear that day will never be."

Swift they turned, so pale and quiet,
watched, and tried to understand.
Soon Tan Tchi unwrapped the package:
—dynamite was in his hand.

All the officers were screaming,
lunging forward on their foe,
but he smiled, and then, like thunder,
fire dealt the room a blow.

Tzu-Lin-Yu was in her kitchen
when she heard the roaring blast.
While she wept about her husband
Japanese were coming fast.

From the street she watched them running,
swift her pulse, her brain, her feet;
now she heard them shouting vengeance,
swift the furnace-flame she beat.

Through the door she heard them surging;
bombs into the blaze she threw.
Now they saw her in the kitchen,
saw the tiny Tzu-Lin-Yu.

"LONG LIVE CHINA!! LONG LIVE CHINA!!"
While they reached and clutched her then:
suddenly the stove erupted
smashing hut and girl and men.

From the hills beyond the village
as the sun was sinking low,
China's Eighth Route Army listened,
heard the crash, and watched the glow.

When they saw Japan's battalions
fleeing scattered from the town,
strengthened now, the troops of China
from the hills came marching down.

Through the silent empty village
with its tiny homes they passed,
till they came where Igasuki
and his friends had drunk their last.

Thirty officers were counted;
of Tan Tchi they saw no trace;
—then they found his shattered body
with a smile upon its face.

On the morrow, when the people
came back gayly to Luchu
they were told the tragic story
of Tan Tchi and Tzu-Lin-Yu.

And the great beloved commander,
while the folk began to cry,
proudly spoke: "With such defenders
can our China ever die?"

Maria

1.

Sighing, Maria rises
from her bath of soapy foam,
and steps from the tub as grandly
as an Empress of ancient Rome.

With a huge, a purple towel
she dries her back and sides.
She weighs her breasts proudly—
they're heavy enough for a bride's.

Her flesh is so raw, so eager
from the water's passionate scorch
to be stroked by strong man-fingers,
to be nude on the windy porch.

She wipes a cloud from the mirror
and begins to tame her hair
that runs down wild and golden
until her breasts are not bare.

There is no more purple towel,
but a scarf hanging limp from her head.
Maria's a Persian dancer;
great princes offer their bed.

A scarf is the purple towel
flung out by the whim of her hand.
Crowds grew hoarse with cheering
Maria over the land.

She is long and white in the mirror—
all unblemished, curved.
Sighing, she yields to her clothing,
and the supper will soon be served.

2.

Boris, Maria's brother,
gulped his milk and ran.
They heard him jump from the porchway
away with another plan.

Night flowed in through the windows
quickly: they tried to knit
by the moon and the distant fires;
they tried to silently sit.

"Mother." "What." "The machine-gun
is making too little noise.
You should have stopped Boris."
"He's just outside with the boys."

"Mother." "What." "I'm worried.
We still have time to go."
"Go then. I'll stay in the village
though they burn me head to toe."

There was no sound in the village.
They could hear a mile away
the fires greedily eating
as though the houses were hay.

Maria counted by a window.
Outside the silence mounted.
Boris crashed through the porchway
and they forgot what they counted.

"Hide! Maria! Mother!
The Nazis—they are here! they've come!"
The mother held on to her needles
as though her hands were numb.

"Under your bed, Maria!
It's you they'd be wanting most."
"I'll kill them all!" said Boris.
"No, son. You'll be the host."

3.

They were very efficient. She listened,
afraid they would hear her heart.
They stamped and yelled 'til the wallbeams
threatened to fall apart.

They visited every closet,
the cellar, the bathroom, the hall.
Not a dresser-drawer was neglected,
not a match-box was too small.

They were very efficient. Two Nazis
crusaded up the stairs.
Her heart boomed out in the bedroom
"Never be theirs, not theirs!"

They had taken a thousand houses;
their hands were not surprised.
They dragged her out by the nightgown
and her scream hung paralyzed.

They smiled at the gift of her beauty;
they felt her thighs, her breasts.
She ran to a window, but quickly
they grabbed her with oaths and jests.

They lay her down on the mattress,
but she kicked at one in the groin.
He crushed her face with an elbow,
and the other flipped a coin.

They ripped away the nightgown.
Maria locked up her eyes.
The loser held her fastened,
and the winner gripped her thighs.

His mouth drooled blood from her kicking,
but the thighs were slowly spread.
She shrieked at the first intrusion,
and welcomed the night to her head.

4.

The day is sunny. Three cloudlets
harmlessly graze in the sky.
Maria finds a berry
whose brothers are all too shy.

The berry melts to sweet wine
on the patient bowl of her tongue,
while Nazis whip to a crevice
the village old and young.

She cannot believe the purpose
that blazes in Nazi eyes.
The day is sunny. From somewhere
a bored old rooster cries.

If the sky were cracked by lightning;
if rains were whipping the corn,
she might believe; or if whirlwinds
were making the willows mourn.

Slowly she counts the village:
not one has been left behind
of all the old and infant,
of all the crippled and blind.

But the Nazi faces are worried.
A new machine-gun song
grows like fire in the distance.
Maria is suddenly strong.

They are stood by the crevice horizon;
everyone's hands are high.
They watch, and the Nazis are watching,
three cloudlets become the sky.

"Fire!" they fall, and "Fire!"
until the horizon is clear.
The Nazis run with their rifles,
and the song of guns grows near.

5.

When Maria woke, the half moon
had no smile on his face.
He watched her slowly remember
the bullet-pain, and the place.

The crevice was shallow; she knew it
from picnics and berry-hunts.
A little farther Stepan
had clasped her tightly once.

She turned each face to the moonlight
'til she reached her mother's head.
She pressed an ear to the body,
but the heart was silent as lead.

She turned each face to the moonlight
'til she reached her brother's head.
Only the moon and Maria
were silent but not dead.

Sobbing, she clasped her brother,
tied to the ground like a stone.
She begged the strength of the bullet
"Let me die, and not be alone!"

A rifle cried at the stillness;
a song of soldiers awoke.
Maria climbed from the crevice
and saw her village in smoke.

Suddenly she remembered
the blaze in Nazi eyes.
Clutching her bleeding shoulder
she ran to the rifle-cries.

6.

"What do you want?" said the captain
as soon as her shoulder was bound.
"I want to fight in the Army."
"How old are you?" he frowned.

Fifteen—she remembered the birthday.
"I'll soon be twenty-one."
He looked at her face and believed it.
"Do you know how to use a gun?"

"I'll learn," she answered quickly.
"Before we get too far,
you should know that war's no picnic.
We go where dangers are.

"We cannot stop for rivers,
we cannot hide in a storm,
we seek no shade in the Summer,
our Winter is never warm.

"We go where cannon are sleepless,
where the living lie with the dead.
Do you want to join our Army?"
"Yes," Maria said.

France

1. THE HARVESTING

Out of their hovels, shadowful and worn,
down to the fields all glamorous with corn,
the reapers come with baskets at their side.
     Oh throw your baskets down awhile, and dance!
     Rich is October flowering in France.
     Outshine the harvest sun that bursts with pride!
The reapers bend like broken grain; and throw
their load ungently to a waiting cart.
No laughter rips the pantomime apart.
     Why are your children timid as the crow
     that sees a figure dangling on a log?
     Why is there silence, heavier than fog?
This harvest seems an alien in their hands.
Above the corn a German soldier stands.

2. THE SOWING

The Square lies pounded by October rain.
Women run, covered up in shawls of pain.
At the foot of a guillotine three faces bleed.
     Blow, murderous wind, sharp as a plough!
     Tear off our fruit, unripened, from the bough!
     Long was our winter; we are ready for seed.
Long was our winter under a false sky:
the shawls hung black, the window-shades were drawn;
guns were the father of our bastard corn.
     Dumb as the earth we watched our children die.
     Three faces lie on the Square: three seeds to sow.
     Rise, river of blood, and overflow!
Our eyes are eager for the glory of France;
Our feet are aching for the harvest-dance.

Sunrise in Paris

Hideous night rolls off our city's heart.
Dimly behind the sunrise grumble volleys
from stubborn shadows making their final fort
some dog-deserted garbage cans in alleys.

Now girls open their closets, lifting out
scarlet blouses, and shake away the dust
gathered so long.
                     Emerging from our throat
the *Marseillaise*, no longer locked in a nest
at secret meeting-places, publicly leaps
over the roofs: a wild, gigantic swan.
And hope, grown tenderly like precious grapes,
beneath our riotous feet bursts into wine.

Such miracles the hideous night has done!
Our eyes, that never wept, weep at the sun.

Victory Comes to the Unbombed Cities

Flower, factory, face—all high, unhurt.
What fierce armada flew? what mutilation
reached down invisibly, ripped us apart,
that bells now bathe our wound in celebration?

Was dancing bold here, a forbidden sport
yesterday? Were song and laughter rationed?
Did windows wait—bitterly shaded, shut,
that all at once they shriek in celebration?

What bloodstain seeps in secret through our shirt?
What cripples crowd the Square with exultation?
What ruined city roars up from our heart
to catch confetti hurled in celebration?

The Real Ogre

Not in a fairy-tale city,
not on a fairy-tale street.
This house becomes cold in his shadow;
this pavement recoils from his feet.

He crawls through the lips of a statesman;
he squirms in the ink of a pen.
We thought we had slain him forever—
but look! he is growing again.

The oceans seethe cold between peoples
who yesterday warmed one another.
A man is forbidden to smile at
the man who last year was his brother.

Machines that should clothe us and house us
are singing his anthem instead;
and vessels, now full of his wishes,
bring bullets to lands without bread.

Those few who arise to defy him,
who rip off the mask of his lust,
are silenced and flogged by a Justice
that only the blind can call "just."

The whole earth is cold in his shadow—
the whole earth recoils from his feet:
this Ogre, this Vampire—the warbeast
who waits in the shade of my street.

Panic

Run home from the field!
            run home from the mine!
The Ogre is thirsty for human wine . . .

Put out the lights!
            get under the bed!
The Ogre is hungry for human bread . . .

Lock every shutter!
            bolt every door!
The Ogre is knocking—the Ogre War!

Prayer

Among her dolls my child lies dreaming.
Before she wakens, join with me:
enough of pain, enough of worry,
enough of ambushed friends to bury,
enough of hopes that cannot be,
enough of hate, enough of scheming!
The world shall be no cemetery—
destroy the Ogre and go free
before she wakens from her dreaming!

Efstratia Nikolaidu

It happened in December
when winds, like police,
drove through the trembling
cities of Greece.

Despite strict orders
for all flames to die,
somewhere one
still lit up the sky.

Till it were tracked down
and choked—having sinned—
there'd be no respite
for a Greek wind. . . .

It happened in December.
She was fifteen years old.
New breasts sampled
by the lecherous cold,

measured by the rifles
of Salonika jail—
was it fear or hunger
that turned her pale?

fear—or hunger?
She sang to the guns:
"Fire! Of your bullets
I will bear sons!" . . .

Girl, can a poet
reach where you are?
I have two daughters,
each bright as a star.

If one of my stars
needed a name
I'd give her yours,
girl of flame.

More than my own life
do I love these two—
yet I would have them
blaze like you.

The Tinderbox

(Based on Hans Christian Andersen's story)

Forests and fields are tinder dry, and the
danger of fire hangs heavy over the land.
   —Nick Kenny, *New York Daily Mirror*

Among ash-trees in the forest,
gray and thin, with furrowed bark—
sang an old, dishevelled giant
whom the ravens had mistaken
for an ash-tree in the dark:

*"From the heart of a rotten tree
that once was fruitful and green,
cut out the bitterest part—
the splintered core of its heart.*

*"This is the wood that once
was loved by April suns,
that dimly recalls the story
of its primeval glory.*

*"This is the wood that knows
a forestful of woe.
This is the wood that remembers
a chronicle of Decembers.*

*"Shamed by the staring stars,
it hungers for a spark—
so that the skies may admire
a towering tree of fire.*

*"If so much flame you need,
seek out a rotten tree
seasoned by lightning and thunder.
Its heart is perfect tinder."*

Among ash-trees in the forest:
gray and thin, with furrowed bark—
sang an old, dishevelled giant
whom the ravens had mistaken
for an ash-tree in the dark.

Neither snow nor rain could budge her
from that melancholy place.
Even when the woods bent double,
straight she sat—as though December
had no power against her face.

Many passersby she'd halted,
hoping each would be the one—
till along the road one twilight
marched a grim-faced little soldier
shouldering a rusty gun.

"Here! you're not in any hurry!
Put the rifle down and stay!
If you're brave and fond of silver
I can tell you where to get some
in a quick and easy way.

"Underneath you lies a chamber,
bursting with its secret store.
Take as much as you can carry;
then, as soon as you have spent it,
come again and gather more!

"Do me only one small favor:
you will pass a cobwebbed shelf;
bring the tinderbox you find there
back to me! As for the silver,
you may keep it all yourself."

Half a night she waited, trembling,
in the quiet, in the mist—
till she heard his climbing footstep,
and at last he stood beside her.
"You were quick enough!" she hissed.

"Now that you have all the silver
you can carry—where's my fee?
Surely you did not forget it
on the shelf among the cobwebs?"
"Here's the tinderbox," said he.

"But before I let you take it,
tell me what it does for you!
Why are you so wild to have it?"
"Never mind!" the woman shouted,
"it will do what it will do!"

"Well, I've fetched enough for others;
now I'll do myself a turn.
Since you'd rather keep the secret,
I will keep the box of tinder.
On a cold night it may burn."

*The story begins. You are safe. It is of a distant land long dead, its
tyrant king, his daughter Beauty—loved by the people and locked
from them, a soldier full of wounds, and a box of forbidden tinder.*

The princess watched from her window
all through a night and a day.
Her bed stayed cold, her broth grew cold;
she frowned her mother away.

Late on the second evening
her nurse besieged the door:
"Beauty! your father wants you to smile.
Here's good news from the war:

"Our troops have taken the city,
the haughtiest city of all.
Its elders whimper for mercy now:
on humble bellies they crawl.

"Look—you can see from your window
the far-off victory flame.
No land is left that will not bow
at mention of his name."

The princess watched from her window
until she could not see.
At last she turned to the door, and sobbed:
"Bring no more news to me.

"Go tell the king how happy
and proud appeared his child.
Go to the king and tell him, nurse,
that at your news I smiled."

In triumph the army marched through the capital city, but some
who leaned from windows sang not in time to the drumbeat.

The wood awakes,
the flags are in bloom—
yet our streets cling to
their wintry mood.

The kingdom grows,
but our places shrink.
We are in great danger
of vanishing.

Each one of us,
alone in his room,
has a secret hunger
more than for food;

a secret thirst
more than for drink.
These are souls, not voices,
whimpering:

Light, oh sweet light!
discover our gloom!
Laughter, seek out
our solitude!

Quickly—two arms
before we sink!
Before winter kills us
come quickly, spring!

A woman moved along the line of march, searching in vain for her
unreturning son, and paining with her questions all who would
listen.

Here are three riddles, not so deep,
    yet no one cares to try.
I promise there'll be prizes—
    but you stare, and turn away.

When is a day like midnight,
    though the kettle-drums rejoice?
When every face is on parade,
    except the dearest face.

What is the town that won so much,
    yet lost more than it won?
It is the town that lent my child,
    and has him not again.

How can a king, a haughty king
    with hundred ears, be deaf?
Because he does not hear my heart
    beat out his epitaph.

At the head of the procession rolled the royal chariot; but for all her
finery the princess could not hide the lamentation in her eyes.

Improper tears are on my cheek;
improper sobs instead of cheers.
Had my grief the knack of speaking
you would smite it with your spears.

I hail the very walls you hate,
and curse the conqueror you hail.
List my heart among the traitors!
Set a spy upon its trail!

Confetti fell for hours. Then there were no more troops to hail, except the unreturning who march without trumpets at the end of all victory processions. So the people turned, and went home.

When the drumbeats marched into murmurs, when the cheers
  dispersed like a crowd,
when evening made of the banners one giant fluttering shroud,
then shadows lined the sidewalks, and a leaf in the wind was loud.

"You're tardy—three minutes tardy! Come in and bolt the door;
waste neither time nor motion—you may spare your knee the floor.
Just part your lips and tell me the truths I've waited for!"

"Your Majesty is in humor—what truths have I to tell
beyond what even the blind know, and you know doubly well?
There was never a day like this one—my head's a ringing bell."

"Oh, save your lies for the people! D'you count *me* among the
  blind?
Shall I look when the lips are grinning, and not when a cloud's in
  the mind?
—How many frowns did you ambush? How many fists did you
  find?"

"At every glimpse of the carriage, the roar of the throng was great—
farmers are said to have heard it ten miles from the city gate—"
"The princess was riding with me; her they do not hate.

"Since you have nothing to tell me, listen while I tell you:
twelve windows hung no banners on Liberty Avenue;
eighty-nine women were silent; one laughed, and I know who."

"Your Majesty is a keen man—none say it louder than I—
yet something I did encounter, that should not pass you by:
it was an old soothsayer, with his chin touching the sky.

"His white lips wove a nightmare that ruined the trumpet's blare—
a frenzied, impossible fancy, that only a fool would share—
yet people turned to hear it, and soon it was everywhere.

"We seized him, the mad old prophet; outside in a trance he lies,
murmuring still of the princess. At your command he dies."
"Bring him to me!" cried the monarch, and covered up his eyes.

Led into the chambers of the king, the prophet told his dream.

I dreamed our city tore
the kerchief of night from her head;
and her million windows, like eyes,
opened—blinked at the sun.
For miles around, in her honor,
a carpet of green was spread—
as though the triumph of triumphs
had finally been won.

Every street, as by magic,
turned into festival ground:
high-hung banners swaying,
taffeta tempting the breeze.
Laughter began—and in tears
strangers embraced at the sound.
Then drums took up a dance-beat,
and bugles waltzed with ease.

"What joy is this?" I wondered,
"that such a city can share,
whose only share has been silence,
darkness and cold till now?"
Then all at once I arrived
at shadowy Gallows Square
(whose cobblestones so long
have been paved across my brow).

It was a wedding feast!
Thousands battled for room.
Our eyes surrounded the lovers
with a garland that laughed and cried.
A soldier, with flame for his fortune,
appeared to be the groom;
and, healing more wounds than his,
your daughter was the bride.

Enraged, the king threw off his hood of dignity; but the minister
sought to calm him.

Why do you suddenly quiver—
you, whose banner is known
to the spray of ocean and river,
to palm and to arctic snow?

Why should you stamp and stammer—
you, whose word can awake
scythe, or musket, or hammer,
whose bugler announces fate?

Why have your features whitened?
What does your fury mean?
Can such as you be frightened
by one poor prophet's dream?

Back and forth strode the king, bellowing decrees at which the lamps
and the minister nodded.

Block off the neighborhood whose air was poisoned
by this mad mouth! Let anyone who dares
to speak of dreams be instantly imprisoned!

Send back the soldiers! We can find them wars . . .
If one among them is not eager, seize him!
Our dungeon-walls cry out for prisoners!

When there's a handshake, tiptoe close and listen!
Disperse them harshly if a third appears!
Whoever walks at night must have good reason!

Set guards to guard the guards at all our doors!
Search every passerby: the sick, the wizened!
Put smiths to work on bolts and window-bars!

Fasten your telescopes on the horizon!
Let not a cough, a sigh, slip past your ears!
Report at once a pair of eyes that glisten!

Blow out the luxury of lamp-post flares!
Whoever lights a candle reeks of treason. . . .
Send dogs and children scampering upstairs!

And you, mad mouth, may find my power pleasing,
if you exalt me in the public squares
and call your dream a lie. . . . But I am raising

a row of gallows where were once held fairs.
If it's the *dream* you cling to—say your prayers!

But the prophet smiled, and spoke:

Pluck out the tongue that told a dream—
without a tongue it still can gleam.
Condemn the prophet to be slain—
his sacred dream will start again.

His sacred dream will start again
for all your promises of pain.
His sacred dream will not be sold
for all your galaxies of gold.

Beyond the shadow of your throne
it has a kingdom all its own.
It flutters past your raging hand.
It is not subject to command.

It is the sap within the tree
that hears and mocks the wind's decree;
because it knows that unaware
the wind will have a seed to bear.

*When the princess learned what the dream was, of him who climbed
so surefootedly to the gallows, she sat many hours at her window, till
the dream become her own.*

A man of wounds shall be my groom:
with lungs of death and lips of death;
and I shall blow my April breath

215

into the breast that is a tomb,
    that is a tomb. . . .

And I shall warm him night and day
with magic on my fingertips;
and when his wounds cry out like lips
I'll suck their agony away,
    night and day.

Soon the soldier, with the tinderbox forgotten in his pocket,
approached his city—unseen except in visions through the long war.

Beloved housetops:
my eyes, like the sun,
kiss you tenderly:
one by one.

Did the winds beat you
while I was not here
to drive them away
with my dreaded spear?

Under your wing
did young ones burst
out of their shells
with bewildered yells?

What death-bed groan
did you alone
hear? What heartbreak
went up in smoke?

Tell me, tell me all
gables and eaves
that came with me
on a highway of graves!

Have you changed a little?
Are you somewhat shaken—
roofs that came with me
where nothing was unbroken?

216

Tell me, tell me all;
but ask nothing in return.
A word is on my tongue
that you would not wish to learn.

*A gang of children heard him, and danced around him with new
words to an old song.*

There was a little soldier came home from war;
(Turn, turn, run into the woods!)
he thought his city was just as before;
(Turn, turn, run into the woods!)

He greeted the roofs, and asked them to say
(Turn, turn, run into the woods!)
had anything happened while he was away;
(Turn, turn, run into the woods!)

The roofs had plenty of news to tell,
(Turn, turn, run into the woods!)
but there was a law against tolling the bell;
(Turn, turn, run into the woods!)

*Strange words they were, but the tune was of his childhood, and
made him thirst even more for a sight of the beloved streets. In
through the gates he wandered—but, instead of an organ-grinder's
melody at the well-remembered corner, he heard chains. Then he
came to a street on which he had often played hide and seek—but
now it was no game.*

LIGHTS OUT! they are riding: the raven-hooded three!
Before the hooves of their horses, moonbeams scatter and
    hide.
Which one of us this evening shall their pale hostess be?
Not me, thank God, not me! They cross to the other side. . . .

They kick in a door without knocking; soon the woman
    shrieks.
Away rides one too many—one who is gagged and bound.
Now she crawls down the stairs.
        (Is it her *mouth* that speaks,
or have her *eyes* the message more thunderous than sound?)

Along the street, and up into the night air, went her lamentation.

    Lost to my pillow are the lips that love;
    a voice has vanished, and my rooms are bare.
    Now grief is all the property I have:
    my bread, my lamp, my mirror, and my chair.

    Out of this empty house, then, I must move
    and seek a shelter for my grief somewhere
    high on a hill, or deep within a cave,
    and slowly turn into a tigress there.

    Good neighbors: do you watch me? do you grieve?
    or can you sleep, as *I* slept, without care?
    (At sunrise, may *your* love still be alive!
    May the swift riders never seize your hair!)

    Lost to my pillow are the lips that love;
    a voice has vanished, and my rooms are bare.

Sobbing, she sat on the steps of her house. One by one the neighbors
came out and stood around her.

    Once the shattered wing of a bird
    pulled our pity to the ground,
    and we wept—we wept for a sound
    that would never again be heard.

    Now we neither bend nor weep:
    what can be happening to us?
    Night after night is murderous,
    yet we stay desperately asleep.

Who knows what loved-one's lovely face
our shoe may tread upon today?
Each dawn fresh corpses line our way,
but staring straight ahead we race.

Straight ahead to our tasks we go,
as though the streets are no-way strange.
But if you cannot see a change
ask the raven and the crow.

They have good reason to be loud.
All night they feast, all day they sing
an anthem to our murderer king.
They are his patriots—his crowd.

Stepping out from the shadows, the soldier came toward them.

Is it as cold for you as for me?
Is it too dark for you to see?
Or am I alone pursued by wind?
Or am I alone becoming blind?

I have a box of tinder here.
One spark: the night grows warm and clear.
Now we read one another's eyes.
Now we avenge one another's sighs.

He struck fire. Some in the crowd shrank toward their doors.

What's wrong with you, boy—have you given up reason?
We've jollier damsels than death to be teasing.
Blow out the blaze! put your tinder away,
or the guards win a medal today!

The law's printed clearly: "A threesome must never
be caught on a thoroughfare speaking together!"
If *that's* not enough, you're a soldier besides:
for *this* they'd be after our hides!

They'd claim we were weaving a web for your senses,
until you had no other wish than the princess;
until you'd be ready to tear through the sky—
until you'd be ready to die.

Your eyes begin gleaming—that isn't permitted!
We're mad to have told you—forget it, forget it!
Quick! blow out the blaze that can only destroy—
and the tinderbox, bury it, boy!

Holding aloft the tinderbox, he scoffed at them.

You—whose throats no longer
remember the bliss of speaking
(except in whispers);
whose eyes are dying of hunger
for a day that's late in breaking;
whose griefs, in clusters

of three, at dusk assemble;
whose ears (like a doe's) imagine
the hunter's bugle;
whose fingers guiltily stumble;
whose dreams are a school-house pageant:
loyal and legal;

you gape at me in wonder—
as though it's I who am altered;
instead of burning,
your blood is alarmed by tinder;
—go, get your windows bolted!
I bring the morning.

*As he turned to leave, the ones who had not fled looked up from
their grief and beseeched him:*

Forgive the frantic, who crawl and cower;
forgive their whining, their helpless wringing
of hands, their stupid ways, their small ways!
each of them's tinder just the same.

Bring Beauty back to us from the tower
where only winds partake of her singing!
Bring Beauty back to our gloom-heaped hallways,
away from the tower which traps her flame!

She shall remind our limbs of their power,
remind the muted bells of ringing,
remind the dawn that night is not always—
and we shall remind her of her fame.

They told him of the beautiful princess, barred from her people by
the tyrant, and of the dream for which many had died. They hid him
in their homes, and taught him a new song.

Not always will Beauty in private be grown,
that long has been gracing your gardens alone.
Not always her laughter will ring through your days
to ease you and charm you like ripples of praise.

Not always will Beauty be mourned by the stars:
their brightest young sister surrounded by bars!
Not always her music will waft you at night
beyond where the eagles abandon their flight.

The planter of barley who pines for her now
will have her at harvesting some day, somehow.
The builder of castles, embittered and cold,
will bloom at her coming, will dance as of old.

In spite of the lock, and the moat, and the gate;
in spite of the sentries that everywhere wait;
in spite of the gallows, in spite of the swords,
not always, not always will Beauty be yours!

All day he gazed through half-drawn blinds toward the castle-tower
in which the princess was held.

Into my brain a rumor creeps—
like sunrays into a grave
at which the corpse in wonder gapes,

dreaming he's still alive.
—Oh I am sick of death's white lips—
a tenderer breast I crave. . . .

Into my brain a rumor creeps
of hair the wizards wove,
a voice like wind on golden harps,
two eyes that shelter love.
—The cloak of death from my shoulder drops,
and I am almost brave. . . .

The next night, when none but the moon and he seemed awake, the
little soldier slipped past the guards and scaled the palace wall.

Two conspirators, we travel
softly through the night:
one on outlawed walls, the other
flaunting outlawed light.

Every pillow has its dreamer
properly at home;
but the moon deserts her pillow—
she and I must roam.

Let the limbs that ache from labor
have a turn at sleep!
Let the eyes have rest from landscapes
that have made them weep!

Night's a time for castle-climbing,
for the moon to gleam.
Night's a time for kings to tremble,
and for slaves to dream.

Now he reached a balcony outside the princess' window, and saw her
asleep within.

Always through glass they glowed,
the golden things I wanted:
since the first year of life
beyond my price.

High on tip-toe I stood,
dug out my coins and counted—
they never were enough
to melt the glass.

Why then, oh foolish pulse,
is now your speech unsteady?
Wild at a window-pane
why should you pound?

We know that someone else
shall win this golden lady—
one who counts coin on coin,
not wound on wound.

Golden (the pulse replied)
aye, more than gold is golden!
In through your eyes she came
and makes me wild.
Coins are with her no good—
tap at the window, holding
your wounds out. They may seem
better than gold.

She slept, and he gazed in at her, and behind a crack in the wall
waited the crone who never slept, who spun and wove by day,
watched and listened by night.

More softly than woodworm or mole,
the carpenter'd burrowed a hole
where, waiting unseen,
two ears that were keen
might listen, two eyes might patrol.

Forever two ears and two eyes
recorded her frowns and her sighs;
each far-away look
marked down in a book
by dressmakers turned into spies.

A hesitant rap at the pane.
What was it? the wind or the rain?
From restless repose
the princess arose
and hungered to hear it again.

For this they had patiently spied:
this waking, this tapping outside!
And now, at a knock,
she ran to unlock
the window—and opened it wide.

The moon gave its comrade away:
a uniform, shredded and gray;
a visage, not hard,
yet shadowed and scarred;
two eyes like the trumpets of day.

Then scurried the watcher to ring
alarms in the ear of the king.
One word was enough.
The blankets came off.
He fled like a wasp on the wing.

*Before permitting the little soldier to be seized, the king put an ear to
the keyhole, so that he might hear what they were murmuring to one
another.*

Now that I see you close enough
my pulse comes suddenly to life—
but call your guards, and let me be taken!
The law of a great king is broken.
    *Not so loud or someone will hear!
    every crack in the wall's an ear.*

What right have I to see you so close?
If you saw me, you'd wake the house.
You'd call your guards, and have me fettered.
—I'm only a soldier, scarred and tattered.
    *The moon touches you, shows who you are:
    every tatter and every scar.*

224

I thought you would be afraid of harm.
I was afraid you might not climb.
Night after night the silence taunted:
"What makes you think that you'd be wanted?
Why would he climb—with the swords around?"
Because you are not on the ground.

"How could he want an unseen face?"
That which I'd seen I wanted less.
"Death is the punishment for coming."
Death was my bread before I came climbing.
—And you, why did you wait for me?
Because of a kiss that will set me free.

At the word "free," the king tore open her door and entered.

Would you be free of eyes that know and love?
Would you be rid of all the good you have?
Would you be gone and leave this place a grave?

You have belonged to me since your first hour:
my crown's top gem, my garden's foremost flower,
my banner's emblem, and my tower's tower!

I'd sooner let your lips by worms be kissed,
sooner your limbs by shadows be caressed,
sooner your maidenhood by death possessed,

than that a common soldier's breath be near
enough to feed on yours or that your hair
allow his greedy eyes a golden share!

But Beauty replied:

I am not yours, although you own me
the way you own a field or town.
If you had ever loved me, known me,
you might have cared less for your crown.

I am not yours, whose servants chide me
for frowning when I should have smiled.
Murder's the son that grew beside me,
and he has been your favorite child.

I am not yours, who seek to save me
from sunlight's touch, from love's embrace.
I am not yours, but theirs who crave me,
who risk your guards to reach my face.

I am not yours, though bars surround me.
Not yours! My pulse is free to shout.
At last the eyes of love have found me,
and they've a flame you can't put out.

"Take him!" commanded the king—and when the little soldier had
been dragged away he turned to the princess.

At dawn a hundred messengers will bring
the news to yawning town and countryside:
"The villain's caught, who impudently tried
to steal the dearest treasure of our king!
Come to the Square!" they'll cry, "and watch him swing!
Come see what happens when a law's defied!"
—And you'll come, too, you wretch, you soldier's-bride;
the gallows-bell your own soft hand will ring.

Wait till you hear the cawing of the crowd,
more hungry than myself to have him hang!
Wait till you see a crow enjoy his tongue!
Wait till the eyes of love are raven's food!
Then home you'll crawl, wretch, with a sweeter song.
—Dare me no more! Who dares me is destroyed.

The soldier was thrown into a dungeon to await his punishment. At
first the silence and darkness oppressed his spirit, but then he
remembered the box of tinder. Striking fire, he saw that others stood
around him, each startled to discover himself not alone. Slowly their
whisper turned into a song.

Where murder shows a proud and proper face
to cheering multitudes across the land,
there prison is a comfortable place
and chains are comfortable on the hand.

Sob, if you must, uncaptivated lark,
for them whose manacles are on the brain:
the daylight crowds—alone and in the dark—
who sing while they are set upon and slain.

O lark without a warden, waste no sob
on us who are alone in darkness bound—
our hope has saucy wings, and our hearts throb
so loud, a tyrant trembles at the sound.

At the hanging hour, Gallows Square was more crowded than ever
before. People craned their necks to see this man who had dared to
make real their most forbidden dream. He climbed the gallows-steps,
took from his pocket the tinderbox, and struck fire.

My heart is willed to Beauty,
the rest of me to the crows.
To you I leave, good people,
my only other prize.

It is the box of tinder
that has brought me where I am.
For all my deeds of mischief
its brightness is to blame.

This evil box of tinder
showed me what none should see:
a king who steals from his castle
each night in search of prey.

I might have found among you
a pillow soft and safe,
and scarcely have felt the vampire
sucking away my life.

I might have dreamed that Beauty
was turning my room to gold,
and not have ached for the tower
in which her warmth is jailed.

This tinder is the culprit:
judge it in my place!
Curse it, spit at it, stone it!
Bind its flame in the noose!

His speech was ended. Now only the fire spoke from the box.

Louder by far than trumpets, a silence rocked the Square.
Taller by far than gallows, a wonder blossomed there.

The tinderbox made planets more plentiful than the sky's:
its blaze went out to the people, and fed their famished eyes.

Down through their veins it travelled, the long-awaited spark,
and set their hearts on fire, that had beat so long in the dark.

Pale on his rubied platform quivered the tyrant king.
"Put out the flame!" he shouted, "and let the villain swing!"

"Put out the flame!" he bellowed; but even the guards stood still.
"Blocks of wood: do you hear me? It is your sovereign's will!

"Do you forget my favors? Do you forget your vow?
Traitors to one another—do you betray me now?

"Is this your thanks for the glory I've brought upon the land?
Put out the flame!" he thundered; "*It is your king's command!*"

The blaze-touched swords of the guardsmen turned glittering and
      grim.
The blaze-touched eyes of the people at last surrounded him.

Were these the fluting shepherds? Were these the gentle flocks?
On fire! the Square was on fire!—a giant tinderbox!

Like a conflagration the people arose and destroyed whatever was
hateful to them. Over toppling gallows, over the king huddled with
his henchmen and spies, over all his murderous monuments they
raged, and wonderful to the stars sounded their song of flame.

> *Burn to the ground, you spires of greed:*
> *tyranny's hall and hatred's temple!*
> *Too long we've trembled in your shade—*
> *time now for you to tremble.*
>
> *Burn down, you rotten citadels*
> *where death sings and the raven hatches!*
> *We'll make a sunrise of your walls,*
> *an April of your ashes!*

END

The Rebels of Greece

Three years you've hunted us from hill to hill,
hanged our best brothers in the public squares,
gorged every jail with us—and now, how fares
your government? Does Greece at last lie still?
Not yet! not yet! There's more of us to kill
this day, than when you started! Neither prayers
nor punishments can purge you of your cares—
for all the ill you work must work you ill.

Gather your wise men—ask them to explain
this weird new law that contradicts all laws,
so that our every casualty's a gain,
so that your every victory's in vain!
Are we immortals—or is it our cause,
our cause that turns your bullets into grain?

To a Dark-Skinned People

You are the latest on a list of shame
that shadows me: a dark inheritance
since first the European cast his glance
westward, and gave his greed a lofty name.
Cloven the footprint of his proud advance;
rabid his torch that fouled the nights with flame;
the soil was rich enough before he came,
but with the flesh of tribes he fed his plants.

Roll him aside! Aye, send him reeling home,
and let his hot mouth know for once the taste
of ruin! Though the Pequot long is dumb,
the Mexic towers long toppled, and erased
the Tagal might—through me those radiant ghosts
beg vengeance of you, bless you at your posts.

Newscast (April 20, 1967)

First came news of the war: "our" bombs had struck
targets hitherto spared; with a clean-cut grin
one pilot described how "beautiful" had been
the raid, thanks to fair weather—a stroke of luck!
Homes had been hit (not many) but how else win?
Then came news of midwest tornadoes: a truck
flung on its face, children unable to duck
from the wind's road, hospitals caught in the spin.

I did not like to see that wind destroy
the open streets of a town in Illinois
—although from one of them may have sprung the boy
beneath whose grin the Haiphong streets lay broken;
I did not like to think some god had woken,
and leaned over my scarless land, and spoken.

PART 11
Journeys

After the Tour

Somehow, after twenty-one days,
the key still fit the lock;
but I was too full, too empty for subtle surprises.
Only now, moving from room to room,
putting out the lights,
do I contemplate the strangeness.
Twenty-one days of palazzi
have, naturally, transformed my living-room . . .
not that I like it less, or am ashamed
to find the floors wooden rather than tiled;
it is, simply, different . . .
as the stove is different
after Livia's kitchen on the Palatine,
as the bathtub is different
after Caracalla,
as the desk is different
after Mrs. Browning's in Casa Guidi,
as the panels are different
after Monreale,
as the street below is different
after Venice . . .
and, finally, the bed, my wife upon it,
my arm around her,
we too—till when I cannot say,
in what way I am not sure—
are different
after the sarcophagus in the Villa Julia
atop which, bliss in their orbless terracotta eyes,
recline the young Etruscan and his bride.

A Good Buy

Oh yes, it was a good buy for the money.
To have eaten calves' liver in the shade of the Rialto
or veal, Genoese style, in the sun of Portofino
is nothing to sneeze at;

to have seen Chianti fields from Siena's tower
or from Milan's top spire a sea of roof-gardens
was worth the trip.

Listen—I can tell you what cafe to shun in Bologna,
what pensione to try in Taormina.
I can draw you a map of the Villa Borghese
so you won't get lost looking for the museums,
and I can reel off the bus-schedule for Pompeii.
Would you like to know where the most Tintorettos are,
the best Berninis?
how to say "toilet" or ask the price of gloves?

Listen—in Naples, about a block from the station
(ferrovia, they call it)
a ragged old woman sits all day against the wall.
In her lap are four pairs of shoe-laces.
She waited for me. She waits for you.
At 3:25, in Siracusa,
a guide at the Fountain of Arethusa
(he has a crew-cut and dark-rimmed glasses)
leans toward the most promising turista
and murmurs: "Your skin is like magnolia."

In a bit of field between Verona and Vicenza
(as the Venice express roars by)
a castle shell far off, fresh baby linen on a nearby line,
two old men together stoop,
broad hats close and parallel,
fingers earthward, tactful, knowing,
at the start of a long row.

What hour did they begin? how far
will they get by nightfall? what
was their ancestors' fate? what hope
have they for their descendants?
what have they ever said? what
does one prepare to tell the other?

I know only that they are there:
motionless, silent, at 1:20,
stooped in an attitude of prayer
or sharing a tableau, consciously composed,
along with the overworked hills beyond
that once were mountains,
along with the lines of ballerina vines—
petite, Degas vines,
holding hands, poised—
awaiting you, as they awaited me.

Last Night in Brussels

Not saucily, like Brussels' mannikin,
eternally bright Flanders, for whom years
are nothing, at my midnight font again
I stand, over the Boulevard Jacqmain.

Our last night bawls away on a loud collision
of cobblestone and beer-truck; into my ears
blunders a drunken song that wakes a vision
of blotched eyes ripe for Boschian derision.

I envy the drenched blindness of such singers,
for neither Belgium's quaintness nor her beers
have quenched this crazy thirst of mine which lingers
despite all guzzling. Flanders flows through my fingers.

I'd hoped that, with one hour of concentration,
the Groote Markt would rock once more with cheers
as ghost by ghost old Bruges' population
roused to some ceremonious occasion.

Instead I hear behind Tournai's Te Deums
Huguenot shrieks, and under the veneers
of haughty colleges lurk mausoleums,
and in the galleries of great museums

Rubens shows Pilate smirking from the castles
of Flanders at the sight of Antwerp spears
plunged in the side of Christ—Van Eyck's apostles
rush hounded up the alleyways of Brussels.

So, finished, of this boulevard accursed
I beg forgiveness, though nobody hears—
despite much drinking, drier than at first;
clutching at Flanders with my crazy thirst.

The Last Supper

Who but Leonardo could conjure me onto his wall,
choosing, of all traumatic moments, my very worst?

Years he wrought, till even he was satisfied
it really was I who sat there
central amid the apostles, tranquil-faced
while storming them with my charge of betrayal.
It seemed the Master had worked with hammer, not brush,
nailing me there, dooming me
ever to hold the aspect of calm
though never again in this life would I sup.

But backed by plaster and paste
my tempera being took hope.
By 1517 (thanks to Milan's humidity)
I felt myself peeling free.
By Borromeo's time I was so far gone,
the Cardinal ordered a copy made;
and when Torre in 1674 sighed "Lost!"
I, half-reascended already,
could hardly restrain my lips from an alleluia.

Then it began: two centuries of crucifixion
sans tree, hill, or nails:
restorations, alterations
limply pinning me down to the plaster—a me
ravaged and scarcely me;

till at last, at last, in August, 1943
(as the German guide tells it, without identifying the planes)
"*wurde das Refektorium*
durch Bombenwurf schwer beschädigt
und blieb ohne Dach und Fenster."

Cursed be the miracle that spared me
as I was positioning for ascension!
Three walls gone, and the roof,
while we, unbudged, kept at the wine and meat!
What use to pray
that in rain and heat
I would at last go loose?
Just as from the start I could have guessed
Judas' deal and all the rest,
I knew my "friends" would soon be back
busy with new techniques,
putting the refectory together again,
strengthening my entrapment,
with a Mauro Pelliccioli in the end
to lift the botchwork
from my agonized tranquility.

—Thus move the pale lips of the Christ.
But his story takes too long.
As he gauges the agitation of his followers,
a Japanese couple peer at a map of the city, arguing,
coldly a Frenchman takes flash pictures,
a Swede, unasked, explains the "composition" to his wife,
a victorious Italian writes down a girl's address,
and I, desperate for a stirring of the blood,
stand there, stand there, until it strikes me
that what he has finally resigned himself to
is not so much his passion as his mission:
probing the treacheries of our devotions, paling
year by year in the humidity of Milan
and in the glare of our predatory lens.

On the Way to Palermo

I.

On the way to Palermo stood, first of all,
Emilio Zappa's mother, a ruffled bird, under our window,
hands on hips, cawing her toothless good morning,
and Vince Cavataio's father
impartially gentle amid his family and fig-tree.

Next came Caruso
afire with Lola, false to Santuzza,
doomed by the bells of Mascagni's square:
Damon, despite Schiller's robbers and rivers,
thrashing his way to the gallows
to teach Dionysius truth;
Shakespeare's twins
bewildered in a harbor booming with cargoes, whores and decrees.

On the way to Palermo
deadpan cinema henchmen, biting cigars,
poised for the decisive nod;
in ritual tabloid towns
clans warred over wooing and rape.

On the way to Palermo sat Aeolus
not a hair disturbed by the wildness in his cave;
Vulcan, ecstatic of hammer, half-visible through the sulphur;
Charybdis and Scylla, twins of untiring vigil,
each with its special trick;
the Sirens, so powerful in song,
Ulysses had to stuff his ears,
fasten his limbs to the mast, while sailing by.

II.

If the sun were on Messina's gables,
if grimness were not on the waves and mountains,
I might have simply crossed.
But sulphur was the ray that reached me.

III.

On the way to Palermo, mulling guide-books,
peeling maps, chewing time-tables, we sit
looking out seldom, and then
in hope of the picturesque:
a citric thirst pulls us, as Carthage
and Rome were pulled
to Marsala's sweet wine, Trapani's tuna,
Gela's cotton, Paterno's oranges,
the asphalt and cheese of Ragusa,
the olive oil of Messina,
the mineral waters of Termini,
the almonds of Avola;
and we hope to carry away
in the suitcases of our Kodak brains and intestines
whatever is Neolithic in Buscoli, Siculian in Thapsos,
Greek in Selinus, Arab in Buccheri,
Norman in Cefalù, Spanish in Augusta—
plus the rocks of Ognina, the stalactites of Mondello,
the legendary springs of Arethusa and Ciane,
the colors of the sea,
the foliage, beaches, panoramas, and air,
marionette shows, underwater festivals,
saint's day parades;
and around the corners of gaunt streets
(which, if quaint enough, we will also carry away)
pasta con sarde, sfincione and cassata
await the open shelves of our stomachs,
while painted toy carts drawn by costumed toy donkeys
await the shelves of home.

IV.

On the way to Palermo the *Tribune* cries: "Beware!
The South blazes! rocks rock the air!
Fighting erupts at Castel Volturno;
police are on stretchers in Villa Literno;
Molotov cocktails scatter the pigeons of Mondragone;
at Trentola they have torn a Roman Temple into barricades;
bankrupt at Casal di Principe are the windowframes of banks;

directors attend a funeral of promissory notes;
no travelers' checks will be cashed today, my friend!
at Calatafimi, teargas or no, the roads stay blocked;
where shall the Mayor dictate to his secretary?
like tongues from his windows the insolent streamers flap!"

"Perhaps," sighs the wife, "we should stay in Firenze . . ."

Stay if you must, dear, with David's
delicate profile and genitals;
I'm for a David in trousers, lips roughly apart,
loading his slingshot with stones for a Roman temple!

CAOS! *Tribuna* bellows,
CAOS IN SICILIA!
TRAFFICO FERROVIARIO BLOCCATO
A SIRACUSA ED A PALERMO!
PARALIZZATA LA VITA NELLA DAPITALE DELL' ISOLA!
SIAMO ALLA MERCE DEGLI AGITATORI SINDACALI!

"Perhaps," she warns, "we should stay in Taormina . . ."

Stay if you must, dear, with the bi-weekly saint's procession,
stereo hymns in excelsis fluttering praises;
I'm for a march of crater jaws unlocking sulphur,
spokesmen for shrunken guts!

V.

Sulphur screams from Etna's
two hundred and sixty mouths.
Two hundred and sixty widows
beseech me
not to shoot them
in Kodacolor again.
When I ask how they came to be widows,
a sulphur silence issues from their jaws.

VI.

I should remove my shoes
and walk lightly.
It seems, on the way to Palermo,
that Sicily in fact is not a lemon
but a raw, convulsing heart
which should be held in the hand tenderly,
not stepped on or squeezed—
a raw heart, this planet's heart,
my own.

VII.

Scampi and octopus, octopus and scampi!
All night they nibble at my shores.
I am Sicily—what else?
Tremors—oh, what tremors!—every so often seize me.
From two hundred and sixty orifices
lava, like sweat, explodes.
Scampi and octopus nibble,
gods drop tears for the missing parts of their temples.
A busy night, a night without slumber. Cities moan.

And when, at two A.M., she asks, "Why do you toss so?"
shall one say that cities moan?
that Aeschylus' stage is laid flat to make room for lions?
that the pool in the anfiteatro thrashes with crocodiles and slaves?
that Enna, whom Ceres blesses but cannot save,
falls to the Siracusans?
that Trojan Segesta, Dorian Selinus
grapple long and well at one another's throats?
that Rome sacks the one at last, Carthage the other,
leaving lone columns to mark their passion?

One mutters: "Scampi! octopus!
I was a fool to eat them . . ."

VIII.

Amid octopus and scampi, on the way to Palermo,
kids guffaw and splash.
She who hangs old clothes to dry
swells with new life;
three of her walls clutch
the fourth, beheld by Carthage eyes.
Amid igneous rock which sits like giant paws,
high-rise apartments ignore the craters behind them.
Peasants, stooping to their meager rows,
ignore the omnivorous breakers before them.
On the railroad platform, facing sea and sun,
atop a base of lava a flower-pot stands
from which a flamboyant geranium
sings.

IX.

Palermo, I saw from the outset
what your strategy would be:
the tourist office would be shut;
there would be no busses running;
nobody we met would understand us;
a window would open and a bag fly past;
beggars would tear at us with ferocious lamentations;
the hotel would be third-rate—no toilet-paper, roach-marks on the
       wall.
You wanted to test me, to see if I would know you
despite your slut's disguise,
or ram your harbor, suck your female riches,
like all the rest.

X.

When those mosaic eyes had followed me
past the open confessional where a child whispered her sins,
past the eighteenth plundered Roman column,
past the cloister of unbenedictine meditations,
past the panoramic view of Palermo
raped for her golden gifts through every gate,

past the grim windings of Monreale astir with Arab ghosts,
past the great dry womb, the Conco d'Oro, emptied of its load,
past the phantom walls of Palermo
through which like a ramrod we tore
onto the Via Roma, road of spiked boots—
then I knew I was under suspicion
like all the rest.

And when I could explain
neither to Christ nor to my wife
why we were here
if not for the Baroque facades, the Neo-classic pillars,
the Gothic courtyards, the Arab-Norman campaniles,
the Renaissance fountains, the Byzantine mosaics—
then the time had come
for my own eyes to follow me,
because we were here for something:
a thirst drove me;
parched I stopped at every cross-street;
parched my eyes demanded of those we passed;
parched I listened to the silent towers;
parched I arrived at Verdi's prophetic statue.
—There, behind a screen of loose reeds,
loving the campari for its bitterness at last,
I discovered the truth of my coming.

XI.

Where do your ominous clusters ripen
for a new Garibaldi?
And oh you bells in all the towers of Palermo,
when, when shall you be heard?
The powerful expect you, at night they tremble;
is it not time, past time,
for Sicily's new Vespers?
How long amid the rotting corpses of trawlers
must boys splash merrily?
How long from bomb-halved buildings on the waterfront
must women lean, not bellowing,
but drying shirts and sheets?
How long, with even temper, must your donkeys

spruced up like courtesans in lace and spangles
drag miserable onions through the streets?
How long must none but Paladins
painted on carts
do valiant battle?
Where are the blocked trains? the swirling mobs?
I want to tell them . . . that they have my approval . . .
that their bitterness is my campari . . .
that if for their barricades they need another temple,
let it be Roman—what else but Roman?—I shed no tears
for Roman temples on Sicilian soil!

Avenge the murder of Archimedes!
Avenge the murder of your brilliant cities!
Avenge your noble isle turned citrus grove!
Avenge your ancestors turned harbor slaves!
Avenge your uprisen, pinned to the rocks of Lipari!
A Roman temple for your barricades!

XII.

The sun sinks to Palermo, Palermo to the sun.
The window-panes of City Hall stop blazing.
There at last we find them: terrors of the headlines—
gently peeking out of the Mayor's window
to watch us drink the slogans of their placards.
Six gather round, argue their case gently:
ten days they have stayed here . . .
what they want is work, pay,
and—for their children—hope.

We understand not much of what they tell us;
and they, how could they understand
that I am Timoleon, freshly arrived, scourge of oppressors,
in need of a city purpling with ominous clusters?

At least they seem to guess our love.

We shake hands. In wretched Italian
I wish them *bona fortuna*.
Their answering smile both parches and quenches:

it is not the smile of Etna, of Easter Monday, 1282,
but of long-dead Mrs. Zappa, hands on hips,
cawing her toothless good morning,
long-dead Mr. Cavataio, impartially gentle
amid his family and fig-tree.

Victoria Station

Gatwick at two A.M. lay so forsaken;
a train pulled in; we thought it best to go.
All the way to Victoria a Jamaican
raved about London, especially Mme. Tussaud:
"You fear that at your touch the wax will waken!"
But came Victoria, her clammy glow
told us at once our hope had been mistaken:
here was no life, but a gray-blue tableau.

The Grosvenor Hotel, in mournful neon,
soliloquized on its more gorgeous youth.
Two yellow clocks had managed to agree on
a joint communique, a common truth:
"It's forty-three past two!" With Ponce de Leon
absent, the Bar gleamed like a last gold tooth.
None of those waiting wished his looks to be on
such prints as proffered by the Photo Booth;

none—not the creature, drowsing or fordrunken,
curled in midstation on a ledge; the pair
entwined in lust or weariness, deep sunk in
an alcove's shade; the crone crouched as in prayer
for life, or a locker to leave her wretched trunk in;
nailed uncomplaining to a bench, arms bare,
the frost- or palsy-mastered girl; half shrunken
nearby, the fellow with a sad affair

where nose and chin should be—burnt or a leper—
who turned revulsion into a career
by vending bits of turquoise-festering paper
at five pence each; the luggage folk, with fear

or longing sculpted faces, London's caper
or nightmare finished or to come, now here
museumed in Victoria's pre-dawn vapor
no matter how they did or may appear

on other days, now here, no animation
of limb or lip. Suddenly, from far tracks,
a rush of wheels; ears wake; but the vibration
rings hollow: four carts, tumbrils heaped with sacks,
are ferried vulgarly across the station.
Though on the Board nor time nor destination
is legible, enough illumination
falls on the bench, toward which, in widening arcs,
forever supervised by those two clocks,
the tumbrils roll, atrocious transportation,
heaped high, it seems in that half-light, with packs
of mail, or persons yellowing into wax.

My Mexico Is Not Your Mexico

(On Sept. 15, 1810, in the vilage of Dolores, Padre Hidalgo issued his
Grito, his great cry for freedom, and headed a small band of
Indians toward San Miguel. There they were joined by the
revolutionary forces under Ignacio de Allende. They captured
several towns, finally storming Alhondiga, Guanajuato's fortress,
allowing the soldiers they seized to be slain. Spain avenged itself
with a massacre of innocents. Hidalgo and Allende were executed;
for eleven years their heads hung on hooks from the walls of
Alhondiga as a warning. After Independence, in 1821, the two
martyred leaders became national heroes, and over the city of
Guanajuato towers a statue of Pipila, the miner who died battering
down Alhondiga's last door.)

"Consider the weather. Eleven months of the year it's mild and
dry—delicious breeze from the hills—no rush, no tension—a
psychiatrist would go broke. The corn gives them zing; the chili
kills their germs. The world's their kingdom—they kid around, sing.
It's poverty, sure, but a *happy* poverty."

My Mexico, age fifteen, having somehow secured five pesos,
matches wits with Redford and Mostel for a stolen diamond
on handsome Fifth Avenue—his eagle heart rising, rising
for two hours to the topmost story of the topmost skyscraper
then stumbles—a pigeon—broken-winged, sun-blinded,
out into San Miguel, birthplace and tomb . . .
on his way home counts adobe after gnawed adobe:
bought, cored of its past, innards removed,
turned by Who's Who in Architexas into House Beautiful . . .
A conquest!—thinks the boy, while answering my *Buenos dias*
through his teeth—*a new conquest . . . bloodless (as yet).*

My Mexico is not your Mexico. My mosquito likewise.
My mosquito, alert and skilled and violently nationalistic,
having waited all day, bombards me the instant the light goes out
with a buzzing more terrible than an iguana bite,
while in every nook of this malignant pre-Independenzia room
termites, gnats prepare for my head to hit the pillow.

Though gallantly under the sheet I trench
with only nostrils exposed,
though my embattled hand takes its toll,
on, on they come, entire legions, Hidalgo and his legions,
with that termite, superwing Allende, in the van.
Now I see—eyes shut I see—that the supposed mosquito
at my left ear is in fact Pipila
still charging ahead of the rest, happy to be smashed
if need be in the final glorious assault
that will burst through my defenses, my Alhondiga . . .
It is of him, having drawn oppressor blood, of him
a statue will be raised on the highest peak of Guanajuato!

In the Geneve Lobby: Mexico City

After six blocks of rain
over, under, around and through the bones of
these foolishly sandaled feet,
you clop-clop finally past the great front doors of the Geneve,
wait in line for the room key,

then start your long trek through the lobby
where dry guests wet their gullets: chatting, idly staring . . .
until you want to yell out: Hey!
Don't you see that I'm drenched to the skin,
that my socks hold a pailful of icy water each! . . .

And you feel that even if you came in with a head
half lopped off and bleeding,
they would still chat, sip, stare idly—
that even if you never made it back
through the great front doors
but melted into one of the beggar women
or cripples out among the puddles
the dry scene would go on . . .

And you realize that this is the way,
that to batter against the way would be childish, useless,
that these chatters, sippers in the lobby of the Geneve
are not among the worst but the best:
they do not kick or rob the beggar women
or curse the cripples silently
for spoiling the gay streetscapes of the Zona Rosa;
no—they are the very ones whose heartbeat
gives a beggar cause for hope day after day;
and, besides, that you're no better, if as good;
that, were you among the dry at the Geneve
and one came in with a drenched yell,
you too would idly stare . . .

And so, the length of the arrogant public lobby,
a loneliness develops inside you and envelops you long before you
      arrive at the elevator,
the stapled aluminum box
that will take you three floors closer
to the God they have agreed upon,
and it comes to you that out of such loneliness
they created him—
as if he, who flooded us in the first place,
would care beans about our drenched yell!

And why should a god,
chatting, sipping away in the long lobby of space,
stare any less idly
than they among whom you are walking,
you their own born brother?

Mycenae: On Brushing One's Shoes in Athens

So: as I feared, she finally did speak
about my shoes; and actually I must
brush off these particles before they crust
as particles will do in one dry week.

But not so easily from off my cheek
shall vanish the descendant of the gust
that brought Mycenae tidings of Troy's lust
for Helen. On his tower I stood, his shriek

came at me from that bathing room; I trust
that war, that homecoming; and—though I seek
no quarrel with my wife, having grown meek—
my dust has mixed with Agamemnon's dust.

Location

"How was the hotel?"
One grew accustomed to St. Pancras' bell
at the left eardrum every quarter hour;
the narrow tub turning one's shower
into a hero's test;
the cold, limp breakfast toast;
the bankrupt bathroom light;
the clock
that had apparently gone into shock
one morning or one night
at five past seven;
and at the register the white-haired female raven.

What one never grew
nor ever shall grow quite accustomed to
were (just across the lane) a pair of dates
marking the residence of Yeats;
and halfway down the street
a sacramental plate
from Abrahamic times
plus more
in that museum on the second floor;
and next to Pancras' chimes
a stop for buses
to Shakespeare's crones, and Chaucer's bones, and the king's
        crosses.

At Four Minutes to One

It is four minutes to one.
As the tourbus makes its final turn,
San Miguel suddenly rolls out before them
its quaint adobe streets and graceful domes
—a sight to remember, they decide—
and the clocktower tells them
it is four to one.

Four to one.
A plain old Indian
enters on her knees the plain old church of la Salud
and on her knees approaches the poor altar
as an aged man
with back irreparably warped
fumbles in his rags for a coin,
drops it in the wooden box,
and hobbles forth
mumbling a faint appeal.

At four to one
on the main square, the Jardin,
a huge man from Texas
buys up loud bouquets

at which his señorita, smiling, scolds
and he orders them
the most expensive lunch
while squatting at the gutter
inert except for hand and mouth
a shawled squaw draws chunks of moldy bread
from her miserable bundle
and stuffs them through her jaws
as if to gag a scream.

At four to one a makeshift bus,
not riveted but stapled,
provided not with windows
but with toy saints
and *Perdóneme, Dios!* scrawled (just in case)
above the driver's wheel,
prepares (unlike Allende timeless on horseback near the bus stop)
to set out
with fourteen drab-eyed, gaudy-fabricked Mexicans
for mysterious drudgeries
amid the monster cacti two miles out of town
and a Manhasset couple
on their way to a private locker room with Roman tub
beside the healing waters, the hotel.

At four to one,
far from the tourist office, the bookstore, the malteds,
against an egregiously rotting wall
which this claptrap bus is about to pass,
three rotting dogs
put spiritlessly each his nose,
then each a lifted leg
while in the shallow end of a long pool
soon to be stepped into by the Manhasset couple
five chubby corporation children from Mexico City,
each with five names,
coaxed by grandmama for one more swim before *comida,*
join hands, led by their governess'
professional smile,
in a photogenic ring-around-the-rosy.

And at four to one, a Norte Americano
about to join the bus for Guanajuato,
the first-class bus with stuck toilet door,
the bus now making its final turn,
buys up every copy of that picturesque card
showing San Miguel
precisely as the passengers see it—
adobe streets and graceful domes—
precisely as he has decided to remember it after one day's
        "research"
while a student from St. Louis,
just seventeen today,
whose first pot—imperfect but unique—of Mexican clay
will be drying soon on a rack at the Instituto,
whose apprentice rug—of Mexican lambhair—
is about to begin its slow blue song on a Belles Artes loom,
voyages her soul
away from the traffic policeman,
the long-distance phone booth,
the Banco Commercial,
down its first side-street
slipping at times on the rain-slick stones
that have not quite washed away the dog-droppings,
frightened less each time she slips,
each time a sombrero's shadow touches her,
adding San Miguel to her soul, cobble by cobble,
adding her soul to San Miguel, cobble by cobble,
finding at last, near the fourth crossing,
her true birthday gift—
not the tin mirror in the store-front,
though she may buy it,
but her own searching eyes
reflected in the pane.

Macedonia

1.

I bought a ticket to Byzantium;
I boarded a bus to Istanbul.
I bought a ticket to the Blue Mosque,
Topkapi, St. Sophia,
Leander and Hero ablaze in her tower,
the sinister windings of my dream-bazaar,
and all the goldsmiths hammering the Golden Horn of Yeats.
I boarded a bus in a real Thessaloniki thunderclap,
farewells really wept,
the electrical storm catching up at Kavala,
darkness choking us, rain stoning us, lightning and thunder
aimed at us like judgment from divine Mount Athos,
a judgment on me (hinted my wife)
for dragging her off to Byzantium (ha!)
though we'd probably be dead before the border.

As I slid still lower in my seat,
so as not to be noticed by an irritated god,
the driver, whose windshield wipers showed
two feet of wet death ahead,
started a cassette; at the first measure
a clapping began, a singing, a dancing of arms
aloft in the lightning,
and so till the tape ended.
Then quickly, outwitting grimness,
a voice began, insolently calm,
a raconteur risen from the storm, as Venus from the sea:
each tale applauded with lessening laughter
as the wind's noose tightened.
One more cassette:
the clapping defiant now, first seat to last,
as the bus groped forward, five miles an hour, toward Turkey,
toward a three-hour probing of luggage and passports,
toward Istanbul, from which hate had driven them,
toward the mother with risky blood-pressure,
the father whose business still broke even.
And now, since *such* could sway in time to melody and storm

as if the windshield wipers were metronomes,
suddenly the thunder was Persia's hooves
about to learn Samothrace;
the lightning was Turkey's blades, at last contrite
inside Topkapi Palace;
the rain was Hitler's bullets,
four wars back.
Greekly I thrust my arms aloft, and clapped, and sang.
Thus the night grew meek ahead of us.
Unscathed, we passed to Xanthe, slept like babes
in a Class D, backstreet hotel.

2.

Next day, exactly as my wife predicted,
our bags were lifted out
on both sides of the border,
sifted, shifted, strewn about
in orderly disorder,
every page of every passport scrutinized
backwards, forwards, every face inspected
as if cunningly disguised.

Then Istanbul: daylong, nightlong, tranced in the honk
of cabs, the insolence of clerks,
trouble,
roared bazaar-arrays of gem and junk,
Topkapi's welcomeway a growl of rubble,
the Golden Horn a fly-mad sump of rotted arks,
at the Blue Mosque
a crippled beggar picturesque
in his wheelbarrow, postcard-barkers thick as worms
at St. Sophia's corpse—and fears
of Hero's tower likewise ringed by souvenirs:
cheap poems
baked on tiles . . .
cheap styles
"hand-etched in Anatolia" . . .
—Byzantium, ha!

Grandparents in London

We are aging,
gripped
by bitterness, by doubt.
My camera sets her raging.
When asked to comment on her hair,
I blurt out:
"Nondescript."
And we're beginning to forget
when we were where.
By Tuesday both are in a fret
as to which restaurant
we tried
following the Sunday sail to Greenwich.

If after two nights' sleep we can't
remember on which side
of Thames we supped, how shall we manage
to separate this London stay
from any other?
Shall we say
it was the time
we started to display
the typical deportment
of grandfather-and-mother,
plucking from Oxford Street a prime
assortment
of rattles, books, and dolls?
Shall we say it was the time we gaped not at St. Paul's
but at Paul Scofield; not at Parliament but the Proms;
hosted not by Carlyle and Dickens in their houses
but by once-gracious monarchs and their spouses
at Windsor?—two finally fiftyish Americans
nearly found by Irish bombs
at Euston Station,
nearly lost by meeting plans
that never went awrier: she
joyless at Keats' House, expecting me,
I in the lobby of the Tate,

from 3:15 to 4,
afraid to quit the door—
wild with the long wait
for public phones,
messages no one would deliver,
imagined moans,
imagined leaps into the river—
finally, frantic with waiting,
hating
the stupid camera still in my grip
whose click, throughout the trip,
from Haymarket to Hampton Court to Bath,
had roused her wrath,
ready now to smash to smithereens
the lens that had focused on so many scenes,
now focusing on, imagining everywhere
as the cab rocketed from Square to Square
one subject only, one half-gray head of hair.

Nafplion: Snapshot

It is far from dark
but already the sun
has built his arc
over Nafplion.
We make our choice
of foods, pretending
no inner voice
declares: *It is ending.*

Four days welded together, a fifty-face centipede,
crawling out of and into museum, restaurant, bus,
crisscrossing the melon-ripe, spectacular Peloponnese,
we'd stood with Apollo's ghost, beheld Clytemnestra's blood,
bathed in the Gulf of Argos, over an aged bridge
entered Arcadia just as a shepherd was guiding his flock
toward the slope of Mt. Erymanthus, gazed into pans for our pick
of lamb-stew, moussaka, vine-leaves, okra, learned to lodge
at hotels named Oracle, Pericles, Halcyon (all night long

trucks rolled over our visions, toilets spasmodically flushed),
learned to emerge from a shower half-frozen, half-burned, half-
    washed,
after the seventh playing learned which tune would be sung
next on the guide's cassettes, learned gradually which name
goes with a face, which are in pairs, in threes, and who
comes from Toronto, from Budapest, Turin, who's probably gay,
who teaches music, psychology, who remains in her room.

        Tables propped
        together, they smile
        at my Kodak, grouped
        family style,
        having just skoaled
        with retsina wine
        a two-year-old
        granddaughter of mine.

Behind the fortress hill of Nafplion painfully sets
the sun: if the picture happens to turn out well, which is doubtful,
I promise solemnly, head by head, there'll be a hatful
printed and sent aloft to each of our argonauts.
—It is ending, no doubt of it, ending—more than this dinner party.
The talk grows closer than ever, tomorrow's a word that hurts,
but it will come; the bus will start, and perhaps, when it starts,
some will agree to meet on the Parthenon steps at nine-thirty
to drink the full of the moon; perhaps they really will meet;
but inwardly the scattering will have begun already:
after five days on the road we'll be feeling soiled and seedy,
we'll be seeking unruined showers; gradually, with regret,
as the bus nears Athens, we'll think of differences; the trip
will fall into focus; our minds will return to family faces,
flight confirmations, a tour of the islands (as good as this is,
we hope); for awhile we may hunger to see one another take
    shape . . .

Thessaloniki: Three Sleeps

1.

I don't blame you that my first night's sleep was fitful;
deep inside your womb you nestled me well
in a back room on the seventh floor—
not like those tour-towns swaggering till four A.M.
No, you are a town of workfolk,
take your sleep to heart,
get up at six.
But how, even in your stillness, could one stay asleep
surrounded by your swarms of lively ghosts:
those of your old town, high near the wall,
and of the older town, its agora half-showing;
Alexander himself on horseback ready to explode south;
Dimitrius, bleeding forever in the heavy embrace of your shrine;
the janissaries butchered all at once in your round tower;
Ataturk, new-sprung from his mother's womb and yours,
opening for the first time incendiary eyes;
Hitler's hostages—300 Greeks per German;
and all your Jews, sixty thousand,
saved from the Inquisition once, but now
proceeding with packages again, to a "better location";
Efstratia Nikolaidu, fifteen years old,
who would now be thirty-nine,
shot down in your prison-yard, fist high.

2.

In the afternoon of the second day,
filled with your ancient marble finds
and the feudal weavings of your artisans
and your waves, winds, sunrays washing through us
and your octopi dancing on the line, hung out to dry,
and your fresh-caught mackerel, tenderly fried to order,
home, exhausted and full, we came to our seventh-floor room
and lay down on your good large bed,
and as we worked at the crossword puzzle
something better crossed our minds.

Let the young in Crete, in Athens, packsacks on their backs,
think what they think of grayheads, whom they pass without a sign.
Afterward we slept beyond dreaming for two hours.

3.

The second night was different.
What woke me was, I guess, your deep-fried pastry
(corkubinia, they called it)
of which I'd had two wildsized helpings.
How, even in your stillness, could one stay asleep?
It is not every man who has a ticket
for the next bus to Byzantium.

Dogs of San Miguel

By night, by day, though next to hopeless
you force your buckling legs
down the exhausted ways of San Miguel,
led on by clues left against walls
by despondent cousins
like messages of explorers vanishing in the Antarctic.

Inspired by despair, your teeth wrestle from the stones
whatever human noses have missed
or fingers been too feeble to displace,
and for a long moment,
chewing what perhaps contains your death,
you lift your heads as if in triumph,
pretending to yourselves that what you have is food.

Facing away from one another,
you couple at high noon right in the Sunday market
unabashed either by first-class Yankee tourists
or by fifth-class buses heading for near towns
—ensuring a new mongrel agony next year;
otherwise you get out of the way at once
when anyone passes, even a small child,

as if grown wise after kicks and rocks enough,
as if afraid of offending for the space you occupy.

How many of you are there now, this day, without collars?
Do you keep statistics?
Can you wonder why seventeen sunrises have passed
since you sniffed a particular urine?
Have rumors reached you concerning poison campaigns
against the collarless?
Could one of you comprehend and translate for others
what the white lady said
in your presence, coolly, in English,
about trucks soon coming by
with gentler, discreeter, more total solutions?
Do you worry?
Or is there within you by now,
side by side with your zest for every new sun,
a surrender, a prayer
that the next cob of corn you attack
will be poisoned,
the next truck that quietly pulls up beside you
will waft you away with your cousins
to Auschwitz, if not to Nirvana?

Some of you seem to have awaited us.
You watch us approach on our way home from the singing tavern
as if midway down that desolate midnight lane
was our appointed rendezvous,
and you join us on the final lap
halting when we halt,
taking far-fetched encouragement
in our not shooing you off,
fantasizing that we will at last be the ones
to recognize in you the dog of our life
—until the great hacienda doors
half open to let us in
and we succeed in not looking back to meet your eyes
as the doors shut.

But what about you—you three—
three of differing shapes, colors, sizes,

perched like lookouts on the roof of the corner shoppe:
were you hired to guard the fifty-peso ornaments at night,
or is this where you have climbed to take your final stand
after all the rest are wiped out
—like the boys of Chapultepec,
like the warriors atop the last flaming tower of Warsaw's ghetto?

Sometimes I imagine that you are preparing
to howl forth a galvanizing alarm
which we two-legged ones will not at first understand
but at which every last remnant of your legions
will lift his head
and emerge from the shadows:
     Enough sniveling! enough self-loathing!
     enough thanks for being cursed instead of kicked!
     enough willingness to stay asleep
     with flies at our open sores
     as if we were quartered melons in the market!
     as if this were not *our* ancestral pre-Columbian soil!
     as if the planets had not sung promises at *our* birth!
     Enough!
     Better to go down at once,
     head lifted, eyes burning, teeth asnarl,
     than slowly, with our tails between our legs!

And go down you will, under machine-gun fire . . .
but for one day at least
the two-legged
will not enjoy the luxury
of ignoring your mangy sides,
your inconvenient brown heaps of defiance.

Dogs of San Miguel—
you that are ghosts already,
you that look like ghosts,
you whose ghostly doom is on the humane society's timetable—
even I who care most
am forbidden to be haunted by you,
to groan at sight of your rotting ribs
outside the novelty window
where well-stuffed button-eyed pups

await the next tourbus explosion;
my concern must be for the one-eyed Indian woman
so disturbing to the charm of San Miguel,
withering in her dark shawl,
who may be next on the timetable.

I am forbidden, forbidden to be haunted by you;
get one of your own to howl.

Visiting Hour: At the Swanholm, St. Petersburg

Despising the driveway's allure, the tree-guised
parking-lot, the spruces' fraudulent greening,
the front door's hail, bright as a tart's lips—
one says the stark;

one says there is no afterlife, no guerdon
for the good, no fire for the fiendish, all
are only inventions to keep the outrageous
in check—and you agree;

one says no human weave, not even
the most colossal, is sturdier than a spider's,
connecting ever fewer, held finally by one,
then none—and you agree;

and you agree that nothing of crowning importance,
nothing that either proves or questions
is likely to be done or said in one of these
nursing homes

where, even if you looked quite hard at the faces pinned
to a pillow or drooped forward in a wheelchair,
you couldn't readily notice there'd been substitutions
since last night;

and you agree that the odds are against its being
worth the effort to lean encouragingly

toward her whose singing white strands of autumn
now sit shorn

so that she's a triplet between shorn neighbors,
a rough-smocked, expressionless threesome who, never daring
to ring for the brash attendant, surrender at last
to wetting themselves;

she will probably, in an hour, have forgotten that it was
you who bothered to visit, that the flowers
are hers; and . . . you see . . . she cannot even decide
what year she was born . . .

or can she? . . . Yes! it was '89—she's certain!
her mumbling begins to be easier to decode:
she's a girl in Russia, with clothes so ragged,
it keeps her from school;

and mother sends her across the fields to grandpa,
who's quite well-off, and quite well-known for his books:
Show him your rags, say you need clothing—
money for school . . .
and he, the pious, the prosperous, praised by all
the village, he for whose soul no Kaddish
has sounded in fifty years, whose well-gnawed gravemark
Hitler trod,

suddenly bursts from between his grandchild's bloodless
lips, entering you: *Take a*
potato sack, and cut your legs two holes,
and go to school!

Sunday in the Square: San Miguel de Allende

Arm half-raised, about to summon from their stumbling
knees, their crumbling stalls, their grumbling countrysides
the great-great-great-grandchildren of his Revolution,
astride his steed Allende rides.

Circling him slower than the hand of a gigantic
clock, an ancient man who does not openly beg
hobbles by; gripped by its best remaining bristles,
an ancient broom is his third leg.

A dried-out woman bending to the dried-out pavement
keeps arranging, rearranging her fourteen
dried-out avocados, facing toward the sunlight
those which are still a little green.

A blind man, not yet twenty-five but pulseless, drowses
too far forward into noon; the deep tin cup
spurts from his fingers; through gray lips a thankyou barely
crawls for the two coins gathered up.

And though Allende's stallion strains, it's no more likely
than the five-peso one a lad struggles to pry
from its onyx base, to break loose and fly forward
with the old enflaming cry.

Gilbert and Sullivan Night at the Proms

Of course, it included the women's section, gaudily
gowned, seated now motionless, still hearing
(despite an intermission) spectacular
passages of their hymn to Princess Ida;
but that wasn't it; nor was it the males in somber
attire, straining like cocks now to declare
that they indeed, definitively *are*
gentlemen of Japan; nor the soloists
grinning into the pit where growths of hair
bobbed up and down, straw hats came off and on,
Union Jacks and balloons took attitudes
suitably "queer and quaint"; of course, it included
all that, but that wasn't it; nor was it just
the being in Albert Hall, the acoustical bigness,
the adoring hush, tier upon tier, of twenty
thousand, sucking eighth-notes like hard candy,
though certainly it included that; nor was it

the seventy-year-old organist from Ipswich
whose son was to meet her midnight train, who'd helped
defend her airdrome from the claw of Hitler,
who was born, along with thirteen brothers and sisters,
in a thatched house they couldn't afford to buy,
who remembers rising at 5 A.M. to help
her mother bake bread in an old brick oven,
whose mother ("the finest woman I ever knew")
lived to a hundred and three, who didn't know
why she was telling us these things—though surely
that too was part of it; but it was mostly
another perfect night, five years before,
when Romeo leaped and Juliet whirled away
their childhood and all eyes in Covent Garden
caressed their fragile ecstasy. Even then
I had known it included more, included the fragile
ecstasy repeated in all eyes,
that instant when I'd gathered in the whole
audience, like a grandfather observing
cherubic skaters on a lake who laugh
as if the blood will never turn to ice,
as if the ice will never turn to blood.

Toluca: The Friday Market

How, since it is Friday,
can you not take the bus to Toluca?

Though the old paths from stand to stand
are paved,
still the flimsy bits of canvas tenting,
jeered at by wind and sun,
attempt to do their work with dignity
—unlike the Aztec, an infant humped on her back,
whining a willingness to hear your mean price
for her masterly baskets;
still a child, three huge disoriented chickens
slung upside-down over her head,
buckles and runs, runs and buckles,

reaches her family and collapses;
still the splendid and atrocious wares
forever waiting, waiting side, by side:
the cactus leaves, cooked into goodness;
the deep-fried surreal stomach-walls of cows;
the dozen tacos, desperate for attention,
forced finally into a buyer's bag.

How, since it is Friday, your one and only Friday,
can you not take *something* from Toluca:
if only a machine-made leather belt (well haggled down)
and eleven slides
which may or may not develop three weeks hence
into the bright garb, the drained life
of the clusters you interrupted:
faces suddenly appalled,
afraid you have stolen their soul
and are carrying it home in your camera
without even bargaining for it;
not even leaving—
as would be proper for these ancient bartering grounds
haunted by so many ravished souls and prices—
yours in exchange.

Delphi: Slide 62

I know we're only one day into the tour;
I know it's nearly eight (you've checked your watch
three times); I know, no matter where we're at,
the slides come off, TV comes on at half
past eight. Last night you bristled at my hint
that all the slides of Greece were home, and all
in order, and we hadn't seen them yet.

Still, though you didn't ask, let me explain
this one your mother's after me to scrap.
You see my profile downcast toward those streaks?
You see the four girls grinning? We had just
caught up with them, and in the nick of time.

While seven gems of the museum posed
for me (the ones you saw just now in seven
seconds—seven!! for the Sphinx of Naxos,
the Charioteer, the War of Gods and Giants!!)
off to Castalia'd gone the bus—from there
whoever was missing could *walk* back to town!
What happened next was not your mother's fault.
She'd climbed her soles off on that holy slope
which was, to her, not holy. Had I said:
"You take the bus. I'd like to stay awhile"—
she'd not have balked; she knew what the book told:
how pilgrims cleansed themselves in it before
facing the word of Pythia, she who drank,
then prophesied. *One still can recreate*
that world of oracles by drinking from
the old Castalian spring, the landscape too,
and all the glories of the sacred grounds.

No need to wake her smile—or, worse, her yawn—
by adding what Castalia meant to *me:*
fount of the Muses, drink my veins have craved . . .
And she'd been quite a sport, hobbling all day
in step with kids a third our age. So, swinging
her hand, I said, "Let's catch the bus, okay?"
—We strode! Each sign along the road, however,
pointed Castaliaward, pulling my soul
that way. There sat the bus! time still to drink . . .

The girls—you see them grinning? They'd just watched
this weird expression cross my profile downcast
toward the dry well that Homer, Sappho drank from
in dreams, that Pythia in her exultations
drank from in fact, then uttered prophecy!
These streaks were all *I* found of it; the girls
pointed "up yonder" where they'd had a drink.
No time to seek it. The bus snarled. Time only
for one slide: the dry basin, my weird face,
and the girls grinning as I mumbled something
about how I'd been waiting all my life
to slake my thirst here.

Back at the Hotel
Oracle (next to the Pythia, by the way)
sipping my coke—a favorite drink in Delphi—
it struck me that I'd come five thousand miles
for nothing . . . *should* have said "I'll stay awhile . . ."
and sought the spring! Well—six weeks have gone by;
the hurt is down (though I may, after all,
remove Slide 62). And in one way
it's for the best. If inspiration fails me,
I can explain it as Castalia's failure.
How could one possibly excuse himself
if there *were* water, not just wretched streaks;
if one *had* placed his lips where Pythia
placed hers before her chantings rocked the world?

Herakleion: The Hidden Beach

There was this taxi driver
who fast-talked an "arrangement" from the airport;
the official who coolly beheld us
buckling under gray hair
and luggage and the lack of a room;
the hotel desk arrogant
in seven languages;
the vendor whose peaches doubled
when set on a tourist scale;
the Class A *mädchens* strawing
lemonade on the roof
who answered in ice-cubes: *Nein,*
I could *nicht* be their scrabble partner.

So we fled to the life-giving sea.
Safe in the lap of the fortress,
safe from the eyes at the roof-pool,
safe in the arms of the reefs,
forty-five bathers reveled—
splashing each other, gorged
on honey-soaked Saturday pastries
sold from a makeshift half-wagon:

one Stavros so fat, his suit
was a blown-up tube, one Kostas
so scrawny, his ribs were a sunlit
squadron, a girl unconcerned
that her playful right breast had almost
slid free of the bikini,
an infant shedding his fear
step by step, hand in father's.

As we peeled and slowly got into
the Creteness of our first peach
careful to drop not even
a bit of its skin on the rocks,
a soldier forgetting Cyprus
for one delirious moment
stealthily looked around,
peeled off all but his trunks,
rolled up his uniform, hid it
in a crevice, and—awkwardly plunging,
his humanhood slowly reviving—
sank himself in with the bathers.

To put it one way: you turned
a corner unmarked on the map,
and there in the sea, in the sun,
forty-five Saturday swimmers
suddenly came into being.
Or, to put it another way:
as we swam in our sea, sun, laughter,
there suddenly came into being
in business trousers and shirt
with his hat-and-handbag wife
one of that passing kind
in bus-windows, airports,
who ate, however, part
of a Cretan peach, instead
of our hearts, and trained on us
not a Kodak cannon
but the trembling lens of love.

Reunion

I don't know what it meant for sure, but this is how it went:

eve of Cuba's twelve-abreast victory-cry—the star had survived
twenty years, and we had survived; on the top floor
of Havana's top hotel, waiting to be tabled, we found each other:
nearing sixty, hair thinned or faked; amazed that the names came
     back,
we circled the buffet, griped about the food, the three hours' wait at
     customs,
with one light finger tapped each other's biography:
each had come tiptoe here for one more sip at the old seduction.

I don't know what it meant for sure, but this is how it went:

eight Russians deigned to drop a *spasibo* into the pianist's lap
for belting out one of the tunes that used to move us;
then it was our turn: *Fly higher!*—we circled the piano,
amazed how the text came back, and even some of the fervor;
—it *was*, after all, Havana; below gleamed the Morro Castle;
Cuba had made it, and we, and there'd been wine,
and there sat the grim round Russian faces.

I don't know what it meant for sure, but this is how it went:

maybe a requiem, maybe a beginning . . .
maybe there could be found, here in Havana, its twentieth New
     Year,
a new year for us, still passionate enough to clasp
a vision, a more palpable vision, a vision worth giving oneself to
without ever again risking cap and bells . . .
For a moment anyhow, as the pianist took command of the
     keyboard,
our voices, our fists: *Fly higher!*—took command of the night over
     Havana.

I don't know what it meant for sure, but this is how it went:

it was Mayday all over the world and we marched twelve abreast
with all that was marching into all the Squares
three times the number announced by the police in next day's
    Times;
ours the streets that day, ours the times to come,
—not a scrawny little bunch nearing sixty
reflected in the pane of a great Carib window,
dancing in the nose of the Russians high over the Bay . . .

—not a scrawny little bunch soon to lug through customs
a growl about food, about unsyntactical guides,
slides of a hospital, a school, anniversary gods a hundred feet tall:
—Revolution Square!! into which, two days after our departure,
the young of Cuba twelve abreast would pour
fists raised, eyes glazed: *Fly higher!*

Indigo

Maybe there is, after all,
something behind it—
something that summons me
out of a deepening blue
and chooses me to choose
not the "wingding climax"
of a '59 thriller,
but JAPAN'S LIVING TREASURES:
the grower of dreamwild paper,
the potter afire with his kiln,
the poet of pleasurable dolls,
the sire of ninety-six bells
each with its soul, its cry,
the prince of Kabuki,
sixty-eight, at the mirror,
who makes himself maiden.

Then suddenly
(maybe there is, after all,
something behind it)
she, nearing ninety, I

nearing sixty, the age of her daughter,
lean toward each other:
she unmindful of lensman, I of screen.

One more thaw, alone, she has sown it;
one more fall she forces her bones to earth,
pulls back the bedding of straw:
yes, it is waking;
though daughter may lend a hand,
great-grandson be led, be shown,
Mrs. Chiga it is
who, hunchbacked, bends to the making.

Now four great indigo spindles,
her harvest, her doom,
rage blue in her nightly sleeps, only hers;
day after day at four she stirs;
with dawn's first ray she leaps at the loom;
fingers of parchment, shuttle of rust,
old mates, they know the way,
but always the thrust, the throb is new,
once more a begetting, once more a breed of blue.

Now four generations, she leading,
flow to the river; the blue is rinsed,
it will live a hundred years, will deep and deep.

Then suddenly
(there is something)
I am told:
"Mrs. Chiga died on March 28th."

For the death of a stranger, ninety years old,
I need not weep;
as for the indigo rows, she sowed them in time;
they have bloomed, been reaped;
the loom is not widowed; it knows,
they know, the way: one lent a hand,
one looked, all flowed to the river;
but oh (I pray) the blue rage

that summoned her day after day before day—
let it be mine again, not ever to lose!
mine, oh you something!
why else would you choose me to choose?

Flood

> Nature hath shouldered Cornwall into the farthest
> part of the realm, and . . . besieged it with the
> ocean . . . a demi-island in an island.
> —Richard Carew, *The Survey of Cornwall,* 1602

"The Lionesse was destroyed on 11 November
1099," the *Chronicle* sobs: a region
wondrously fertile, inhabited by a race
of comely people,

builders of gleaming cities, a hundred forty
dream-high churches whose bells in the clear of summer,
in the blue, in the rock of waves, can still be heard
gently tolling.

Once, as Lyonesse slept, the riled Atlantic
lifted a vengeful fist and, flooding over
all but her highest peaks, engulfed the towns
in swift succession.

On a still night—Mount's Bay fishermen tell you—
house roofs can be seen beneath the water.
On a June day, at low tide, you may glimpse
the ghost of a forest.

At neap tide it is possible to gather
beechnuts, and cut wood from trees embedded
in sand. At Trewa, tin-stream works decay,
older than Cornwall.

Each year at springtide's lowest ebb the children
of all Perranuthnoe, in hope of finding
treasure, flock to the sand 'round Cudden Point
(some are rewarded).

Into this parish, aided by the swiftness
of his white horse, before the wall of water
Trelawney (or Trevelyan) fled—they two
alone surviving.

And what of Lelant? Aye—and what of Phillack?
Were not they meadowland? Were they not smothered
by sand in one night? Were the ancient towns
not somewhere seaward

of the Black Rock? Was not old Lelant churchyard
washed away? Are human teeth not sometimes
discovered even now, after a great
undertow scratches?

Night floods Newquay (new in 1640!)—
Newquay, with its famished high tides daily
munching on beaches, eyeing this hotel
for a real dinner.

Night floods Newquay, and I clutch the bed frame
so as not to be washed away, as the old harbor—
somewhere seaward of these toffee shops
and tour charts—vanished

one night . . . or century . . . away with the bustling
mines, market towns, pilchard vessels,
crosses, customs, words for hello, goodbye,
a washed away Cornwall.

PART 12

The Map of Spain

In the Land of Olives

In the land of olives, and of warm, rich wine;
Of rich, deep soil, and of a warm, red sun;
Of warmer hearts, where there's no "me for mine"
But only "I for you, and we for everyone";

In the land of love, of star-seen serenade;
Of haunting, heart-made melodies, heart-sung;
Where aged architecture did not fade;
And where the rich, warm, Spanish blood is ever young;

There can I see no scene that is serene;
(Though last year there was beauty dressing Spain)
There can I see no grass fields that are green . . .
Nothing that has been saved from slaughter and from pain;

No castle stays but keeps as souvenir
A half-torn tower, or a blood-filled moat.
No face that has escaped a trickling tear . . .
No crime done but made many weep, and few men gloat.

No warm sun comes but soon is hid by planes . . .
No melodies but dirges for the dead.
Nothing of that great land in fact remains
Except the rich, warm, Spanish blood, that is so red.

Except the hearts, so brave, whose steady beat
Leads on the march for life, of battling men;
The driving force that does not know defeat,
And will not rest until it takes its Spain again!

Smiles and Blood

Smile at me again,
And tell me how unpleasant is the bloody War in Spain . . .
Say that all is night,
And nothing there is worth the poem I will write.
Shudder in your plea,
And say how far from poetry the Civil War must be.

And smile again.
—Forget the men
That die each day
And are reborn—
Oh, smile away!
A heart is torn
In sunny Spain—
A land gone grey.
A million mourn,
And your sweet smile:
—A mocking thorn!
So deadly, vile. . . .

They're writing a wonderful poem in Spain,
And you would not hear it.
The grandest endeavor—a portrait in pain;
An epic of courage, of deathless men slain . . .
And, smiling, you fear it!

Oh, hear it!
Oh, bear it!
A blood-stain has come on the earth—I must smear it.
I can not erase it;
You mustn't replace it
With smiles that will not hide the fact that you fear it.
I'll spread it
I'll wed it
To bravery—till all the world knows of the monster that shed it,
— —And all the world knows of the "poet" who fled it.

Smile at me again,
And tell me how unpleasant is the bloody War in Spain. . . .
Say that all is night,
And nothing there is worth the poem I will write.
Shudder in your plea,
And say how far from poetry the Civil War must be.
— — —I'll smile, too, as you rave,
And think how great the poem is: the spilt blood of the brave.

García Lorca

He felt a wind upon his face never again to feel,
and eighteen moonlights, thin as lace, stood in a line of steel.
Eighteen men were dumb as rock, the trees were loud with wind,
and far away, like a flock of stars, lamps in the village dimmed.
They shrank from the moon all swollen white, far from the lights of
    town;
beneath a tree they watched his eyes until their own turned down.
"Oh shoot me, brave young men!" he spoke, looking at every one,
"and hide my grave with stone before the night gives way to sun.
"Wake the town with drunken yell! Dance, and believe your dream
that Spain is safely under stone, and cannot lift a scream!"
"Fire!" four times the captain barked; thrice no pistol stirred;
then eighteen bullets found their mark, and not a groan was heard.

Blood and wind and moonlight cooled on García Lorca's face;
the soldiers quickly drove away, as from a haunted place.
No one dared to look behind—they drank themselves insane.
They heard his poem rising up, and spreading over Spain.

Barcelona Celebrates Three Years of Franco

Over the sunless ways of Barcelona
Franco rides upon a proud white horse.
Behind him come the generals, that force
the blackness of their banners on the breeze.

279

Mother, this day is not for counting beads.
How can you lock your door, while Barcelona,
flushed like a maiden with festivities,
throws flowers at the leader's lifted head?

Three years ago the ways of Barcelona
opened themselves to Franco's triumph-tread,
and on the gutters empty guns lay dead.
Always counting your beads, have you forgotten?

Even the lock upon my door, the cotton
stuffed in my ears, allow this day no dimming.
Here is the room my bravest son was shot in.
He fell on the same day with Barcelona.

Let Franco fill his eyes with crowds of women
that dream of spitting where his horse has gone!
This room's the temple that I sing my hymn in,
and here I count the beads for Barcelona.

How glad I am that not a ray of sun
blesses the flag of Franco! Oh great owner
of farm and city—when our counting's done
we'll drive your shadow out of Barcelona!

Guernica

(Holy city of Spain destroyed by fascist bombs)

Dead, Dead. Every child. Shriek out
from the stormed park, the smothered school-yard.
                    Shout!
because this quiet shocks the sky as much
as the first roar of the bombers.
                            Noise became
expected: ears survived. Even the touch
of shadows changing, that had stayed the same
for hundreds of holy years, became expected.

But the planes went, and all unresurrected
lies the city. Not one sudden wonder
has risen to mock the bombs.
                              Are you afraid?
Those were no eagles; all their titan thunder
was made by human hands.
                              Grant Icarus shade
or he will fall again! Mothers, grow wild!
shriek out! Dead. Dead. Every child.

Tidings from Spain

I thought it was over: May after May on the train
sending my senses desperately through a wood
I begged the brook on parole, the bough all bud,
to magic me into merriment again;
but nothing altered—it was as if April's rain
had reached all roots but one, and after the flood
one fruitless tree in a lush forest stood
fettered by wintry spells. Then I heard: "Spain!"

How could such sound not turn the trick for me?
If a whole land, swaddled in years of frost,
can rise from its swoon—frightening as a ghost
that frolics for its murderer to see—
why need April's rain forever be lost
to the parched root of one bedeviled tree?

Barcelona

I handled Barcelona rather well, considering;
held back the tremolo when telling friends
it was there we would head from Madrid.
The mailman heard no thud in my heart
when I took from his hand the hotel confirmation,
the envelope marked "Barcelona."
The clerk at the airport received no sign

that anything more than two persons and two bags
were being weighed in.

Metallically the stewardess announced
Barcelona, on this particular trip,
would be less than a destination
—merely a stop on the way to Vienna.
But her words, "We land in five minutes,"
were finally more than I could handle.
I myself was startled at having to turn from my wife
precisely as she complained about the nescafe.
Noticing my biscuit crumbs,
she added them to her complaint:
they would go all over my trousers.

Tenderly, as if they were petals,
I scooped them into the dish.
Even she could not guess
that what I had come to was not *a* city but *the* city,
not *a* city with a reservation at the Hotel Continental,
but *the* city which—look, it's been only thirty-nine years,
there are millions still alive who understand me—
the city which taught us what it means to stand,
            fall, rise again.

And if I sat speechless beside my wife,
unable to see the biscuit crumbs,
how could I tell the taxi driver,
knowing it was a tip he awaited, not a speech,
that he had brought me—to the Plaza de Catalunya, yes,
to Las Ramblas #138, yes,
to the crowds, stores, posters, restaurants
I hoped I might come to love, yes,
but also to something alive under the sidewalk,
something I wished to caress
and would, in broad daylight, if one could,
more passionately, more purely,
letting the luggage look foolish,
than the city in which I and my children were born,
in which I have sung the dirges and the praises
of my father and Barcelona.

Madrid: Coming Home

Though I admire the turning of one's cheek,
Christ's is no easy life to imitate.
I did, I did
resent the fact that Franco's death was late
and gentle, that the tyrant lay in state,
that History did not wreak
vengeance before my coming home, Madrid.

When finally the plane fare had been paid,
blizzards and other business ringed me round.
The marvel slid
out of a brain that otherwise could pound
into submission the most pompous sound
December ever made:
"July will bring me home to you, Madrid!"

Each bough of April dipped with bugle-beaks;
"The time is near!" they probably declared.
But I, amid
their music, was more readily ensnared
by mutterings of mischief hatched or bared;
whole days went by, whole weeks
without the gasp: "I'm coming home, Madrid!"

Halfway through June, the sundeck's peeling red
entranced me, and the failing lawn. In dreams
I still bestrid
legions of dandelions, that mocked my schemes
and slaughters with their green, defiant screams.
Not once in my June bed
did I sit bolt upright and cry: "Madrid!"

Even as the airport's bulletin board
proclaimed that 904 would leave on time,
a bawling kid
caught at me, then the headline of a crime.
Dialing a sick aunt with my last dime,
I did not say one word
about my coming home to you, Madrid.

At dawn Iberia hove in view. I should
have risen with an inward shout, at least;
but we were bid
pull out our tables for a final feast;
poor sense, poor nerves, poor nescafé increased
the toilet lines; I stood
in place and heard: "One hour until Madrid."

Coruña passed; the cockpit spat a name:
below there . . . by that river . . . what? León?
Valladolid?
No matter—all at once we had been drawn
into the Guadarramas, flushed with dawn
peak after peak, and came
at last into the outskirts of Madrid.

All new . . . all prosperous . . . all rearranged . . .
Only the hills stayed firm. It made me feel
the way El Cid
might, if by miracle he found Castile
after nine hundred years: automobile
stampedes, where lambs had granged . . .
all changed . . . estranged . . . all but your name, Madrid.

Two hours I benched on your most populous street,
searching each passer's brow: perhaps in one
the stanzas hid
of what I hummed—your song, "No pasaran!"
Perhaps the book-clerk, when she saw me run
toward Lorca's shelf, would greet
my eyes with eyes of welcome to Madrid.

Of all who—with bare fist, back to the wall—
had stopped the tanks, was not one witness left?
Had Franco rid
your air of its best echoes, set adrift
your loveliest phantoms? Were you too bereft
of memory to recall
what lodestone drew me home at last, Madrid?

Nightfall. I lug to the eleventh floor
my bones and questions. In the looking-glass
under each lid
a bag sits brooding; sideburns (thick as grass
above stopped mouths that howled "They shall not pass!"),
run gray. . . . Who was it swore,
the day you fell, he'd yet come home, Madrid?

Sevilla: July 18th

We arrived
not on the birthday of Bizet or Byron,
but on July 18th, the anniversary
of Franco's fist.

> Awaiting the menu del dia,
> while sipping your charm, your sangria,
> we watched on TV, Sevilla,
> the matador's ritual call,
> the crowd's *Ole! ole!*
> devouring—one and all—
> at five in the dying day
> the ear of an outmatched bull.

Although suspicious, Carmen of the world,
I let you try seducing me:
> such plazas, barrios! your Santa Cruz!
> Giralda, long-necked flamenco dancer
> about to set her pious skirts awhirling at the first bell . . .
As a cocotte still in her prime leans under a street lamp,
you leaned your whitewashed face with dark wrought-iron balcony
     lashes,
waiting, if not for me, then for another,
success a million times proven.

Below your mantilla of towers, below the lashes and skirts,
I smelled you out
as Lear smelled out his daughters:
But to the girdle do the gods inherit,
beneath is all the fiends' . . .

As we filled on your fruit, your tortilla
and asked for the bill, Sevilla,
the bullring of Madrid
filled with a bullringful
of your Guardia Incivil—
eighteen thousand—enough
to do as their grandfathers did,
to play it equally rough
in the name of Colón and El Cid—
to work their patriot will,
to show their matador skill,
come in for a scarlet spill
and fetch home as souvenirs,
at eighteen to one, the ears
of a thousand Lorcas—*ole!*
as eighteen marched him away . . .

You pretended not to know of it, Seville,
fanned yourself just a bit more swiftly;
—who, after all, expects a Carmen
to be mixed up with such things?

Now your official guidebook in four languages repeats
your every charm as Lorca sang it, now his poems
in sumptuous leather, like the prize ear of a bull,
keep the pesetas rhyming in your pocket,
while everywhere the posters, everywhere
graffiti of that special kind one comes to recognize,
honor his killers and their grandsons
who itch to leadpipe from their doors at night
the new "traidores y perjuros":
VIVA FRANCO! VIVA POLICIA! ADELANTE LAS
FUERZAS NACIONALES!
ARRIBA ESPANA! ARRIBA EL 18 DE JULIO!
ARRIBA DIGNITA, HUMANITA, PAZ ETERNA!

I look you over, smell you out a day or two,
hum you a new habanera:
> *there's hell, there's darkness, there is the sulphurous pit,*
> *burning, scalding, stench, consumption; fie, fie, fie!*

Cunning city, bent on winning me
one way or another!
On the last day I push through surrendering byways;
your Civil Guard salute me;
your grocers come out of their shops
to repeat with Franciscan patience
which are the turns to the Charity Hospital;
your nun there, proud
of every brushstroke by Murillo and Leal,
leaves us alone with her treasury of slides and books;
on the way back to the hotel, your families love-touch,
two grown girls, each with an arm inside grandfather's arm,
share with him, from your merchant's makeshift bag,
a 1/4 kilo of cashews.

—Giralda's bell strikes three . . . perhaps now she is whirling . . .
Is it that which wakes me, or the air conditioner,
or the vision that carries over from my sleep?
> Once again there rounds a corner,
> face full of peace and white beard,
> a slow Andalusian, savoring his path, a boy beside him . . .
Suddenly I know: this would be Lorca now,
if, as his friends begged, he had fled:
> just finishing a jug of sangria, pointing to a disciple
> the special charms of the Plaza de la Falange,
> which will soon have its old name again . . .

> O city of souvenirs!
> O city of bullring cheers!
> Strike your castanets hard!
> Keep, for the time I stay,
> their slashing tread from my ears:
> eighteen, still marching away
> on the night of the grimmest day
> of Granada's grimmest of years
> her proud, imprudent bard

            to make him decisively pay
            for "The Song of the Civil Guard."

I will not return, Seville; you are bad for my blood pressure.
It is hard to love and hate at the same time—
enough that I have my own town to deal with:
the same dark rumblings, still hidden in its skull,
shrieked forth in black graffiti from your whitewashed walls.
If I stayed one more day and were true to my best self,
eighteen bullets would find me too.

Granada: The Rose

You leveled with me, Granada;
you didn't once overcharge;
you walked out of your way to show me my way;
you really meant it when you said *De nada!*
—so I'll level with you.

Of course I loved your beauties—Lorca taught me how;
but neither Alhambra's picturesque wealth
nor Albaicin's picturesque poverty brought me,
neither the gypsies' hot freedom on their hill
nor the cold imprisonment of Fernando and Isabella.

I came, after forty years,
to find the center of Lorca's life
and leave a rose there.

At eleven this morning I shall board the bus for Málaga
having left no rose,
although I know where it should be placed.
Perhaps it was the fahrenheit that stopped me,
or my wife's plea that I do nothing "controversial."

But in fact at the end it grew clear
that Lorca needs no flower;
his name bursts richer than the gardens of the Generalife.
It was I who needed to bring it and find its proper place

—I, whose mouth opened because his was shut,
I, whose weakness feeds on his strength.

And you, Granada, you need it
—though I am a small poet, seldom anthologized,
and one rose more or less is perhaps not important
in a city of many roses.

When you have erased the name of Valdes
from that street behind the post office,
when you have finished with the statue of José Antonio,
when you have renamed the Square for him whose eyes caressed it
at all hours from the Acera del Casino window,
whose shoes increased its price each time he stepped across it—
then I will come again;
I have learned how to wait, but this time
it will not be for long.
I will come to you, Granada,
and place my rose at the feet of his statue,
for whatever one rose is worth.

Málaga: A Prayer

Into a great firefly, without guile
alighting on this long gray stem of shore,
Málaga turns, mile upon brilliant mile,
suddenly, and for a little while
dances defiance of the sea's dark roar.

The lighthouse beams a vessel toward its dock:
this night no mariners are to be lost.
They disembark as mindless of the rock
as motorists are of the moon-round clock
that tries to warn what hour it's forty past.

Touched by such light, all shades of voices, faces
blend for one moment. Ah! the breeze!—whose promise
drew us together from those parched, far places . . .
Málaga, firefly, do not vanish from us!

Córdoba: Nocturne

Now, in the dog days of July
(the dog nights too) there's not a breeze
for Córdoba to lullaby
her overnight dependents; these,
having no choice but to comply,
accept the brash disharmonies
of plodding bus and prodding car
and squalling square and braying bar
a mile from Mosque and Alcazar.

They sleep. But sometimes an unease
wakes them. They wonder: Where am I?
For which hotel have I the keys?
Is this Madrid's, Toledo's sky?
It comes to them: Maimonides,
Lucan, and Seneca let fly
their lightnings here; and not so far
from where those lucent phantoms are
Gabirol blazed; here set his star.

Granada

It is possible to reach Granada
in the dead heat of siesta
yet two hours later,
sure that for the next days here on Lorca's street
sleep will be out of the question,
sink into slumber
—having brushed off a dark child's palm
gnawing at the corner of one's vision
like a fly on the tortilla,
—having measured Isabel's cathedral, her marble song
of triumph over the Moslems soon to be shoved out of their city,
and beside it the chapel of her boxed-in power,
she and her empire gorgeously domed forever:
eagles, pennons, coffers, crown,
—having had all one's questions about Lorca finally answered:

the house of his birth, the street of his singing,
the date of the fusillade,
all except a tomb for his bones, a doorway for one's rose,
—which scarcely matters,
since it is the Queen who belongs to the past;
the future is Lorca's;
he needs no tomb;
if the stars that honor their poet
were twice as high,
the dome would still not be pretentious.

Madrid: The Ghosts of Its Defenders

This boy with shirt half-open
who scooters into the dusk
clutched from behind by his girl—
where did he start from? I don't mean today . . .
today he started from one of the balconies off in the suburbs.
His granny, I mean—
did she bleed? did she hunger?
did she lullaby first his father, then him
with a hushed No Pasaran?

All three million—
who were their ancestors?
Here and there, like hen's teeth, I meet a gray head.
How I wish I could stop them: *Por favor!*
Where were you, granny? what were you up to when the city fell?
You can tell *me;* I won't take down your name . . .
Were you in the clasp of these hills that day,
or did panic drive you from the dying farmlands later?
or did they bring you, by bus, by railway, later,
with Franco chairs, Franco beds, Franco tables
to fill an empty place,
to stroll, chatter, urinate
over the ghosts of its defenders, drown out its NO PASARAN
with your migrant tunes, as bulldozers
swept away its splendid rubble, as grand hotels
squatted heavily on its heart?

Barcelona: The Last Night

I am lying past midnight
thinking not of a woman but of a city.
I have always been susceptible to cities—not all:
some I hate outright: the arrogant ones,
the ones who want my money,
the man-eating ones—
from them it is bliss to escape!
some I both hate and love,
including the one that cradled me;
of those I love
I touch not a hair
—they never suspect I am there.

It is not blind love, Barcelona.
I took note of the driver
who doubled my fare,
the guard at the beach gate
who denied me a glimpse of the sea.

But inside the cathedral a Sunday handful responded
in sweet Catalan (forty years outlawed)
to the priest's chant;
while out in the square, hands linked,
defying a hostile high noon,
four rings of gentle sardañas
revived with each cool flow
from the gaily umbrella'd musicians;
and the side-street one-man show:
juggling oranges four at a time,
blowing Ping-Pongs ten feet high
and homing them in his mouth like doves,
coaxing frail melodies
from Catalan veins around him,
catching them one by one in his trumpet
and blaring them back full-fledged
into the veins that had nested them;
and the multicolored cartoons

turning old walls into young screams for freedom;
and the lad in the bookstore, the crone at the hotel,
eyes flashing, back stiffening:
"Of course I am Catalan!"

Madrid: July 1978

All day I staggered about, unable to shake off those three
visions of Goya: the white-bloused Palace defender, arms wide,
     about
to join his comrades heaped under conqueror bayonets;
the Infant Time beheaded by his Father's teeth; the things of night
leering their black mass of triumph . . .

All day I staggered about, unable to shake off the posters
summoning Spain's "New Force" into Madrid,
into the bullring wide as Saturn's jaws
to tear at the frail new day, to hymn July 18th: when bayonets
pointed at the north, the Palace.

Now, back in bed, I am reached
by a rumbling from a region, of a kind, unknown.
You might call it the whir of nightlife traffic;
for me it is once more the insurgent artillery
closing in on the city . . .

But a loudspeaker reaches me too—enflamed, enflaming—
protesting yesterday's army attack on Pamplona,
passionate as that which bloomed through the last nights in '39,
saying there's sap in it yet; after thirty-nine years
it could bloom again!

And I, who came to salute ghosts, salute Time instead:
Saturn's new child, unawed by his brothers' fate.
If, as the grafitti around the corner threatens,
the army will strike again, the "Fuerza Nueva," rumbling
even now into Madrid

in caravans of cars trailing red and gold streamers,
black-massing even now in the bullring, tucking chains
and batons into their trousers along with what's already
there risen and ready, Time's new city
will not lie back and take it.

Granada: First Showing

No, we did not join the pilgrims
plodding heavenward (by taxi)
to the caves of Sacromonte.

No, we crossed the street for tickets
and in sweltering Granada's
lobby, pressed by youthful speech and
flesh, grew faint, before at last the
doors creaked open, and a Spanish
Gary Cooper, Ingrid Bergman
mimicked forth in large, dynamic
motions what had truly happened
eight kilometers from where we
sat, up there in the Sierras
forty years ago, which parents
could not murmur, poets would not
sing, remembering foolhardy
Federico's riddled body.

Better than the best flamenco
to be found on Sacromonte
was the silence of Granada
rising row by row and bearing
home the shriek of Ingrid Bergman.

Córdoba

No sulking terminal weak in light but powerful in urine,
no dragging of luggage up long shadeless ways,
no disappearance of passports—
no! Straight from the bus one should enter the Sultan's gardens
out of whose shrubs the sweets of de Falla pour;
deep in the Mosque, that awesome confection of marble,
around its striped pillars,
should creep like rays through a many-mythed window
the most reaching notes of *Iberia* . . .

My Córdoba neither sang nor danced.
Outside El Corte Ingles, in Saturday brilliance,
a blind girl chanted lottery tickets.
Outside my meditation
the synagogue caretaker paced his toothless craving for lunch.
Inside Isabel's most forbidden of nooks,
around her decaying bathtub,
a gang of guttural wisecracks splashed like mud.

On the second and final day
the museum was locked but the fountain ran free in the plaza;
the market sprawled dead,
but the balconies laughed geraniums;
on the inside lane of my nerves a midnight scooter braked,
but a girl hopped on
and off they zoomed inventing a breeze.

So up to the sixteenth-story roof I came
to give Córdoba one last chance.
There below in the darkness floated her lights.
Without strain I lifted them into me, one and all,
along with an illegal pup and its walker
I had suddenly embarrassed near the ledge.

PART 13

Runes, Riddles, and Darkness

The Flowers of Georgia O'Keeffe

A lady treads our bleakest thoroughfares,
listening to the curses and the sobs—
at every alleyway she stops and stares,
climbs a dark staircase, turns one of the knobs,
stands blinded in the blackness of a room
till slowly she begins to recognize
the wan-faced children, wasted before their bloom:
blue fear, blue pain, blue hunger in their eyes.

Then out the door she rushes with her grief,
down the dark staircase, the bleak thoroughfare.
Away to a meadow rushes Georgia O'Keeffe,
to a meadow, a park, a garden—anywhere—
takes up the first white flower, the first leaf,
and flaunts it like a banner in the air!

His Something

It wasn't as if the phone had stopped ringing,
as if no hand turned the knob of his door,
as if the postman of late had been bringing
messages to his box no more.

It wasn't as if what he'd drunk when younger
won thanks no longer from his thirst,
as if what food once reached his hunger
failed now where it succeeded first.

It was only that somehow he'd crossed a border
into the bleak, unbearing lands
from which his something, in wretched disorder,
fled despite the clutch of his hands.

Lesson

Into the land of the raven
where little is loved but the dark
there came once, hoping for haven,
a daylight-trumpeting lark.

Loathed was that skyward clarion
till kindly a hoot-owl spoke:
"Here, one must feed upon carrion,
grow midnight feathers, and croak."

Lines on a Museum Postcard

The old Jew, playing Rembrandt's Noble Slav,
Cezanne's young apples, immortally disarrayed,
and Egypt's emperors, glaring past their tombs,
all ask me to deliver their regrets.
Your eyes have much too long been missed by them.
The same goes for the trees in Central Park,
as well as their reflections on the lake.
I've taken it upon myself to pledge
that you'll come soon; while they, in turn, have vowed
to stand exactly where they are—and wait.

Midsummer

Half awake on a midsummer eve
I heard a singing too lovely to believe.
and could not say, so subtle was the chime,
whether it was distant in space or in time.

Half asleep on a midsummer night
I saw a darkness more lovely than the light
and could not tell, so clouded was the face,
whether it was distant in time or in space.

Air for Bagpipe

From Carlisle north to Edinburgh
the way goes uphill, winding, narrow;
and on that road, and in between
the flocks of wool, the fells of green,
there rides and grows and sits unseen
the Groaning Bliss, the Grinning Sorrow.

The Redwing's Cry

Sharp and silver
and mislaid these forty years
suddenly through my ears
comes the redwing's cry,
turns the lock
that held back the river;
it is six o'clock
and I . . .

I do not stop to wonder whether I am in the valley
or the valley is in me.
Dew soaks my sneakers.
Everywhere a scent of rising, opening creatures
halloos me and my heart trumpets.
Longer than widest armspread can encompass
flows the river toward mysterious turnings
past Cornwall in the south and in the north the burning
windows of Newburgh; but whatever lies
within the compass of arms, of eyes,
is mine today, mine forever,
the river in me, I in the river.

A long time I lie still,
as if the roar of hair against pillow
will ruin the redwing's work, return the terror
of rising to meet a mirror . . .

till I'm uncertain
whether I heard
an actual bird
or a fiction,
and, if real,
whether it will sound again;
whether it came as ordeal
or benediction.

Falling Asleep

Right now in every corner of the planet
one by one the billions are falling asleep
hungry or full, in hate, in love, in trouble;
even, at last, the ones who meant to keep
vigil all night beside the wife, the husband
assigned tomorrow afternoon at three
for more sophisticated tests and X-rays
because today's were not as they should be.
        Later, somehow,
        even those
        drop into calmness
        and their eyes close.

Night Thoughts

"Died in his sleep . . . so lucky!"—How do you know?
You had no attack last year, nor afterward
with friends sat mute, death-still; yet even you
have lain for hours counting your dearest in coffins,
imagining them and finally you among them,
your name above-ground gradually fading
to less than the whisper a branch outside your wall
will send somebody else not caring whether
that somebody has an ear as loving as yours.
For hours you've lain without an eyelid stirring,

so as not to disturb your wife, and if she does
wake for a moment, how could she know that you
are anything but asleep? and how could his wife,
who knows more than the rest of us put together,
know he was lucky, know he died in his sleep?

PART 14

Poet's Work

Neruda in Hiding

The tyrants of Chile are hunting Neruda:
they've ordered police to the sea and the plains.
They pray that his throat may be locked in a dungeon;
they hope that his wings may be harnessed by chains.

The tyrants of Chile are hunting Neruda:
they halt every train, and examine the cars.
The hero that finds him will be well rewarded
with praises, and *pesos,* and bright golden stars.

The tyrants of Chile are hunting Neruda:
his face is in hiding—his voice can be heard.
Go look in the forests—perhaps you will find him
on one of the branches! Go look for a bird!

The tyrants of Chile are hunting Neruda:
they ask, "Have you seen him?"—and everyone smiles.
Ah yes, we have seen him, we know where he's hiding.
Fly after him, fellows! He'll mock at your miles.

The tyrants of Chile are hunting Neruda:
Come look in our hearts, say the poor and the weak.
Come look in our hearts, with your chains and your dungeon!
It's here that he's hiding—the eagle you seek.

Singing

At last the hand of night is thrust away
and through my window leaps the morning light:
I hear a roar of boys at battle-play,
an airplane ominously taking flight—
but from the branches not a note is heard
announcing day—
as though a music-hater in the night
had ambushed every bird.

With no one singing, how can day begin?
What breakfast, till the fast of song be broken?
What other key can let a new day in?
(The wind knocks, but my heart's door will not open.)
—The first dawn I remember was with song,
and I have been
listening for each day's melodious token
since then, when I was young.

(Wait! for a moment I can almost hear
my mother humming at her wash again;
my father—operatically clear—
joining his voice to hers in a refrain.
So the days started; I recall them yet—
and would pay dear
if his dead lips, and if her lips of pain
could blend in one duet.)

The trees are bare of music as of leaf,
and without music I am motionless.
He wished me dead who was my music's thief;
and though till madness I have tried to guess
which enemy he is—of this I'm sure:
he loves my grief,
and hates all songs, for in their loveliness
my strength begins its cure.

Listen, my enemy, wherever you are—
in spite of all your plots I shall not die.
Even this day, with trees made bare by war,
must have its song—if others dare not try,
then I and mine will make the tune we need,
and if you'd bar
that composition from the public sky
then you are doomed indeed.

For I'll not be that poor Pacific thing
who sang on a green island all alone.
Lovely of lung he was—but weak of wing—
to no one but himself and scholars known;

until a warship anchored there, and rats
—hearing him sing—
rushed from the hold, devoured him beak and bone,
then supped on fruit and grass.

I'll be the peg-leg sailor without name
who every winter limped across the South
singing to young black men at night the same
melody, till it rooted in their mouth.
That song was cursed by many a cotton-lord,
for when spring came
a hundred slaves had found his peg-leg path
and followed *The Drinking Gourd.*

Threnody

The time of year is green, but black's my color;
cloudless the sky, but in my skull a cloud;
I harvest nothing, though the hayloft's fuller,
and have no tune, although the day breaks loud.

Loud breaks the day—and I, a lark but lately,
crouch wingless, tuneless, on a bare tree's bough
as though it were a day of death, and rightly
a song of death should be my music now.

O friends, I tell you this: no face is finished;
no sea has drawn a body to its bed;
no stone's been cut, no stone to mark what vanished—
only the dream by which I lived is dead . . .
And I, that bellowed so, must learn to be
silent—except for this one threnody.

The Widower

I woke one morning: lifeless at my side,
after much agony, lay my belief.
Long had I kept her closer than a wife,
and many nights had wept to see her bleed.
My songs were all for her. The dawn she died
I sang once more, one final chant of grief,
then buried both—as though beyond her life
my music had no living mouth to feed.

Five years have I, a faithful widower,
brought flowers to her grave, and seldom sung;
but black's not right for me: I still am young;
longer than she loved me, did I love her.
Now disbelief lies warm upon my bed;
for her I'll sing, till one of us be dead.

And I Looked, and, Behold, a Whirlwind

Poet: do you hear, do you see
how winds, at eighty miles an hour,
carry death across the Atlantic
while behind you, like chubby moles,
Mr. Jones and Mr. Smith are digging
—camouflaged by smiles and garbage cans?

(He leans far out over the river,
listening for the pulse of his next poem,
watching his lone, grotesquely rippled face;
this he hears, this he sees.)

Ah, poet: on behalf
of the bridge, so delicately poised,
on behalf of the trees
—like virgins fearing attack—
on behalf of the buildings
filled with precious footsteps,
on behalf of the one child in a hundred

who might some day read your poem
and the other ninety-nine who are that poem—

turn your ears to the wind of death,
your eyes to the derricks of death!
shout BEWARE! BEWARE! as if Ezekiel
stood again on his street-corner in Jerusalem . . .

Dialogue

I masquerade in clothes
more fireproof than prose:
a scarf about the ears
to stop the roaring years;
a cap above the eyes
to stop the skies.

Pale leaves, about to fall,
gape down at me and call:
"Who bids you flutter past
unfriendly, and so fast,
not turning once your head
to mark our dead?

"Have you no mass to sing
for every death-touched thing,
oh laureate of leaves?
Are you not one who grieves?
Have you forgotten how
we greened the bough?"

"Ask not if I forget;
nor name me laureate!
You have mistaken me:
I neither hear nor see.
The one whom you await
is likely late."

But what I say deceives
not me, and less the leaves;
and what they, dying, said
comes with me to my bed;
and I take off my clothes:
the scarf, the prose.

The Count

Sometimes a fellow, victimized by theft,
instead of reckoning his loss that day
invents a dozen causes for delay
and never knows of what he is bereft—
as if he hopes that goblins, kind and deft,
will visit on tip-toe (the very way
the robbers did) and, coming to assay
his fortune, he will find that much is left.

Ten years ago I too began to miss
a treasury—not coppers, but a creed.
It was—don't ask—a frightening amount!
And ever since, because my cowardice
could not endure the knowledge of such need,
I have been careful to avoid the count.

To Himself

Finally it will not matter
how many kicked, how many kissed him—
how many rooms there were, how many rumors—
how many poisons were offered, or prizes—
how many salvos, how many silences.

It will mean nothing, nothing at all
whether anthologies nested his poems—
whether a critic called them bright birds—

whether they soared across heaven-smooth pages—
whether slumberers leapt at the tune.

Nothing will matter, nothing at all
except that his heart maintained its own beat,
his face its own hue, his foot its own thud,
his night its own vision, his soul its own heat,
his hand its own touch, his tongue its own word.

This will be all, on the day of days.
But meanwhile, what is a man to do—
a man, like everyone, flesh and blood?
How many times can he say to himself:
Hush, fool, hush! it will not matter,
not matter at all, not matter at all . . .

Sunday Morning

There
with his dog
on the road
under their favorite tree
stands the poet
ready for new visions.

A station wagon slows and halts:
which way to the tunnel?
"Left . . . then right . . .
then past two traffic lights . . .
a pharmacy . . . a movie-house . . .
follow the signs—you can't go wrong."

The driver: balding, pale, strong-boned.
Between him and the woman
two blonde thumb-suckers.
Behind them—
cousins, uncles, aunts,
one grandmother;
all smiling, nodding, waving

as they disappear
toward the tunnel.

Across the river,
the poet remembers,
is a green and shady park—
right for lolling, ball-throwing,
hide-and-seek.

Past the park,
a boardwalk and a beach—
right for shouting, splashing, snoozing,
castle-building.

The family waves thank you and so long
to the dog-walker;
they have no room for anyone else—
especially a stranger—
in their car.

Yet he has made room for himself somehow:
goes through the ominous tunnel,
(seeing each face, though one can't see the others')
comes out into the boisterous day,
is It with whoever is It,
hides with whoever hides,
splashes and is splashed,
and more . . . much more . . .

rides home with them after the sun goes down,
kissing grandmother and cousins goodbye
at their corner;
rides on to the graduation of one blonde thumbsucker,
the wedding of another,
grandmother's funeral,
cousin's departure for war,
father's last ride down a hospital corridor,
and more . . . much more . . .
before the dog is finished
and they turn from their favorite tree.

The Swan

(FOR BORIS PASTERNAK)

Suddenly, poet, your season of brooding is ended.
The egg, secretly guarded, is hatched. Now high
over your countrymen's heads, on wings that are splendid,
the swan of your sorrow and theirs is beginning to fly.

Thinking of you, poet, and your creation,
I pray it may happen also here, where I live,
a swan like yours will sing such lamentation
which those in power, paling, can not forgive.

To the Countrymen of Alfred Kreymborg

(written three weeks before the poet's death)

When one informs you that the cry-filled eyes
of Kreymborg are not yet entirely shut,
his rill-pure voice still trickling, with surprise
you shake assassin heads and murmur: "But
we thought the man was dead . . ."
                                Aye—well he might;
long since, you nailed the coffin of his name;
long since, his song you buried from the light.
Aye—but his breath moves feathers just the same.

And let me add, while yet those feathers move
ever so lightly, that his lyric breath
more durable—in the long run—may prove
than yours, which feed upon a prophet's death.
His faltering pulse, from Stamford by the Sound,
across this poet-choking land will pound.

315

Not Being Yevtushenko

Not being Yevtushenko has its advantages—
although one envies his vivid arms and throat,
his large editions, interviews at airports,
listeners bursting to lip the hem of his coat.

Unknown in a dusk where even shadows are audible
beats being taken and tossed from town to town,
forever bellowing his bellow, forever
the same dance of his arms upbeat and down.

It is preferable to drink more than reflections of
one's own fine face in every passer's eye,
more than acoustical reverberations
of one's own cry, more than the bravo cry.

Not being Yevtushenko is better than slumbering
late, untroubled by matters of menu or rent;
the son of Pushkin, grandson of Jeremiah,
should be obliged to no man, no government.

To the White Minority of South Africa

Open the Book of Time, if you have eyes;
turn to your page, and know it.
The State that slays its poet swiftly dies,
but never dies the poet.

Paul Celan

(at rest in the Seine, April 20, 1970)

He must have experienced bursts of shaping
power . . . accorded only to the greatest of artists
(eighty-one poems between June 1967 and January
1968). He must have heard inside himself those
storms of light of which Rilke spoke when the famous
breakthrough came to the *Duino Elegies.*
   —George Steiner

So yours was the breakthrough that should have been mine—
climbing, climbing from good to fine—
clawing, clawing from Apennine
to Alp to Parnassus, from fine to sublime—

while I, by a soft green lake below,
venturing in to the depth of a toe,
risking not even a glimpse at your snow,
fashioned my tune of a ripple's flow.

No peak was peak enough for you
till you sucked of the Dawn her first, best dew,
till wingwords flew as the eagle flew,
till the clouds broke and let you through.

Yours the breakthrough, yours the bliss,
Apollo's blessing and Muse's kiss;
yours the leap from abyss to abyss;
yours the snow-crowned precipice.

Twenty-five years have passed since then,
since you broke through again and again,
fire on the tongue, fire from the pen,
fire quenched in the lake-deep Seine,

while I, each year of the twenty-five,
toe in the lake, was at least alive.
I am good, I am liked, I am busy, I thrive,
fashioning tunes that will not survive.

If, as advised, I had bolted my doors
to wife, to children, and waged high wars
till the soul was a lump of bleeding sores,
might mine be a breakthrough such as yours?

If I, a thousand midnights awake,
abjured all joys for the music's sake,
might mine be the breakthrough? might I break
through to the groin of a Seine-deep lake?

Notes to the Poems

PART 1: A CONSUMER CULTURE

"See America First"

First published in *The Thunder of the Grass* (1948) in a group titled "Advertisement," this poem was later translated into Urdu by Zainul Abedin and published in *Afkar* [Karachi] 14 (1959).

"Switch to Calvert"

A popular and inexpensive blended American rye whiskey, Calvert "Extra" was named for the Calvert family that founded the Maryland colony in 1632. Calvert "Extra" was heavily advertised during the 1940s, especially on CBS radio by Edward R. Murrow. Kramer rarely drank alcohol.

First published in *The Thunder of the Grass* (1948) in a group titled "Advertisement."

"Encyclopedia"

First published in *The Thunder of the Grass* (1948) in a group titled "Advertisement."

"Treatment"

First published in *The Thunder of the Grass* (1948) in a group titled "Advertisement."

"Prayer"

First published in the *Arkansas City Star,* August 4, 1963.

"Progress"

First published in *Visions* 20 (February 1986).

PART 2: NEW YORK, NEW YORK

"Esmeralda"

First published in part 2 of "Coney Island" in *'Til the Grass Is Ripe for Dancing* (1943).

"April on Avenue C"

First published in *The Tune of the Calliope* (1958).

"Carousel Parkway"

A shorter version of this poem first appeared in *Modern Poetry Studies* (Autumn 1975). This revised and expanded version was initially published in *Carousel Parkway* (1980).

PART 3: THE POETRY OF WORK

"Ballad of Tom Mooney"

Thomas J. Mooney (1892–1942) was the central figure in the most notorious case of a frame-up over a labor dispute during the first half of the twentieth century. Mooney served a substantial portion of his life—some twenty-three years, from 1916 to 1939—in prison for a crime he did not commit.

Mooney grew up in a left-wing family, the son of committed socialists. At only age fifteen, he won a trip to attend a conference in Switzerland sponsored by the Second International. He campaigned actively for the Socialist presidential candidate Eugene Debs, edited the magazine *Revolt,* and became a genuine force in the San Francisco Bay Area labor movement. He also opposed U.S. involvement in World War I. But it was his labor activism that drew the anger of allied businessmen, politicians, and police forces in California. Mooney worked hard to organize the car men of the United Railroads of San Francisco and became a clear leader of the California Federation of Labor.

In 1916, at a July 22 Preparedness Day march in San Francisco, a bomb exploded killing ten people. Perjured testimony placed Mooney and several of his friends at the scene, though evidence soon surfaced that he was actually some blocks away. Mooney was convicted, though soon afterward the conservative federal Wickersham Commission judged the case a frame-up. Then the trial judge and jurors admitted publicly that they had made the wrong decision. When President Woodrow Wilson joined the protest, Mooney's death sentence was commuted to life imprisonment, but Mooney was not actually released until 1939. His health destroyed, he died a few years later. Among the worldwide protests were the poet Lola Ridge's 1935 *New Republic* poem "Stone Face" and Kramer's September 26, 1937, *Sunday Worker* poem reprinted here.

"Thought on a Train"

First published in *Brooklyn College Observer* (November 1937).

"The Shoe-Shine Boy"

First published in *Sunday Worker,* August 22, 1937, as "Poem."

"Work Day"

First published in the *Brooklyn College Observer* (March 1941).

"Unemployed Song"

First published in *The Glass Mountain* (1946).

"Help Wanted!"

First published in *The Thunder of the* Grass (1948) in a group titled "Advertisement."

from The Minotaur: *"Eight O'Clock Whistle"; "All Hail!"; "A Trick on Nick"; "In the Lunch Wagon"; "The Trap-Door Shuts"; "Five O'Clock Whistle"*

First published in *Roll the Forbidden Drums!* (1954). Several sections were set to music by Michael Cherry in 1976 and by Ronald Armanini in 1986–87.

"Song No. 1" from Santa Fe Night (a hobo fantasy)

In 1960, Kramer contributed about twenty lyrics to a musical composed by Arnold Black based on play by Albert Bein. Titled *Heavenly Express,* the musical was optioned but never produced. Under a new title, *Santa Fe Night,* seven songs appear in *Moses* (1962). The Library of Congress incorrectly credits Lehman Engel with the musical settings. Granted the University of Michigan Musical Theater Award, April 1978.

"Nick"

First published in *The Brooklyn College Alumni Literary Magazine* 1.1 and 2 (Spring–Summer 1981).

"Elegy for a Carpet Boy"

First published in *Outlook* (July–August 1995) and *Long Island Quarterly* (Autumn 1995).

PART 4: AFRICAN AMERICAN HISTORY AND STRUGGLE

"Paul Robeson"

Paul Robeson (1898–1976) was a singer, a stage and screen actor, a Communist, an African American, a civil rights advocate, and a spokesperson for revolutionary cultural and political change. He possessed one of the most powerful singing voices of the century, along with a personal presence and aura of courage exceeded by no one.

Robeson's father was a North Carolina slave who escaped to freedom at age fifteen, went to college, and became a minister. Robeson's mother came from a prominent black family in Philadelphia but died when Robeson was only six years old. Robeson was class valedictorian and an All-American football player at Rutgers. He earned a law degree at Columbia but changed careers after joining the Provincetown Players, the legendary Greenwich Village theater company codirected by Eugene O'Neill. He appeared in a stage revival of O'Neill's *The Emperor Jones* in 1924 and starred in the 1933 Hollywood film.

During the 1930s, when London was his primary residence, Robeson met and talked readily with the radical philosopher C. L. R. James, befriended the future Kenyan leader Jomo Kenyatta, read widely about socialism, and was gradually radicalized. His first trip to the Soviet Union was in 1934. In 1943, the year that Kramer wrote his tribute, Robeson starred in a highly successful performance of Shakespeare's *Othello* on Broadway. Beginning in 1949 he was harassed by the House Un-American Activities Committee and by the State Department. He was simultaneously blacklisted in his own country and barred from traveling and performing abroad. Many of his immensely powerful recordings survive.

First published as part 3 of "The Steel and the Eagles" in *'Til the Grass Is Ripe for Dancing* (1943).

"Natchez"

On April 23, 1940, the Rhythm Night Club in Natchez, Mississippi, burned down taking 203 African American patrons to their deaths. The dance hall was located in a 200-foot-long corrugated iron building on St. Catherine Street, and its metal skin tended to concentrate the flames within the building while the people inside massed at the only exit. The crowd was larger than usual that night because Walter Barnes and his orchestra had come to town as the featured band.

Two years later the famous Coconut Grove nightclub fire took place in New York. Though both are among the worst fires in American public places, only the Coconut Grove fire, most of whose victims were white, received continuing national publicity. There are gospel and blues songs devoted to the Natchez fire, among them Howlin' Wolf's 1956 "Natchez Burning," but Kramer's poem is unique.

First published in *'Til the Grass Is Ripe for Dancing* (1943).

"Isaac Woodard"

On February 12, 1946, Sergeant Isaac Woodard, a recently discharged African American World War II combat veteran, was returning to his wife and family in North Carolina after boarding a bus in Augusta, Georgia. Following an exchange of words with the white bus driver "over some minor point of racial etiquette," Woodard was forcibly removed from the bus in Batesburg, South Carolina, and then beaten and maimed by the local police chief, Linwood Shull, and his deputy. Woodard was denied medical help until the following day when he was taken to an army hospital. Doctors determined that his eyes had been crushed with the blunt end of a billy club. Woodard was permanently blinded.

Woodard's maiming went unreported until the National Association for the Advancement of Colored People (NAACP) published his sworn affidavit in July 1946. At the same time, Orson Wells discussed the case on several of his nightly radio shows. Wells's outspoken condemnation of Woodard's treatment cost him his show's sponsor, Lear Radios, and ultimately his show, which ABC canceled in October 1946.

As a result of the national publicity, a federal grand jury indicted Shull in the fall of 1946 for violating Woodard's civil rights and brought him to trial in the federal court in Columbia, South Carolina. An all-white jury deliberated fifteen minutes before acquitting him of all charges, and Shull left the courtroom accompanied by cheering white spectators.

"Isaac Woodard," Kramer's response to the tragedy, was written during the events of 1946 and first published in *The Thunder of the Grass* (1948). The poem was set to music first by Moses Chusid (1949) and then by Irwin Heilner, whose "Isaac Woodard" was later published in *Broadside #54* (1964). Woodie Guthrie's "The Blinding of Isaac Woodard" dates from the same time as Kramer's poem.

Ironically, Frank N. Shubert, the historian of the United States Joint Chiefs of Staff, notes that President Harry Truman was "really touched" by Woodard's blinding, so touched that when on July 26, 1948, he issued Executive Order 9981 beginning the total integration of American armed forces, he cited Isaac Woodard's experience as one of the incentives for his signing the order (<http://www.defenselink.mil/news/Jul1998/n07171998_9807163.html>, accessed September 21, 2003.)

"The Seamstress"

Written ca. 1950, "The Seamstress" includes Kramer's note: "(a true incident from slavery times, recorded in B. A. Botkin's collection of ex-slave interviews, *Lay My Burden Down*)."

First published in M. Myers, ed., *Paul Laurence Dunbar: An Anthology in Memoriam (1872–1906)* (Bristol, Ind.: Bristol Banner, 1997).

"Denmark Vesey"

This twenty-six-section poem relates the story of Denmark Vesey (ca. 1767–1822), who was most likely born in St. Thomas, Danish West Indies, although his exact birthplace is unknown. Some suggest he was of Ashanti descent. In 1781 he was sold into slavery on St. Domingue by Captain Joseph Vesey (1747–1835). Joseph Vesey repurchased Denmark in 1782 and then settled in Charleston in 1783, giving up the slave trade for civic affairs.

On November 9, 1799, Denmark won $1,500 in the East-Bay Lottery of Charleston and purchased his freedom one month later. Adopting the surname Vesey, he opened a carpentry shop, prospered because of his artisanship, and married. Despite his freedom, his wife and children remained slaves.

Vesey was a charismatic figure because he was tall and physically imposing, extremely intelligent, and not afraid to argue in the street with Charleston whites. Furthermore, he was deeply religious and an active participant in Charleston's African Methodist Episcopal (AME) church. After authorities closed the church as a potential breeding ground of rebellion and arrested congregants (Vesey perhaps among them) between 1818 and 1820, he probably conceived the idea of an insurrection and mass exodus to freedom in Haiti. By 1821, he had developed the plan in his home at 21 Bull Street, assisted by Ned and Rolla Bennett, slaves of Governor Thomas Bennett; Peter Poyas, a ship's carpenter; and Gullah Jack Pritchard, a "magic man" whose followers considered him bulletproof. The original date set for the insurrection was July 14, Bastille Day. By May, approximately nine thousand slaves were involved in the conspiracy. As with all widespread groups, maintaining secrecy was a thorny problem. On May 22, William Paul discussed the rebellion plans with Peter Prioleau, a household slave of Colonel John Prioleau. Within a week, Peter Prioleau revealed the plan to his master, who alerted the authorities. Learning of Prioleau's betrayal, Vesey moved up the date of the insurrection to June 16, but the frightened whites of Charleston moved more quickly.

Governor Thomas Bennett immediately created a special army regiment to occupy and guard the city. By June 27, Vesey, the Bennetts, Poyas, Pritchard, and more than one hundred others were arrested. Forty-five people, including Vesey, pleaded not guilty and refused to testify despite being tortured. After their torture and a quick trial, Vesey, the Bennetts, and Poyas were hanged on "the Lines," high ground in Charleston, on July 2. By August 1822, thirty-five slaves had been hanged, forty-three deported, fifteen acquitted, and thirty-eight released for lack of evidence. Six informers received their freedom. The Vesey Rebellion was crushed.

Kramer read everything he could locate about Denmark Vesey, including the original trial record. He was such a highly regarded expert on Vesey that Rayford Wilson and Michael Winston, editors of the *Dictionary of American Negro Biography* (New York: Norton, 1982), asked him to write the entry for Vesey.

A number of recent biographies of Vesey exist, for example, Douglas R. Egerton's *He Shall Go out Free: The Lives of Denmark Vesey* (Madison, Wis.: Madison House, 1999). Some recent scholarship, most notably by Michael Johnson, a professor of history at Johns Hopkins University, suggests that Vesey did not organize the rebellion but was merely caught in the mass arrests.

Kramer's "Denmark Vesey" was first published in *Denmark Vesey and Other Poems* (1952). Section twenty-four, titled "The Hanging Song," appeared in the *National Guardian* (July 4, 1952). Sections 3, "Plantation Song," and 15, "A Meeting at Vesey's" (mistitled "Whisper the Word"), were translated into Yiddish by I. B. Bailin and appeared in *Freiheit* (New York) on August 3, 1952. Waldemar Hille set the poem to music as *Denmark Vesey: An Oratorio.* The premiere performance occurred in the Los Angeles Unitarian Church, May 19, 1954. A May 1962 performance in Charleston at Vesey's AME church earned the NAACP's Celia Buck Award.

Alan Wald's "Cultural Cross-Dressing: Radical Writers Represent African-Americans and Latinos in the McCarthy Era," in his *Writing from the Left: New Essays on Radical Culture and Politics* (London: Verso, 1994), contains crucial information and quotations from Kramer regarding the creation and reception of "Denmark Vesey."

"The Bell and the Light"

As Kramer notes, the poem is based on Benjamin A. Botkin's *Lay My Burden Down: A Folk History of Slavery* (Chicago: University of Chicago Press, 1945). Botkin (1901–75) was an influential folklorist who coined the expression "folk-say" to signal his theory that older folklore traditions continue to traverse the modern experience. He is best known for his anthologies drawn from both archival sources and his own fieldwork. In 1938, he became the national folklore editor of the Works Progress Administration (WPA) and in 1941 became chief editor of the Writer's Unit of the Library of Congress Project.

The Federal Emergency Relief Administration began interviewing former slaves in the Ohio River Valley in 1934. The WPA Federal Writers Project broadened the effort to all the Southern states as well as Indiana, Kansas, and Oklahoma between 1936 and 1938. Federal field workers met with people who had worked in plantation fields and houses. Some were but infants when the Civil War ended; others were as old as fifty. Beginning in 1939, the archives were transferred to the Library of Congress.

Lay My Burden Down gave the collection its first major national visibility. Edited from some one hundred interviews of former slaves, the book records their voices as they recall the experience of bondage, the Civil War that freed them, and the decades of struggle that followed.

First published in *Roll the Forbidden Drums!* (1954). "Freedom Song," the final section of the seven-part poem, appeared in the *National Guardian* (July 4, 1954) and provides the title of *Roll the Forbidden Drums!* Incorporated into the final section of Waldemar Hille's oratorio *Moses* and in *The Burning Bush* (1983) as "The Hour."

"Blues for Emmett Till"

Emmett Till was born in Chicago on July 25, 1941. In August 1955, his mother, Mamie, sent him to Money, Mississippi, to spend the summer with family there. A few days after arriving, Emmett apparently whistled at a white woman who owned a grocery store in the town. He did not realize he had violated the unwritten code of the segregated South. Two days later, Roy Bryant and J. W. Milam, both white, kidnapped Emmett from his bed and beat the fourteen-year-old African American boy severely. They then dragged him to the Tallahatchie River, shot him in the head, weighted his body with a large metal fan, and threw it in the river. Despite witness testimony, Bryant and Milam were both acquitted of murder by an all-white jury that September. Kramer published his poem in the November 7, 1955, issue of the *National Guardian*. Two days later, a grand jury refused to indict the two murderers for kidnapping. Bryant and Milam then felt free to tell a journalist the full details of how they committed the murder in exchange for four thousand dollars. Their story was published in the January 24, 1956, issue of *Look*.

"Blues for Medgar Evers"

As he was returning home just before midnight on June 11, 1963, Medgar Wylie Evers, field secretary for the NAACP in Mississippi, was shot in the back. He died a few minutes later. Born to an African American family in a small town in Mississippi in 1925, Evers left school to serve in the army in World War II. The experience of fighting the supremely racist Nazis apparently left a deep impression on him. He completed college on returning home and soon became involved with the NAACP. He began to work full time for the organization in 1954, moving to Jackson, Mississippi, and concentrating both on building membership and on investigating and publicizing the incidents of racist terror that were common in Mississippi at the time. Repeatedly threatened and beaten, Evers nonetheless persisted. In May 1963, a bomb was hurled into Evers's garage. A month later the white racist Byron de la Beckwith planned and executed his murder. Beckwith was tried twice, in 1963 and 1964, but two all-white juries could not come to a decision. He was finally convicted in 1994. Evers's death was one of the key events that galvanized the civil rights movement in the South.

First published in *Freedomways* (Fall 1964).

"Calvary: Philadelphia, Mississippi"

In June 1964, three civil rights workers—James Chaney, Andrew Goodman, and Michael Schwerner—were murdered in Philadelphia, Mississippi. Chaney was black, while Goodman and Schwerner were white. They were in Neshoba County during what came to be known as Mississippi Freedom Summer, a massive voter registration and desegregation campaign. Just days before the deaths of the three men, the FBI had begun a large-scale investigation of the organized burning of some twenty black churches in the state. When the three activists disappeared in June, the agency took responsibility for that investigation as well. Their bodies were not found until August 4. It became clear that the men had been murdered as part of a conspiracy between the Ku Klux Klan and Neshoba County law officers. Seven people were eventually convicted on federal civil rights charges for activities related to the murders and served sentences ranging from three to ten years. National outrage at the crimes helped Lyndon Johnson win passage of the Civil Rights Act in 1964 and the Voting Rights Act the following year.

First published in *Adelphi Quarterly* (Summer 1965) as "Calvary." Retitled "A Ballad of Jesus" in *On the Way to Palermo* (1973).

"St. Nicholas Avenue Blues"

This memorial tribute to Langston Hughes (1902–67) was first published in *Freedomways* (Summer 1967).

"Judgment"

On Monday, October 4, 1984, Elinor Bumpers was killed by New York City police at her apartment in the Sedgwick houses in the Highbridge section of the Bronx. She was an African American woman in her sixties, suffering from arthritis and diabetes, some 5'8" tall and weighing three hundred pounds. She had failed to pay her monthly rent of $89.44 for five months. The authorities considered her mentally ill.

Perhaps frightened when the police officers broke down her door, she lunged at one with a knife. She was killed with a blast from a shotgun, a weapon considered more likely than a revolver to stop a criminal in his tracks. There is good reason to suppose that six heavily armed police officers represented excessive and intimidating force on their own, and reason as well to suppose this woman could have been subdued with less than lethal force.

First published in *riverrun* (Fall 1988) as "Judgment (for Elinor Bumpers)."

PART 5: FRIENDS AND FAMILY

"Mother"

First published in *Another Fountain* (1940).

"The Rockabye Love"

First published in *'Til the Grass Is Ripe for Dancing* (1943) as part 1 of "Love Songs for My Parents."

"Serenade No. 1" and "Serenade No. 2"

Both serenades were composed in 1948 and published for the first time in *The Golden Trumpet* (1949).

"Prothalamium"

First published in *The Thunder of the Grass* (1948) as part of the sonnet sequence "Astoria." "Prothalamium," set to music by Michael Sahl in 1949, was later recorded by Judy Collins and released on her album *Whales and Nightingales* (Elektra, 1970), arranged and conducted by Joshua Rifkin. Barbara Kingsolver used the poem as the epigraph to her novel *Prodigal Summer* (2000).

"Winter Song"

First published in the *Arkansas City Star*, March 18, 1962.

"Dogs"

First published in the *Denver Post,* February 2, 1964.

"Uncles, No. 1"

First published in *Jewish Currents* (March 1967) as "The Sport."

"For My Grandmother"

Part 1 was first published in *Bitterroot* (September 1967); part 2 was first published in *Lyrismos* (Spring 1968); part 3 was first published in *Icarus* (Fall 1974); and part 4 was first published in *The Burning Bush* (1983).

"Homecoming"

First published in the *New York Times,* December 15, 1968.

"Ghosts"

First published in *Arion's Dolphin* (Fall 1971).

"Quebec"

First published in *Modern Poetry Studies* 3.2 (1972).

"Granddaughter on Beach"

It is Kramer's elder granddaughter, Nora Gordon, born in 1973, who is referred to here.

Pablo Picasso: Picasso (1881–1973) lived in Paris during World War II and, hence, during the German occupation.

Maginot: a more than 150-mile fortified network of interconnected bunkers built by France after World War I along its German border to prevent a German invasion.

First published in *Icarus* (Winter 1975).

"Words"

First published in *Islip Arts Review* 1.1 (1975).

"Thanksgiving Day"

First published in *Journal of Humanistic Psychology* (Spring 1978).

"Now, Before Shaving"

Carnovsky: Morris Carnovsky (1897–1992) was a stage and screen actor, briefly associated with the Yiddish theater, who was blacklisted in 1950 for refusing to name names. Carnovsky rebuilt his career in the 1960s by concentrating on Shakespearian roles, especially that of Shylock.

First published in *Carleton Miscellany* (Winter 1979/80).

"Matilda"

Written at the death of Kramer's longtime Dowling College colleague Matilda Salamone and read by the poet at her memorial service, April 25, 1978.

First published in *riverrun* (Spring 1979).

"Phone Call"

First published in *Carousel Parkway* (1980).

"On the Death of Someone Else's Grandchild"

First published in *Lyric* (Spring 1986).

"Home"

This five-part poem details Kramer's reaction to the death of his father-in-law, Jacob Kolodny (1896–1990).

"Schliemann . . . his Troy": Heinrich Schliemann (1822–90) was the German archaeologist who discovered the ruins of Troy in 1871.

"[to] love that well which we must leave ere long." The last line of the poem quotes the last line of Shakespeare's Sonnet 73.

First published in the *Minetta Review* (Spring 1995).

PART 6: ELEGIES

"Ernst Toller"

Ernst Toller (1893–1939) was a German-Jewish dramatist and poet who was exiled in 1932. Radicalized by the experience of thirteen months in the trenches at Verdun in World War I, in which he was wounded in 1916, Toller became a committed socialist and wrote expressionist plays of suffering and revolt against the imperial order. As a result of his role in strikes and antiwar agitation, he was imprisoned for a time. Toller was a leader in the short-lived Bavarian Soviet Republic of 1919. When the revolution collapsed, he was imprisoned for five years. It was there that he wrote his most famous plays, including *Masses and Men, The Machine-Wreckers,* and *Brokenbrow.* His prison poems, first published in 1923, were translated and collected as *The Swallow-Book* in 1924. After Toller was exiled, his life became increasingly difficult. Despite translations of his work by Stephen Spender and W. H. Auden, he remained little known in the English-speaking world. But it was not his career that was his main focus in those years; it was the struggle against fascism. A foe of the Nazis throughout his exile, Toller was the object of especially intense Nazi hatred. He was also deeply engaged in efforts to help the Spanish Republic, and Franco's victory plunged him into despair. Toller committed suicide in New York in 1939. The poet Edwin Rolfe included his elegy to Toller, "May 22nd 1939," in his *First Love and Other Poems* (1951).

First published in *Another Fountain* (1940), which Kramer dedicated to Toller.

"Einstein"

Albert Einstein (1879–1955), the German-born physicist who developed the general and special theories of relativity, the photon theory of light, and the mass/energy equivalence, and who was awarded the Nobel Prize in physics in 1921, died in Princeton, New Jersey, on April 18, 1955. Kramer wrote this elegy immediately following Einstein's death.

First published in the *National Guardian* (May 2, 1955).

"The Consummation"

Kramer wrote this elegy for Ernest Hemingway (1988–61), the American short-story writer and novelist who received the Nobel Prize in literature in 1954. Having left his beloved Cuba after the 1959–60 revolution, Hemingway suffered from depression and writer's block. He committed suicide with a shotgun on July 2, 1961. Four days after Hemingway's death, Kramer's poem appeared in the *Village Voice*.

"Rumshinsky's Hat"

First published in *Fiddlehead* (Winter 1961/62) and set to music by Elizabeth Shreeve (1972).

"The Pigeons of Maspeth"

Arthur Kevess (1917–73) had been a friend of Kramer ever since both had attended a Young Labor Poets workshop in Manhattan conducted by Eli Siegal in 1937–38. A lifetime resident of Brooklyn, Kevess had worked as a linotype operator and a proofreader. He also translated into English and published Yiddish and German folk songs. His wife, Hilde Wiengarten, was one of the artists who illustrated Kramer's *The Tune of the Calliope* (1958). Kevess died of cancer at Memorial Sloan Kettering Cancer Center in Manhattan on June 23, 1973. The occasion of the poem is Kramer's driving home on the Long Island Expressway to Oakdale following a visit with Kevess at Sloan the day before his death. Kramer read "The Pigeons of Maspeth" at the funeral of Arthur Kevess.

Hoboken and Weehawken: towns on the New Jersey side of the Hudson River, across from Manhattan.

Maspeth: Just after leaving Manhattan through the Queens-Midtown Tunnel and traveling east on the Long Island Expressway, one passes through the community of Maspeth, Queens.

First published in *Renaissance Faire* (Spring 1974).

"Uncle"

First published in *Carousel Parkway* (1980) and later translated into Yiddish by Isaac E. Ronch and published in *Freiheit* (May 3, 1981).

"Bella"

First published in *Carousel Parkway* (1980) and later translated into Yiddish by Isaac E. Ronch and published in *Freiheit* (May 3, 1981).

"The Ides of March (for Allard Lowenstein)"

Allard Lowenstein (1929–80) was a New York congressional representative for one term and a leader of the antiwar movement during the Vietnam War. He was the principle architect of the campaign that convinced Lyndon Johnson not to run for a second term as U.S. president, first persuading Senator Eugene McCarthy to mount an antiwar challenge to Johnson. After McCarthy won 42 percent of the New Hampshire primary vote in March 1968, Robert Kennedy entered the race; Johnson withdrew later that month. Lowenstein lost his 1970 reelection bid after being branded the "Viet Cong-ressman" by supporters of his Republican challenger. At the age of fifty-one, Lowenstein was shot to death in his Manhattan office by a mentally unbalanced former colleague in the civil rights movement. Lowenstein's leadership was also critical to the anti-apartheid and gay liberation movements in the United States.

First published in *riverrun* (Spring 1980).

"Elegy for Muriel Rukeyser" and "The Chair: Notes for an Elegy"

From the outset, Muriel Rukeyser (1913–80) was at once a political poet and a visionary. At times, those qualities were intensified and, in those moments, she was simultaneously a revolutionary and a mystic. But to grasp the forces that drive her work—through a career that spanned five decades of American history—we have to come to terms with a visionary impulse rooted in time, embedded in a struggle with lived history. She understood early on that politics encompasses all the ways that social life is hierarchically structured and made meaningful.

Rukeyser was born and raised in New York City and educated at Vassar College and Columbia University. During the 1930s, Rukeyser regularly wrote for Communist Party publications like *New Masses*. She was in Spain to cover the antifascist Olympics in Barcelona when the Spanish Civil War broke out. She described that experience in the long poem "Mediterranean" and returned to the subject throughout her life. Years later, in 1975, she went to South Korea to protest the poet Kim Chi-Ha's imprisonment and anticipated execution; the poem sequence "The Gates" grew out of that trip.

Kramer's *Neglected Aspects of American Poetry* (1997) includes his account of Rukeyser's visit to Dowling College at his invitation, as well as the transcript of the public conversation he conducted with her.

Sections 1 and 2 were first published in the *San Fernando Poetry Journal* 2.3 (1981). The complete three-part "Elegy for Muriel Rukeyser" and section 4, titled "Notes Perhaps for a Poem to be Titled 'The Chair,'" appeared in the *Brooklyn College Alumni Literary Review* (Spring 1983).

"The Death of a Friend"

Kramer's long-time friend Benjamin Spiegel died July 12, 1981, at sixty-five, in Flushing Hospital, Queens, New York. For many years, they had lived near each other in

Astoria, Queens. When he died, Spiegel had been a senior administrative law judge in New York City's Department of Environmental Protection.

In the early 1960s, as a partner in the law firm of Wachtell and Michaelson, Spiegel had written the briefs on behalf of the plaintiffs in *Abernathy et al. v. Sullivan*, the landmark case concerning freedom of speech and of the press that was combined to form the libel case of *The New York Times v. Sullivan*. The case concerned a full-page ad in the *New York Times* entitled "Heed Their Rising Voices" alleging that the arrest of Dr. Martin Luther King Jr. in Alabama was part of a campaign to destroy King's efforts to integrate public facilities in Montgomery, Alabama. L. B. Sullivan, a Montgomery city commissioner, sued the Reverend Ralph Abernathy and other ministers and the *Times* for libel even though he was not mentioned in the ad. Sullivan won a $500,000 lower court judgment but the ruling was overturned unanimously by the U.S. Supreme Court in a 1964 decision that argued in support of "the profound national commitment to the principle that debate on public issues should be uninhibited, robust, and wide-open."

Spiegel was survived by his wife, Pauline; his daughter, Barbara; and his two sons, Michael and Robert, all of whom are mentioned but not named in the poem.

First published in the anthology *Life and Love: Scottish Special and Inter-Continental Poetry* (Madras, India: Tagore Institute of Creative Writing, 1984). Published in *In the Suburbs* (1986) as part two of a poem of the same title. Published in its restored original form in *Indigo* (1991).

"Alfred Kreymborg's Coat"

Alfred Kreymborg (1883–1966), poet, playwright, novelist, and critic, was Kramer's mentor. A professional chess player and founding member of the Provincetown Players (along with Susan Glaspell, Edna St. Vincent Millay, Floyd Dell, and Michael Gold among others), Kreymborg was also extremely influential as a magazine editor. In the journals *Glebe, Others,* and *Broom* (all between 1913 and 1922), he championed and later anthologized new poets like H.D., William Carlos Williams, T. S. Eliot, Wallace Stevens, Muriel Rukeyser, and Marianne Moore.

Kreymborg was, moreover, an early admirer and proponent of Kramer's work. He provided the introduction to Kramer's politically defiant, McCarthy-era collection *Roll the Forbidden Drums!* (1954) and was Kramer's "Uncle Alfred" until his death at eighty-two in 1966.

Commencing in 1950 after he published his last volume of poetry, *No More War, and Other Poems* (which condemns fascism and defends working people), Kreymborg suffered from severe writer's block, as well as from Parkinson's disease, for the remaining sixteen years of his life. So complete was his block that, at the funeral of his friend the poet Maxwell Bodenheim (1893–1954), murdered with his wife in their Greenwich Village apartment by a man who boasted of having "killed two reds," the eloquent and moving eulogy Kreymborg read was not his own words; it had been written by Aaron Kramer, whose supervisor would not allow him to miss work that morning.

Kreymborg's most representative poetry is available in *The Selected Poems of Alfred Kreymborg, 1912–1944*. His early autobiography, *Troubadour* (1925), depicts what the critic Mark Van Doren describes as "a unique record of an important literary generation" (review of *Troubadour, The Nation,* May 6, 1925).

Charles Street: crosses Bleecker Street in Greenwich Village, Manhattan.

Sandburg: Carl Sandburg (1878–1967) was an American poet and biographer.

Crane: Hart Crane (1899–1931) was an American poet.

Dorothy: Dorothy Bloom was Kreymborg's second wife, whom he married in 1918.

First published in *Indigo* (1991).

PART 7: THE LOYAL OPPOSITION
"Have You Felt the Heart of America?"
First published in *The Alarm Clock* (1938).

"The Breeze"
First published in the *Brooklyn College Observer* (December 1939).

"May First 1940"
First published in *Another Fountain* (1940).

"The Golden Trumpet"
First published in *The Golden Trumpet* (1949) and set to music by Michael Sahl (1949) and by Jeff Veryzer (1976).

"Ballad of Washington Heights"
In the fall of 1776, after its stunning defeat by the British army commanded by General William Howe at the Battle of Long Island (August 27, 1776), the American rebel army built Fort Washington on the heights of rural upper Manhattan in the hope of retaining control of that small section of New York. On November 16, 1776, an overwhelming force of British and Hessian troops attacked the fort from three sides. George Washington crossed the Hudson River from Fort Lee, New Jersey, to help lead the 2,800 American defenders. After a daylong battle, the surrounded Americans surrendered. Both sides suffered heavy casualties, including 133 dead and 467 wounded. The British marched more than 2,700 American POWs to prison hulks floating off lower Manhattan. Kramer is alluding to the silence of post–World War II Americans in the face of "new tyrants" inciting the anti-Communist hysteria and witch hunts of the late 1940s.

First published in *The Golden Trumpet* (1949).

"Patriotism"
First published entitled "As Shakespeare Said" in *National Guardian* (August 9, 1950) and then in *Roll the Forbidden Drums!* (1954) as "Patriotism."

"Monticello: A Jefferson Cantata"

First published in *The Last Call!* (December 1951) and later in *Denmark Vesey* (1952) with the first twelve lines omitted.

"The Crucifixion"

First published in *Roll the Forbidden Drums!* (1954).

"New Jersey—December 1776"

Kramer is alluding to events described by the pro-American Englishman Thomas Paine (1737–1809) in the *American Crisis* 1 (December 19, 1776). Paine had marched with Washington's retreating rebel army from Fort Lee, New Jersey, to the Pennsylvania border. Paine excoriates those Americans who, hiding behind closed doors as the army passed, refused to aid in the fight for freedom, calling them "cowardly and disaffected inhabitants." In this poem written in 1953, Kramer metaphorically condemns those Americans whose meekness or deliberate lack of protest or dissent helped extend the duration of the McCarthy era.

First published in *Roll the Forbidden Drums!* (1954).

"In Power"

The speaker is Fidel Castro after he has gained complete political power in Cuba in July 1959. By 1960, he had begun to suppress all political dissent or opposition. "In Power" first appeared in the *New York Times*, June 12, 1960.

"A Man Is on the Hill Again"

The man of the title is the liberal lawyer and activist Mark Lane (1927–) who, in the early 1960s, was a one-term member of the New York State Assembly from upper Manhattan. His vigorous defense of the civil rights of African Americans and of Puerto Ricans as well as his exposing of a construction scandal involving fallout shelters in the city caused him to be attacked regularly in city newspapers. Kramer wrote "A Man Is on the Hill Again" following political sniping at Lane in the *New York Times* during the fall of 1961.

First published in the *Village Voice*, February 8, 1962.

"Des Moines and Council Bluffs"

First published as "Des Moines" in *Adelphi Quarterly* (Summer 1964).

"Lullaby"

First published in *Broadside #75* (October 1966), set to music by Waldemar Hille and then in *Poets for Peace; Poems for the Fast* (1967). The fast referred to in the latter title was a twenty-four–hour vigil at St. Mark's in the Bowery, New York City. Hundreds of poets, including Kramer, read from the pulpit.

"Henry at the Grating"

"Henry" is Henry David Thoreau (1817–62) who, on July 23 or 24, 1846, spent a night behind bars—the "grating"—in the Concord, Massachusetts, jail for refusing to pay his poll tax used to support the war with Mexico. He and other abolitionists regarded the war as unjust and as a pretense for extending slavery westward.

Chapultepec is a hill outside Mexico City from which Mexican defenders vainly attempted to prevent American troops from entering the city on September 12–13, 1847. Vera Cruz is where General Winfield Scott's army landed on March 29, 1847, to begin the U.S. invasion of Mexico. Monterey is the site of the September 20–24, 1846, engagement between American and Mexican forces.

Although all the battles mentioned in the poem took place after Thoreau's night in jail, Kramer uses Thoreau's voice and experience to condemn the war in Vietnam. "Henry at the Grating" first appeared in the *Adelphi Quarterly* (Summer 1968) in a group entitled "War Poems."

"Loyalty March"

"*Die Wacht Am Rhein*": A song composed by Max Schneckenburger in 1840, it consists of seven six-line stanzas, each of which ends with the same refrain: "Land of our fathers, have no fear / Your watch is true, the line stands here." It is conventional martial music that urges Germans to "take sword in hand" and "save the Rhine." Popular in World War I, it took on more sinister connotations when it was revived under the Nazis.

First published in *Lyrismos* (1968).

"The Bloodied Young: August, 1968"

First published in *Henry at the Grating* (1968).

"Considering My Country"

First published in *Adelphi Quarterly* (Summer 1968).

"Fourth of July Dialog"

The traditional Nine Muses do not include a Muse of Politics; however, one may read Polyhymnia (Polymnia), the muse of oratory, rhetoric, and sacred poetry, as fulfilling that responsibility.

"Garrison mobbed": William Lloyd Garrison (1805–79) was an American abolitionist and newspaper editor. Considered one of the great antislavery leaders of the nineteenth century, Garrison was torn from his home in Boston on October 21, 1835, by a proslavery mob. Police eventually rescued him, and he spent the night in jail, the only safe place for him in Boston.

"the Pequod tents on fire": During 1636–37, New England Puritan forces all but annihilated the Pequot (Kramer's Pequod) nation. The greatest slaughter took place on May 25, 1637, when a small Puritan force attacked a Pequot fort on a low hill near Mystic, Connecticut. The Puritans set afire the wooden fort, which surrounded a village of wigwams, burning to death all the warriors, women, and children trapped inside and shooting those who fled. Untold hundreds of Pequots perished at the loss of two British dead.

First published in *Discover America: Poems 1976* (San Jose, Calif.: San Jose State University Press, 1976) titled "Dialog: A Sestina." Later it appeared in *In Wicked Times* as "Fourth of July Dialog," and in *Indigo* as "Dialog," dated "4 July 1976" under the title.

"Seven Days"

Aaron and Kitty Kramer visited Cuba during the late spring of 1979 and participated in Havana's May Day celebrations.

Morro Castle: El Morro is a seventeenth-century Spanish fortress overlooking Havana Bay. Originally built to protect Havana from pirates, today El Morro's few modern artillery pieces point north toward the Straits of Florida, symbolically defying American invasion forces.

Nicolás Guillén Batista (1902–89) is a Cuban-born poet of social protest and a leader of the Afro-Cuban movement that affirmed and celebrated the black Cuban experience. He was committed to social justice and a long-term member of the Communist Party. In 1961, Fidel Castro named him National Poet of Cuba. On his return to the United States, Kramer dedicated two radio programs on WBAI (New York) in July and August 1979 to Guillén, tracing his career from the 1930s through the late 1960s.

Ethel and Julius: Ethel and Julius Rosenberg.

Written in 1979, "Seven Days" was not published during Kramer's lifetime and appears for the first time in this volume.

"In Wicked Times"

As the first section of the seven-part "In the Fortieth Presidency," "In Wicked Times" demonstrates Kramer's intellectual as well as visceral reaction to the Reagan era by his connecting it to the McCarthy era.

The poem was first published in the *San Fernando Poetry Journal* (Fall 1982) as "A Political Ballad," then in *In Wicked Times* as the title poem and in *Indigo* as part of "In the Fortieth Presidency."

"All-Star Neutron Day, 9 August 1981"

A neutron bomb, as opposed to fission or fusion bombs, does not create a huge explosion and blast wave that destroy, for example, a city and leave deadly lingering radiation. Instead, a neutron bomb releases a wave of high-energy neutrons that will kill all humans and animals within its circumference but neither destroy the infrastructure (e.g., buildings, roads, bridges) nor leave any lingering radiation. In other words, the weapon would kill an enemy people but would leave their real estate intact—very appealing to the Pentagon and the government throughout the cold war. During his administration, Ronald Reagan ordered the production of over one thousand neutron bombs. Criticism from European NATO allies prevented the

American deployment of these weapons across Europe. After the end of the cold war in 1991, the first Bush administration is reported to have moved to dismantle the stockpile of neutron bombs.

In the 1981 baseball all-star game, the National League beat the American League, 5–4.

First published in *Visions* 8 (1982) and later in *In Wicked Times* and in *Indigo* as part 3 of "In the Fortieth Presidency." See Kramer's subtitle note for the occasion of the poem.

"Grenada Symphony: First Movement"

Grenada is a Caribbean island that achieved its independence from Britain in 1974. When the government of its Marxist prime minister, Sir Eric Gairy, was overthrown in a violent coup in 1983 staged by a radical group of army officers who were themselves Marxists, the United States saw an opportunity to eliminate a country long aligned with Cuba. Citing supposed dangers to American medical students on the island and the anxieties of other Caribbean nations, President Ronald Reagan ordered the invasion and successfully installed a government sympathetic to the United States.

First published in *Broadside* 154 (August 1984).

"Bitburg"

On May 5, 1985, President Ronald Reagan laid a memorial wreath in the military cemetery in Bitburg, Germany. Among the many buried there are forty-nine members of the Waffen S.S., a subunit of the elite Nazi force that ran the death camps. Although the Waffen S.S. did not serve in the death camps, Reagan's appearing to memorialize and forgive its members stirred deep feelings of unease and anger in the United States. Before his visit, both houses of Congress overwhelmingly passed resolutions imploring him to change his itinerary. Furthermore, public opinion in the United States was strongly against the visit. Reagan, however, refused to change his plans, claiming the ceremonial event was "morally right" and that it celebrated the "miracle" of postwar reconciliation between Germany and the United States. Kramer expresses the revulsion felt by people worldwide concerning Reagan's dismissive approach to the Holocaust and to Nazism.

"Bitburg" first appeared in the anthology *Snow Summits in the Sun* (Cucamonga, Calif.: Cerulean, 1988) edited by Allen Blair and later appears in *Indigo* as part 5 of "In the Fortieth Presidency."

"Bhopal"

During the 1960s and 1970s, India attempted to increase the productivity and self-sufficiency of its agricultural sector through a series of programs it dubbed the Green Revolution. One of the revolution's goals was that India produce its own pesticides. In 1969, the American chemical company Union Carbide received a contract to build and run a pesticide plant in the central Indian city of Bhopal. The facility's site was in a residential neighborhood near the railway station.

On the night of December 23, 1984, the greatest industrial accident in history occurred when, apparently due to poor construction, maintenance, and management, over forty tons of highly toxic methyl isocyanate poured out of a holding tank for two hours, escaped into the air, and spread downwind among Bhopal's 900,000 residents. Within an hour, more than 4,000 people died in their sleep or as they fled in panic from the heavier-than-air fumes. Official estimates of those injured with crippling disabilities or chronic diseases range from fewer than 10,000 to upwards of 400,000.

Separate Indian and American investigations concluded that Union Carbide had tried to hide its poor safety and maintenance record along with other faults in order to continue to operate its deteriorating pesticide plant. To this day, Union Carbide, on its official Bhopal Web page, fails to acknowledge its full responsibility for the incident even though the corporation has paid $470 million to settle claims by those injured.

"Bhopal" appears in *Indigo* as part 4 of "In the Fortieth Presidency." The Pakistani poet Adeeb Suhail translated "Bhopal" into Urdu and published the poem in *Auraq* [Karachi] (November–December 1993).

PART 8: AGAINST McCARTHYISM

"The Soul of Martin Dies"

Martin Dies Jr. (1900–72) was a member of Congress from Texas who became chair of the notorious Special Committee to Investigate Un-American Activities when it was founded in 1938. Dies, who had been a lawyer and rancher in Texas before winning his congressional seat, found the committee chairmanship a perfect means to pursue his two obsessions, attacks on Roosevelt's New Deal and attacks on Communists and their supposed allies. The House committee had been intended to investigate a full range of what were considered extreme political positions. Some supported its creation out of concern for the rise of fascist organizations in the United States. Others expected the Ku Klux Klan to be a target, but Dies was a KKK sympathizer. Dies soon made anti-Communism the committee's focus, successfully establishing the tactics congressional committees would later use more broadly in the witch hunts of the 1950s. These included pressuring witnesses to name associates, slandering witnesses with vague and threatening accusations, and assuming guilt by association. Dies conducted hearings in Hollywood in 1940 that backfired when leaked testimony smearing numerous film industry veterans was identified as coming from an established liar. The Dies Committee's activities were put on hold during World War II.

First published in *Student Outlook* of the American Student Union, Brooklyn College Chapter (February 2, 1940); there, "slow" for "low" in line 23.

"Peekskill"

See the introductory essay in this book for historical background. Less than a month after the riots, Kramer and the Weavers defiantly performed his poem (set to the music of "The Vilna Ghetto Song," the text of which Kramer had translated from Yiddish) at a folk concert in Peekskill on September 30, 1949, and again at the 1950 first anniversary commemoration of the riots, with the actor Frank Silvera as narrator and the Weavers singing section 4.

"Peekskill" originally appeared in the *Harlem Quarterly* (Winter 1949/50). An errata slip inserted following page 28 adds line 6 of section 4, which was omitted in the original printing and properly spaces the third and fourth quatrains.

"Halloween"

First published in *Sing Out!* (October 1950).

"Is This the City?"

First published in *The Last Call!* (December 1951).

"October in 'Freedom' Land"

First published in *Denmark Vesey* (1952).

"Visit"

First published in *Roll the Forbidden Drums!* (1954).

"To the Silencers"

Written on August 18, 1955 , the day that Pete Seeger was summoned to testify before the House Un-American Activities Committee.

First published in the *Hartford Current* (June 17, 1961).

"Called In"

First published in *Visions* 4 (Fall 1980).

PART 9: JUDAICA

"To My People:"

First published in *Another Fountain* (1940).

"The Thunder of the Grass"

The following exchange occurs in a January 14, 1949, *Daily Worker* interview: Asked about the recurring symbol of "grass" in his poems, Kramer said he thought "it signifies to me one of the defiant things of the world. Grass always keeps coming back. It's like people—you can't destroy it forever."

First published in *Jewish Life* (January 1948).

"The Hour"

First published in *National Guardian* (July 4, 1954) as "Freedom Song." In *Roll the Forbidden Drums!* as the final section of "The Bell and the Light," providing the volume's title. Incorporated into the final section of Waldemar Hille's oratorio *Moses*.

"A Ballad of August Bondi"

August Bondi (1833–1907) was born in Vienna, Austria, the child of Hart Emanuel and Martha (Frankl) Bondi, both Viennese Jews. The father manufactured cotton products. Bondi was educated at the Catholic College of the Order of Piarists. As a teenager he began to study English, acquiring a language skill that would, unexpectedly, prove rather useful. As a student he also became involved in the unsuccessful democratic revolution in Austria, joining the Academic League and fighting with Kossuth. The failure of that effort led him to be exiled. In September 1848 his family left for the United States.

Bondi also began keeping a diary, which survives in the American Jewish Historical Society, and which makes it possible to reconstruct his life in some detail. He taught school in St. Louis and in Texas, became an American citizen in 1854, and the following year moved to Kansas, aiming to participate in the vote over whether Kansas was to be a free or a slave state. Bondi was applying the same values that fueled his participation in the student revolutionary movement in Vienna.

It was in 1855 that he also became familiar with the radical abolitionist John Brown (1800–1859), first joining John Brown Jr.'s company and then joining John Brown himself in an engagement at Black Jack, where Brown captured forty-eight pro-slavery partisans. As Bondi wrote in his diary, "We walked with bent backs, nearly crawled, that the tall dead grass of the year before might somewhat hide us from the Border Ruffian marksmen, yet the bullets kept whistling." Of John Brown, Bondi remarked: "We were united as a band of brothers by the love and affection toward the man."

When Quantrell's raiders burned Lawrence, Kansas, Bondi lost a general store he had opened there. Bondi then laid out plans for the town of Greeley, where he became postmaster for a year and maintained the underground railway station until the outbreak of the Civil War. In 1858, he became the enrolling officer for the Eighth Brigade in Anderson County, in what was still the Kansas Territory. Bondi remained in Kansas when Brown left for his famous stand at Harpers Ferry. When the Civil War began, Bondi enlisted quickly, serving as commissary sergeant and then as first sergeant in the Kansas Cavalry. Wounded in several battles, he was most seriously wounded on September 14, 1864. Taken prisoner by Confederate forces, he was left for dead on the battlefield. Bondi was finally discharged at Fort Leavenworth, Kansas, later that year.

It was there he married Henrietta Einstein. They settled in Salina, Kansas, where Bondi opened another store. He also served as probate judge and postmaster, and in 1896 began a law practice.

Section 2 was first published as "Letters from Kansas" in *Masses & Mainstream* (April 1955). Sections 1, 3, and 4 (with a summary of section 2) were first published in *Jewish Life* (May 1955).

"A Word of Thanks"

Babi Yar: This is a ravine northwest of the city of Kiev in Ukraine (in what was then the Soviet Union), where the Germans murdered 34,000 Jews on September 29–30, 1941. Ostensibly a reprisal for an explosion set by Soviet partisan fighters that damaged the German command center at Kiev, this mass murder was carried out as part of the Nazi plan to exterminate all the Jews of Europe. Special killing squads from the S.S. lined the Jews of Kiev up in front of a trench and machine-gunned men, women, and children in such a way that the force of the bullets propelled them into the trench. Two years later the Germans began to dig the bodies up and burn them in the hope of hiding the crime, but the advancing Russian army compelled them to withdraw before the work was complete. The Russian poet Yevgeny Yevtushenko published his poem "Babi Yar" in 1961.

First published in *Village Voice,* October 26, 1961. Addressed to Yevtushenko on his poem "Babi Yar." Some years later personally presented to Yevtushenko by Kramer.

"The Rising in the Warsaw Ghetto"

The Germans began the final liquidation of the Warsaw ghetto in Poland on April 19, 1943. The prewar Warsaw Jewish population was about 375,000. Given the relative isolation of the large number of Jews in the Soviet Union, Warsaw had effectively become the most influential center of Jewish life in Europe. The Germans occupied the city in September 1939. Soon they began to seize Polish Jews for forced labor. By the end of the year, Jewish businesses were closed. The following November the Warsaw ghetto was surrounded and isolated by a high wall. Mass deportations and killings did not start until July 1942. By the following April the Germans were ready to begin completing the project of extermination. The pattern by then was clear, and a growing number of Jews became determined to resist. Organizations planning to fight had formed and obtained some weapons. Bunkers were constructed throughout the ghetto. After the Germans were compelled to fight street battles in the ghetto, they decided to burn it building by building. Numerous German soldiers died in the struggle, and the revolt in the Warsaw ghetto entered history and legend. But no more than 2,000 of Warsaw's Jews survived the war.

First published in *Polish Review* (Winter 1962).

"Night at the Concertgebouw"

"Amsterdam's evaporated Jews": As of 1941 some 80,000 Jews lived in Amsterdam. When the Germans began to occupy the Netherlands in May 1940 they claimed no special measures were planned for the 140,000 Jews of the Netherlands, but before the year was out Berlin sent orders removing Jews from public employment and denying them access to public places like restaurants. The new year began with a key step in preparation for planned removals: all Jews were required to register. The following month 389 Jewish men were seized and sent to the Mauthausen concentration camp. In the summer and fall, 470 more were deported. In April 1942, all Jews were required to wear the Star of David in public. Three months later 6,000 Jews were assembled for the trip to the death camp. That fall the Nazis began seizing from 300 to 500 Jews each night. By the end of the war, the Germans had murdered over 100,000 of the Jews of the Netherlands, the Holland campaign being particularly successful. The Jews of Amsterdam were annihilated.

Millie Perkins: Perkins (1938–) is an American actress who won the starring role in the Hollywood film *The Diary of Anne Frank* (1959), directed by George Stevens. She had been a junior model and cover girl before winning the role. It was in Amsterdam that Anne Frank hid from the Nazis for twenty-five months, beginning in July 1942, before being betrayed and sent to the death camps. It was in hiding in Amsterdam that she wrote the diary that is the single most famous Holocaust memoir.

First published in *Midstream* (November 1968). In musical settings, Irwin Hielman (1971) and Pauline Konstantin (1976) changed title to "The Ghost[s] of Amsterdam."

"Zudioska"

Original version first published in *Midstream* (October 1970) and the revised version in *Carousel Parkway* (1980).

"Gimpl"

Gimpl Beinish is the title figure in a comic strip that ran in the Yiddish language press. He was a *shadkhn*, or matchmaker, who amused the readers of *Die Wahrheit* (Truth), which was edited by Louis G. Miller from 1912 to 1919. Samuel Zagat (1890–1964), the "Z" of Kramer's poem, was the artist. In addition to his work for *Die Wahrheit*, Zagat contributed drawings to other Yiddish publications, as well as the *New Masses* under the pseudonym G. Holan. After leaving *Die Wahrheit*, Zagat headed the art department of the country's major Yiddish newspaper, the *Jewish Daily Forward*, for forty-two years. As the Balch Institute for Ethnic Studies notes on its Web site at <http://balchinstitute.org/index.htm> (accessed September 21, 2003):

> Runt-sized Gimpl was a bearded, top-hatted, beady-eyed, frock-coated busy-body in striped pants. His frantic desire to make a living from uniting the most unpromising single men with unattached females took him to any place where Jews could be mated, however unlikely; from the streets of New York's lower East Side to the Catskills, from parks and beaches to suffragette marches. Though editor Miller supplied the ideas and the text for the strip, Zagat's drawings have a feel for Jewish settings and characters missing from the work of Hirshfeld and other creators of Jewish comic strip characters in the Anglo-American press. . . . The comic strip characters created for the Yiddish press inhabited a more unselfconsciously Jewish milieu than the syndicated Jewish types in the Anglo-American press, less circumscribed by the cartoonists' or the syndicates' taboos concerning immigrant speech and characteristics. The strip characters created for Yiddish-speaking, primarily working class immigrants therefore seem more robustly ethnic, more Jewish even when they do not transcend the broad slapstick farce that was the mainstay of the comics.

First published in Samuel Zagat's *Jewish Life on New York's Lower East Side, 1912–1962*, ed. Ida R. Zagat (New York: Rogers Book Service, 1972).

"A Wedding in Los Angeles"

Temple Akiba: Temple Akiba is a reform Jewish congregation in West Los Angeles founded by twenty-five families in 1953.

sher: This Jewish dance may be an adaptation of eighteenth-century English and French court dances; it is also known as the *Hakhnaah* (Hebrew for "respect" and "fear") because the dancers bowed their heads in a gesture of respect. It is similar to a square dance.

freilachs: This is the major group of dances performed by Eastern European Jews, often at weddings and bar mitzvahs; they are group dances usually performed in a circle or a line.

hora: The hora is a national Romanian and Israeli dance, done in a closed circle; the first Israeli folk dance was the *hora agadati,* choreographed in 1920.

First published in *Passage II* (River Grove, Ill.: Triton College Press, 1976). Awarded a first prize by the editors.

"View of Delft"

First published as "Three Young men" in *Passage III* (River Grove, Ill.: Triton College Press, 1977). Awarded a gold medal in the "Ravages of War" category, All Nations Poetry Contest. Last twenty-eight lines (sans first two words) first published in *Carousel Parkway* (1980) as "View of Delft."

"Tour"

First published in the Conference of Secular Jewish Organizations *Newsletter* (March–April 1978).

"Westminster Synagogue"

First published in *New England Review* (Summer 1980) and in *Carousel Parkway* (1980) as "At Westminster Synagogue."

"The Dance"

Giselle: The title role in *Giselle* (1841) and the role of Princess Odette in *Swan Lake* (1877) are among the great romantic roles in classical ballet. *Giselle,* based on Byron's poem "The Corsair," about a girl in slavery, was choreographed by Saint-Leon. *Swan Lake,* in which the princess turns into a swan, was choreographed by Marius Petipa. In 1905 Mikhail Fokine choreographed a three-minute solo piece titled "The Dying Swan."

Deborah: The prophet Deborah's story is told in the Book of Judges. She is referred to as the "mother of Israel" because of her leadership in the struggle against the Canaanites. In 1200 B.C. she helped raise and inspire an army that defeated the Canaanite army led by Sisera.

Miriam: Miriam was the daughter of Amram and Jochebed, and the sister of Moses and Aaron. Her story is told in the Book of Exodus in the Old Testament. Miriam led the Israelites in singing God's praises as the Egyptian army was drowned in the Red Sea.

Masada: Masada (Hebrew for "fortress") was an ancient fortress atop a mountain in the desert about thirty miles southeast of Jerusalem. After the fall of Jerusalem and the destruction of its temple by the Roman army in 70 A.D., about a thousand Jews fled the city and occupied this mountaintop overlooking the Dead Sea. Led by Eleazar ben Jair, they held their ground despite a two-year siege by the Roman Tenth

Legion. Eventually the Romans constructed an immense rampart and broke through the walls of the fortress with a battering ram. Faced with defeat and enslavement, the Jews chose to die by their own hands.

Bar Kochba: Shimon Bar Kochba was chosen by the spiritual leader Rabbi Akiva to lead a revolt against the Romans in Palestine in 132 A.D. The revolt followed years of religious persecution by the Romans. With an army of 580,000, Bar Kochba gradually overthrew the Romans throughout Palestine. The Roman Hadrian then mounted a sustained counterattack that reconquered Palestine town by town. Bar Kochba retreated into a small fortified city in Jerusalem called Betar. On that battlefield Bar Kochba and a half million of his followers died.

Judith: The Book of Judith is an apocryphal text included in the Roman Catholic Old Testament but not in the Hebrew or the Protestant versions. When her Jewish city is besieged, Judith seeks to save it by assassinating the Assyrian general Holofernes. Pretending to flee her city to befriend him, she cooperates with his offer of a private dinner in his tent. He plans a seduction, but she carries out her own plan, beheading him with a sword when he falls into a drunken sleep. The Hebrews mount Holofernes's head on their city walls, and the leaderless Assyrians are defeated.

First published in *riverrun* (Fall 1980).

"May 4, 1986: Austria Acquits Herself"

When Austrians elected Kurt Waldheim (1918–   ) as their country's president in a May 4, 1986, runoff election, they simultaneously reaffirmed their country's wartime service on behalf of Nazi Germany. Waldheim had served two relatively undistinguished terms as the United Nations secretary-general (1971–81), service that gained him credibility at home as an international diplomat. Just prior to the election, he had published a biography that downplayed his role in World War II. Yet a series of newspaper articles began appearing in March 1986 that showed he had served in a German army unit that murdered thousands of Yugoslav partisans and deported Greek Jews to the death camps. Implausibly, Waldheim claimed he was unaware that these atrocities took place. Many Austrians voted for him out of a desire to rationalize their own wartime guilt.

First published in *The Forward* (June 13, 1986).

"1906"

First published in *Outlook* (January 1995).

"Bath Beach"

First published in *Jewish Currents* (October 1995).

PART 10: A CENTURY OF WARS

"A Song for Freedom"

First published in *Daily Worker* (May 23, 1940).

"The Ballad of Two Heroes"

First published in *Another Fountain* (1940) and, in 1985–86, translated into Chinese by Xiangmin Zhou.

"Maria"

"Maria" exists as a two-page typescript laid into a copy of *'Til the Grass Is Ripe for Dancing* (1943) with Kramer's name at the close of the poem. Thanks to Eugene Povirk of Southpaw Books, Conway, Massachusetts, for providing the editors with this hitherto unknown and unpublished Kramer poem. "Maria" appears for the first time in this volume.

"France"

First published in *'Til the Grass Is Ripe for Dancing* (1943).

"Sunrise in Paris"

First published in *Thru Our Guns* (1945) as part 4 of "Liberation Song."

"Victory Comes to the Unbombed Cities"

First published in *New Masses* (April 9, 1946).

"The Real Ogre," "Panic," and "Prayer"

Sections 2, 3, and 7 of "When Every Tear Is Turned to Stone," a poem of 116 lines in seven sections commissioned by the Film Division of the United Nations.

First published in *Thru Every Window!* (1950).

"Efstratia Nikolaidu"

Kramer's note: "After World War II, a Greek Government of National Unity was re-placed by a reactionary Royalist government. This caused thousands of anti-Nazi guerillas to again take to the mountains, where they were hunted down by the Roy-alists. Efstratia Nikolaidu was captured and executed in December 1948." The fact that Efstratia Nikolaidu was murdered is reaffirmed in Kramer's "Thessaloniki: Three Sleeps" (1977), in which he says, "Efstratia Nikolaidu, fifteen years old, / who would now be thirty-nine / shot down in your prison-yard, fist high."

First published in *Denmark Vesey* (1952) and translated into Greek by Flora Zeipekkis (1985).

"The Tinderbox"

Eight lyrics first published in *Denmark Vesey* (1952) and the entire poem published in *Roll the Forbidden Drums!* (1954). "The Tinderbox" (parts 1 and 2) was presented by the British Broadcasting Corporation on February 10, 1957, with incidental music by Tristram Cary and directed by Terence Tiller. A section of "The Tinderbox" never otherwise published, "A Song Unsung from the Windows," appeared in *The Last Call!* (December 1951).

"The Rebels of Greece"

First published in *Roll the Forbidden Drums!* (1954) and translated into Greek by Flora Zeipekkis (1985).

"To a Dark-Skinned People"

First published in *Freedomways* (Winter 1967) as "To the People of Vietnam." Retitled "To a Dark-Skinned People" for *Adelphi Quarterly* (Summer 1967).

"Newscast (April 20, 1967)"

First published in *Adelphi Quarterly* (Summer 1968) as "Newscast."

PART 11: JOURNEYS

"After the Tour"

Kramer and his wife, Kitty, traveled to Europe for the first time in 1956, touring Italy and England for three weeks.

"Livia's kitchen on the Palatine": Livia Drusilla (58 B.C.–A.D. 29) lived with her husband, Octavian (Augutus Caesar), in a palace on the Palatine, chief of the Seven Hills of Rome. After his death, she lived in the so-called Casa di Livia on the Palatine, the ruins of which contain a kitchen.

Caracalla: This is the nickname of the Roman emperor Marcus Aurelius Severus Antoninus (A.D. 118–217), whose baths are in Rome.

"Mrs. Browning's in Casa Guidi": This refers to the home in Florence in which the poet Elizabeth Barrett (1806–61) and her husband, the poet Robert Browning (1812–89), lived until her death.

Monreale: The town of Monreale in northwestern Sicily, near Palermo, noted for its classical mosaics.

"Sarcophagus in the Villa Julia": The Villa Giulia, a sixteenth-century villa in Rome, houses the Museo Nazionale Etrusco, the largest collection of Etruscan antiquities in the world. Archaeologists and art historians consider the sarcophagus called the Sarcofago dei Sposi (Sarcophagus of a Married Couple), from the sixth century B.C., depicting an enigmatically smiling Etruscan couple reclining together on a couch, one of the collection's masterpieces.

First published in *Flame* (Fall 1961) and later in *Mediterranean Review* (Fall 1970).

"A Good Buy"

Written after the Kramers' tour of Italy and Yugoslavia during the summer of 1968.

Rialto: A bridge in Venice over the Grand Canal.

Portofino: A town in northwestern Italy.

Siena: A city in Tuscany, central Italy.

Milan: A city in Lombardy, northwestern Italy, and a center of Italian economic activity.

Bologna: A city in north-central Italy

Taormina: A town in eastern Sicily at the foot of Mount Etna.

Villa Borghese: A Renaissance villa in Rome designed ca. 1610 by Giovanni Vasanzio. It houses a distinguished collection of Italian baroque paintings and ancient sculpture collected by the powerful Borghese family.

Tintoretto: Jacopo Robusti (1518–94), called Tintoretto, was one of the most important Italian painters of the late Renaissance. His masterpiece is the 1594 *Last Supper.*

Bernini: Gianlorenzo Bernini (1598–1680), an Italian artist, was perhaps the greatest sculptor of the seventeenth century. He is credited with creating the baroque style of sculpture.

Siracusa: Syracuse, a city in southeastern Sicily, was originally a Greek colony.

Fountain of Arethusa: Arethusa was a water nymph, loved by the river god Alpheus, whom the goddess Artemis turned into a spring (located in Syracuse) so that she could escape his pursuit.

Vicenza: A city in northeastern Italy.

Degas: Edgar Degas (1834–1917), French painter and sculptor, was best known for his depiction of ballerinas and of race horses.

First published in *Carleton Miscellany* (Spring–Summer 1971).

"Last Night in Brussels"

"Boschian derision": Hieronymous Bosch (1450–1516), was a brilliant and original Flemish painter of the early Renaissance. One of his masterpieces is *The Garden of Earthly Delights* (1505–10).

Groote Markt, Bruges: The "large market" in Bruges, a commercial, industrial, and tourist city in northwestern Belgium.

Tournai: A city in southwestern Belgium, founded by the Romans.

Huguenot: The Huguenots were French Protestants who suffered persecution and death at the hands of Catholic French forces in the sixteenth and seventeenth centuries.

Rubens: Peter Paul Rubens (1577–1640) was a Flemish baroque painter. Among his masterpieces is *Venus and Adonis* (1635).

Van Eyck: Jan Van Eyck (1395–1441), a Flemish painter, perfected the technique of painting with oil paint. His masterpiece, painted with his brother Hubert Van Eyck, is the Ghent Altarpiece (1432).

First published in *Renaissance Faire* (Spring 1972) as "Midnight in Brussels."

"The Last Supper"

Leonardo: Leonardo da Vinci (1452–1519), was a genius of the Italian Renaissance— a painter, sculptor, engineer, and architect.

The Last Supper: Leonardo's fresco (1494–98) on a wall of the refectory of Santa Maria delle Grazie in Milan. One of the most famous paintings in the world, it has a long history of deterioration due to poor materials and humidity and was badly damaged by moisture-laden bags used to stabilize it during World War II. Modern restoration and preservation finally took place between 1977 and 1997.

Borromeo: Federico Borromeo (1564–1631) was cardinal of Milan. An art patron and theorist, Borromeo was the first to attempt to safeguard the deteriorating Leonardo fresco. He commissioned Andrea Bianchi, called "Il Vespino," to make an oil copy on canvas in 1612–13.

Torre: Carlo Torre was a seventeenth-century writer and art critic whose *Il Ritratio di Milan* (1674) compared the fresco to a setting sun whose "vivid expressions" and "resplendent colors" would soon be lost.

"wurde das Refektorium . . . ": "the refectory was severely damaged by bombing and remained without a roof and window."

Mauro Pellicioli: In 1947, Pellicioli applied a coat of wax-free shellac to re-adhere flakes of plaster falling from the fresco and to revive the painting's colors. He then attempted a single-handed restoration (1951–54) that scholars considered admirable but not successful.

First published in *Renaissance Faire* (Fall 1972) and again in *Modern Poetry Studies* (Winter 1976).

"On the Way to Palermo"

The Kramers traveled in southern Europe during the revolutionary summer of 1968. This poem is Kramer's response to the events and the atmosphere in Sicily as the province experienced the social upheavals of 1968.

Palermo: Sicily's capital and largest city, founded by Phoenicians in the eighth century B.C.

Caruso, Lola, and Santuzza: Enrico Caruso (1873–1921), one of the greatest operatic tenors of all, sang Turiddu, who loves both Lola and Santuzza, in *Cavalleria Rusticana*.

Mascagni: Pietro Mascagni (1863–1945), an Italian operatic composer, was best known for *Cavalleria Rusticana* (1890), which is set in a Sicilian village.

Damon and Dionysius: Dionysius (430–ca. 360 B.C.), the military leader and dictator of Sicily, jailed and condemned Damon, a follower of Pythagorus, who was then saved at the last moment by his friend Phintias.

Schiller: Friedrich von Schiller (1759–1805) was a German playwright, poet, and historian. The reference is to his early drama *The Robbers* (1782).

Shakespeare's twins: *Comedy of Errors* (ca. 1592–94) follows the adventures of two sets of twins in Syracuse, Sicily.

Aeolus: Aeolus was the son of Poseidon and god of the winds. A character in Homer's *Odyssey,* Aeolus rules the island of Lipari, north of Sicily.

Charybdis and Scylla: Charybdis is a monster living on a rock in the Straits of Messina, between Italy and Sicily, who creates a whirlpool to snare unwary ships. Scylla is a monster living on a rock above the Straits of Messina. It has the form of a woman with six dogs' heads around its lower body.

Sirens and Ulysses: Half-woman, half-bird sea-demons, the sirens lured sailors to their rocky Mediterranean island with their music and then devoured them. Ulysses had himself lashed to the mast of his ship to enable him to resist the attraction of their songs.

Messina: A city on the northeastern coast of Sicily.

Carthage: A Phoenician city in northeastern Tunisia, on the African coast of the Mediterranean. From ca. 500 to 146 B.C., Carthage was a powerful military and economic rival of Rome.

Marsala: A city on the northwestern coast of Sicily, best known for its sweet dessert wines.

Trapani: A city in northwestern Sicily.

Gela: An ancient city in southern Sicily that was once a center of power on the island. Carthage destroyed Gela ca. 400 B.C.

Paterno: A small town north of Syracuse, famous for its Norman ruins.

Termini: (Termini Imerese), a small town southwest of Paterno, known for its Roman ruins.

Avola: A small coastal town south of Syracuse.

"Neolithic in Buscoli, Siculian in Thapsos, Greek in Selinus, Arab in Buccheri, Norman in Cefalu, Spanish in Augusta": archaeological sites in ancient or Renaissance Sicilian towns and villages.

Ognina: A small resort town south of Syracuse.

Mondello: A fashionable resort north of Palermo.

Arethusa and Ciane: (Cyane) water-nymphs whose springs are located in Syracuse.

Firenze: Florence, in Tuscany.

Etna: A mountain in eastern Sicily. At 3,350 meters, it is Europe's tallest and largest active volcano.

Enna and Ceres: Enna is an ancient fortified city in central Sicily atop a thousand-meter summit. It was the site of the Cult of Ceres, the Roman name for Demeter, the mother goddess of the earth.

Segesta and Selinus: Rival ancient cities in northwestern Sicily. In 409 B.C., Segesta with the aid of Carthage destroyed Selinus only to be taken by the Romans in 262 B.C.

Conco d'Oro: [Kramer's note] The Conco d'Oro is a large coastal area of citrus groves between Monreale and Palermo.

Via Roma: The main street through the historical center of Palermo.

"Verdi's prophetic statue": A statue of Verdi stands before the opera house (the nineteenth-century Teatro Massimo) in the Piazza Giuseppe Verdi, in central Palermo. Verdi (1813–1901) is the foremost Italian opera composer. His great works include *Rigoletto* (1851), *La Traviata* (1853), *Aida* (1871), and *Othello* (1887).

Garibaldi: Giuseppe Garibaldi (1807–82), Italian patriot and soldier, helped unite Italy under King Victor Emmanuel in the 1860s.

"Sicily's new Vespers": [Kramer's note] The sounding of vespers in Palermo, on Easter Monday, 1282, signalled [sic] a general revolt which swept the French out of Sicily. This event is celebrated in Verdi's *Sicilian Vespers*.

Paladins: Any of the twelve legendary peers in the court of Emperor Charlemagne (742–814) and his personal companions.

"murder of Archimedes": The mathematician and inventor, born in Syracuse ca. 287 B.C., was killed ca. 212 during the Roman sack of the city.

Lipari: The largest of the Aeolian islands, north of Sicily. Ancient Greeks believed the island to be the home of Aeolus. (See note above.)

Timolean: [Kramer's note] Timolean, Greek statesman and general, at the appeal of Syracuse's citizens, led a Corinthian army against the tyrant Dionysius [II, ca. 396–ca. 330 B.C.] in 344 b.c. [sic], and liberated other Sicilian cities as well.

First published in *On the Way to Palermo* (1973); however, the last six lines of "Taormina Dawn," written in 1972 and collected in *In Wicked Times* (1983), appear as the last four lines of section 8 of "On the Way to Palermo." The Sicilian poet Nat Scammacca translated section 7 into Italian as "da: Sulla strada per Palermo," first published in *Trapani Nuova* [Sicily] February 11, 1982, and later in *In Sicilia ed Altri Luoghi Poesia* (New York: Cross-Cultural, 1984).

"Victoria Station"

Gatwick: location of the Gatwick International Airport (one of the three major airports serving London), southwest of London, in West Sussex. Every fifteen minutes, the Gatwick Express leaves the airport for Victoria Station.

Victoria Station: Railroad station in London, just south of Buckingham Palace.

Mme. Tussaud: Marie Tussaud (1761–1850) founded a museum in London in which she exhibited wax figures depicting famous and/or notorious people.

Victoria: Victoria (1819–1901) was queen of England, Scotland, and Ireland (1837–1901) and empress of India. She was the longest-reigning monarch in English history.

Grosvenour Hotel: Built in 1861, the hotel stands next to Victoria Station.

Ponce de Leon: Juan Ponce de Leon (1460–1521) was the Spanish explorer who founded the oldest settlement in Puerto Rico (1509) and later discovered Florida (1513) while searching for the Fountain of Youth.

First published in *Orbis* (Summer 1975); includes an essay by Kramer explaining why "Victoria Station" is the "favorite among his poems."

"My Mexico Is Not Your Mexico"

"Redford and Mostel": Refers to the 1972 motion picture *The Hot Rock* in which Robert Redford and Zero Mostel star as two of a number of inept thieves vying for a large stolen diamond.

San Miguel (de Allende): A city northwest of Mexico City that is home to a sizable expatriate American community.

Architexas: An architectural firm based in Dallas and Austin, Texas, that specializes in restoration and preservation of historic buildings, especially courthouses.

"My Mexico Is Not Your Mexico" provides the introductory frame for Kramer's sequence of the same name. Other poems in the sequence include "In the Geneve Lobby: Mexico City," "At Four Minutes to One," "Dogs of San Miguel," "Sunday in the Square: San Miguel de Allende," "Toluca: The Friday Market" (all in this volume), and "Gringo Insurgent," in *Regrouping*.

Written ca. 1975, "My Mexico Is Not Your Mexico" was not published during Kramer's lifetime and appears for the first time in this volume.

"In the Geneve Lobby: Mexico City"

Geneve: Calinda Geneve and Spa is an older but well-kept hotel in the Zona Rosa.

Zona Rosa: The "Pink Zone" is the main restaurant, hotel, shopping, entertainment, and tourist district in Mexico City.

First published in *Epos* (Spring–Summer 1975) as part of the group "My Mexico Is Not Your Mexico."

"Mycenae: On Brushing One's Shoes in Athens"

Mycenae: Mycenae is situated in the northeastern corner of the Argive Plain in southern Greece. Also located there on a hill among steep ravines is an ancient citadel, traditionally the palace of Agamemnon that Homer describes as "rich in gold."

"Troy's lust for Helen": Helen, the most beautiful woman in the world, was the wife of Menelaus, the king of Sparta and brother of Agamemnon. She ran away to Troy (across the Aegean Sea on the western shore of Turkey) with Prince Paris, the youngest son of the king of Troy, thereby setting into play the events described in the *Iliad* and the *Odyssey*.

Agamemnon: Agamemnon, the king of Mycenae, was married to Clytemnestra, sister of Helen. He and Menelaus will fight in the Greek war with Troy. On his return from the Trojan War, Clytemnestra will take part in his murder.

First published in *Street Magazine* 2.1 (1975) as "On Brushing One's Shoes in Athens," in a group titled "Fragments of a Greek Tour, 1975."

"Location"

"St. Pancras' bell": Part of London's inner borough of Camden, St. Pancras is the home of the British Museum and of a 189-meter bell tower—a major tourist attraction.

Yeats: William Butler Yeats (1865–1939) was an Irish poet, playwright, and essayist. A senator of the Irish Free State from 1922 to 1928, Yeats was awarded the Nobel Prize in literature in 1923.

First published in the *Islip Arts Review* 1.1 (1975).

"At Four Minutes to One"

San Miguel: See the note for "Dogs of San Miguel."

the Jardin: A square, the *Plaza Principal* in San Miguel, called the "Jardin" (the Garden).

Allende: See the note for "Sunday in the Square: San Miguel de Allende."

Guanajuato: A city in west-central Mexico. Situated on the steep slopes of a ravine, Guanajuato once contained the richest gold and silver deposits in the Western Hemisphere.

First published in *riverrun* (Spring 1975) and later in *Xanadu* 5 (1978), part of the group "My Mexico Is Not Your Mexico."

"Macedonia"

Byzantium: Originally a Greek colony on the eastern side of the Bosporus dating from the thirteenth century B.C., Byzantium was the site of Constantinople (after A.D. 330), which was later the capital of the Byzantine Empire, and after 1923, the capital of Turkey, renamed Istanbul in 1930.

Blue Mosque: Beautiful mosque of imposing size with six minarets. Built in Istanbul ca. 1615 by Ahmed I.

Topkapi: The palace across from Hagia Sophia. Built in 1559–64 by Mehmet the Conqueror as the seat of government for the Ottoman Empire, it once housed a sultan's harem. Now, Topkapi is a huge museum containing classical art, manuscripts, armor, and other antiquities.

St. Sophia: Hagia Sophia (Aya Sofya), one of the world's greatest architectural monuments, stands between the Blue Mosque and Topkapi Palace. The immense church was built by Emperor Justinian I in A.D. 537. It was converted into a mosque in 1453 by Mehmet the Conqueror. St. Sophia opened as a museum in 1934.

Leander and Hero: Leander loved Hero, a priestess of Aphrodite. They lived on opposite sides of the Hellespont. Each night, Leander swam the Hellespont to be with Hero. One night he drowned. When his body was found, Hero jumped into the Hellespont and drowned herself.

Golden Horn of Yeats: In "Sailing to Byzantium" (1928) William Butler Yeats (1865–1939) describes "Grecian goldsmiths" creating a device of "hammered gold and gold enamelling" that keeps a "drowsy Emperor awake" in Byzantium.

Thessaloniki: A city in central Macedonia.

Kavala: Also given as Kavalla, this city is in northeastern Greece, eastern Macedonia.

Mount Athos: At 2033 meters, the highest point in central Macedonia.

"Persia's hooves about to learn Samothrace": Samothrace is an island in the Aegean, site of the powerful Cult of Cabiri. This reference is obscure because during the two Persian wars with Greece, neither the army of Darius (490 B.C.) nor the army of Xerxes I (480–79 B.C.) passed through Samothrace. Kramer may mean Thrace, the vague territorial boundaries of which are northeastern Greece (including much of Macedonia), southern Bulgaria, and western Turkey at the Hellespont. The army of Xerxes I passed through Thrace during the Second Persian War.

Xanthe: Also rendered as Xanthi, a small city in Greek Thrace, west of Macedonia, south of Bulgaria.

Golden Horn: Section of the river Heliz that flows beneath the hills of Istanbul and empties into the Bosporus creating a natural, but now heavily polluted, harbor.

Anatolia: The Asiatic area of east-central Turkey and the westernmost part of Asia.

First published in *riverrun* (Spring 1976) as "Macedonia: Bussing to Byzantium."

"Grandparents in London"

Greenwich: Greenwich is an outer borough of greater London and home of the Royal Observatory; longitude 0° passes through the observatory.

Thames: The principal river of England, the Thames flows through London.

Oxford Street: Oxford Street forms the boundary along the north side of Soho, London.

St. Paul's: The great cathedral designed by the English architect, astronomer, and mathematician Sir Christopher Wren (1632–1723) after the Great Fire of London (1666) destroyed the original building. Built between 1675 and 1710, it is now the seat of the Anglican bishop of London.

Paul Scofield: English actor, born in 1922.

Proms: See note for "Gilbert and Sullivan Night at the Proms."

Carlyle: Thomas Carlyle (1795–1881) was an English historian, essayist, and autobiographer.

Dickens: Charles Dickens (1812–70) was an English novelist and essayist.

Windsor: A castle in the county of Berkshire that is the English royal residence.

Euston Station: Railroad station in northwestern London.

Keats' House: Home of John Keats (1795–1821), one of the principal poets of the Romantic movement, during the last few years of his life. Located in Hampstead, northwestern London.

Haymarket: Site of the Theater Royal in London.

Hampton Court: Site of Hampton Court Palace, in Greater London.

Bath: A city in southwestern England with natural hot springs. Romans built baths there in the first century A.D.

First published in *Passage II* (River Grove, Ill.: Triton College Press, 1976), later in the *Journal of Humanistic Psychology* (Spring 1978).

"Nafplion: Snapshot"

Nafplion: Nafplion, or Navplion, is a beautiful town on a small peninsula jutting into the Gulf of Argos in southern mainland Greece. Nafplion contains antiquities and a colorful mix of Greek, Turkish, and Venetian architecture.

Peloponnese: The southern section of mainland Greece, a peninsula comprising the Argive Plain and connected to northern Greece by the Corinthian isthmus. Site of much classical Greek history and mythology.

Clytemnestra: See the note for "Mycenae: On Brushing One's Shoes in Athens."

Gulf of Argos: The gulf is located in southeastern Greece, near the cities of Argos and Nafplion.

Arcadia: A mountainous area of the central Peloponnese, Arcadia is often inaccurately portrayed in literature as an idealized pastoral world.

Mt. Erymanthus: One of the highest peaks (2,220 meters) in the Peloponnese.

First published in *Xanadu* (Summer 1977). In 1985, translated into Greek by Flora Zeipekkis.

"Thessaloniki: Three Sleeps"

Thessaloniki: Also known as Saloniki, this is a large city in central Macedonia that has seen the rise and fall of many cultures: Macedonian, Hellenic, Roman, Byzantine, Ottoman, and Jewish (the latter exterminated during World War II).

Alexander: Alexander III of Macedonia (356–323 B.C.) was known as Alexander the Great. Alexander and his Grand Army extended the Macedonian/Greek empire south to Egypt and east to India.

Dimitrius: Dimitrios was martyred in A.D. 303 and became the patron saint of Thessaloniki. A church, the largest in Greece, built on the spot where he died, bears his name, Ayios Dimitrios.

janissaries: These were members of the Turkish sultan's elite personal guard, from the fourteenth century until 1826 when they were disbanded.

"your round tower": This refers to the White Tower on the sea wall facing the Gulf of Thessaloniki, once a place of execution known as the Bloody Tower.

Ataturk: Kemal Ataturk (1881–1938) was a soldier, statesman, and reformer who founded and was first president (1923–38) of the Republic of Turkey. Born in Thessaloniki, Ataturk modernized and westernized Turkey.

Efstatia Nikolaidu: See the note for "Efstatia Nikolaidu," page 344.

Byzantium: This refers to the Byzantine Empire, roughly A.D. 527–1450, formerly the western Roman Empire and the seat of the Eastern Orthodox Church.

First published in *Xanadu* (Summer 1977). In 1985, translated into Greek by Flora Zeipekkis.

"Dogs of San Miguel"

San Miguel: San Miguel de Allende is a city in north-central Mexico that is the birth-place of the Mexican revolutionary hero Ignacio Allende. It is currently home to a large expatriate American art community.

Chapultepec: This is a hill near Mexico City, formerly home of Aztec rulers and site of a battle on September 12–13, 1847, during which outnumbered young Mexican defenders vainly attempted to prevent American troops from entering Mexico City.

Warsaw's ghetto: This was the site of an uprising and resistance from April 19 to May 16, 1943, by trapped Polish Jews against overwhelming Nazi S.S. forces.

First published in *Xanadu* 5 (1978) as part of the group "My Mexico Is Not Your Mexico."

"Visiting Hour: At the Swanholm, St. Petersburg"

Swanholm: This is a nursing home and rehabilitation facility.

St. Petersburg: This is a city in western central Florida, on the coast of the Gulf of Mexico.

Kaddish: The Kaddish is a prayer for mourners, often recited for eleven months and one day after the death of a parent or other close relative.

First published in the *Journal of Humanistic Psychology* (Spring 1978) titled "Visiting Hours" and later in *Modern Poetry Studies* (Fall 1978) as "Visiting Hour."

"Sunday in the Square: San Miguel de Allende"

San Miguel de Allende: See the note in "Dogs of San Miguel."

"his Revolution": Ignacio Allende (1779–1811) is a hero of Mexico's revolution with Spain. As a captain of cavalry and one of the leaders of the revolution that began in September 1810, Allende fought bravely until Spanish loyalists captured and executed him in Chihuahua in March 1811.

First published in *riverrun* (Spring 1979), part of the group "My Mexico Is Not Your Mexico."

"Gilbert and Sullivan Night at the Proms"

Gilbert and Sullivan: Sir William Gilbert (1836–1911), an opera librettist, and Sir Arthur Sullivan (1842–1900), an operatic composer, collaborated on fourteen light operas between 1875 and 1896, including *HMS Pinafore* (1878), *The Pirates of Penzance* (1879), and *The Mikado* (1885).

Proms: This refers to the Sir Henry Wood Promenade Concerts, performed every summer at the Royal Albert Hall, London.

Princess Ida: This is the lead character in Gilbert and Sullivan's *Princess Ida* (1885), based on Tennyson's "The Princess: A Medley" (1847).

Albert Hall: The Royal Albert Hall of Arts and Sciences, a concert hall in London, was built between 1867 and 1871. It is the home of the Royal Philharmonic and of the "Proms."

Ipswich: Ipswich is a city in eastern England.

Covent Garden: Covent Garden Square, London, opened in 1732. The theater is home to the Royal Opera and to the Royal Ballet.

First published in *riverrun* (Spring 1979) and later in *Whetstone* (Summer 1980).

"Toluca: The Friday Market"

Toluca: Toluca de Lerdo, a city in central Mexico—just west of Mexico City and at a somewhat higher elevation—is the capital of the state of Mexico.

First published in *Carousel Parkway* (1980), part of the group "My Mexico Is Not Your Mexico."

"Delphi: Slide 62"

Delphi: This ancient city in central Greece is the seat of the Delphi Oracle, the most famous and powerful in ancient Greece.

Sphinx of Naxos: This refers to a statue dating from 560 B.C. that appears on a tall Ionic column, now in the Delphi Museum. Naxos is a Greek island in the Aegean Sea.

Charioteer: This beautiful life-size bronze statue, dating from 470 B.C., was excavated at the oracle sanctuary at Delphi. It is now in the Delphi Museum.

War of the Gods and Giants: This second-century B.C. sculpture depicts the giants losing their decisive battle with the gods, who were helped by the mortal Herakles. The piece is now in the Delphi Museum.

Castalia: Castalia was a nymph who threw herself into a spring to escape the pursuit of Apollo. The spring then became a source of inspiration for Apollo and for the Muses.

Pythia: Pythia, near Delphi, was the site of the ancient Pythian Games, which were ranked second in importance to the Olympian Games.

First published in *Carousel Parkway* (1980). In 1985, translated into Greek by the Flora Zeipekkis.

"Herakleion: The Hidden Beach"

Herakleion: Herakleion, in northern Crete, is the largest city on the island and was built near the site of ancient Knossos.

First published in *Passage V/VI* (River Grove, Ill.: Triton College Press, 1980), titled "The Hidden Beach."

"Reunion"

"Havana's top hotel": Kramer is likely referring to the landmark high-rise Hotel Habana Libre Tryp, completed in the late 1950s by the Hilton chain and the site of Fidel Castro's headquarters after the revolution in 1959.

"*spasibo*": "Thank you" in Russian.

Morro Castle: See note for "Seven Days," page 335.

Revolution Square: The Plaza de la Revolución is the governmental center of Havana and the site of Cuban political rallies. The plaza contains a nine-story portrait of Che Guevara and the tower-memorial to José Martí.

First published in *San Fernando Poetry Journal* (Fall 1980) but written in 1979.

"Indigo"

Kramer alludes to the National Geographic Society documentary *Living Treasures of Japan,* broadcast several times on PBS during December 1980. The living treasures, called *Ningen Kokouh,* are practitioners of ancient arts and crafts who are recognized and protected by the Japanese government so that they may pass on the nation's cultural heritage to future generations. The approximately one hundred living treasures practice such arts as paper making, sword making, origami, kabuki, calligraphy, pottery making, koto music, doll making, and bell making, among others.

Mrs. (Aiano) Chiga (1890–1980), one of the original living treasures, was a textile-weaver and dyer. Following traditional methods that include washing the finished cloth in a cold stream, she produced four bolts of hand-woven, hand-dyed indigo cloth each year. Mrs. Chiga's cloth is said to last over one hundred years and its indigo will deepen with age. After the filming of the documentary, Mrs. Chiga died at ninety.

Mrs. Chiga's exquisite lifelong obsession with creating indigo cloth allowed Kramer to explore one of his themes: that the life-sustaining power of artistic inspiration be fervently nurtured, never questioned or taken for granted, and never lost.

First published in the *New England Review and Breadloaf Quarterly* (Winter 1885).

"Flood"

Cornwall: Cornwall, a peninsula, is the southwestern-most county in England.

Lionesse: Lionesse, also rendered as Lyonesse, is the legendary tract of land between Land's End (the westernmost part of Cornwall) and the Scilly Islands. Tectonic subsidence sank Lionesse to destruction in the sea. Lionesse is the homeland of Sir Tristram (see Malory's *Le Morte d'Arthur*).

Mount's Bay: This is a large bay in southeastern Cornwall.

"At Trewa, tin-stream works decay": Tin and, later, copper were mined in Cornwall as early as 2000 B.C. and until the mid-nineteenth century.

Perranuthnoe: This is a small village on Mount's Bay.

Cudden Point: A point of land on the western side of Mount's Bay.

Trelawney: Edward John Trelawney (1792–1881) was English novelist and biographer of Cornish descent.

Trevelyan: George Macaulay Trevelyan (1876–1962) was an English historian of Cornish descent.

Lelant: This is a small village in northwestern coastal Cornwall.

Phillack: Phillack is actually Philleigh, a small village in south-coastal Cornwall.

Newquay: This is a coastal town in north-central Cornwall.

"pilchard vessels": These are sardine (pilchard) fishing boats, usually sailing from the extreme southwestern Penwith district of Cornwall.

First published in *Cumberland Poetry Review* (Fall 1985) but composed in 1975.

PART 12: THE MAP OF SPAIN

"In the Land of Olives"

In a longer historical perspective, one not yet available to Kramer when he wrote "In the Land of Olives," the 1936–39 Spanish Civil War amounts to the opening battle of World War II, perhaps the only time in living memory when the world confronted—in fascism and Nazism—something like unqualified evil. The men and women who understood this early on and who chose of their own free will to stand against fascism have thus earned a special status in history. Viewed internally, on the other hand, the Spanish Civil War was the culmination of a prolonged period of national political unrest—unrest in a country that was increasingly polarized and repeatedly unable to ameliorate the conditions of terrible poverty in which millions of its citizens lived. Spain was a country in which landless peasants cobbled together a bare subsistence living by following the harvests on vast, wealthy agricultural estates. The hierarchy of the Catholic Church, identifying more with wealthy landowners than with the Spanish people, was in full control of secondary education; education for women seemed to them unnecessary and universal literacy a danger rather than a goal. Divorce was illegal. The military, meanwhile, had come to see itself, rather melodramatically, as the only bulwark against civil disorder and as the ultimate guarantor of the core values of Spanish society.

When a progressive Popular Front government was elected in February 1936, with the promise of realistic land reform one of its key planks, conservative forces immediately gathered to plan resistance. The Spanish Left, meanwhile, celebrated the elections in a way that made conservative capitalists, military officers, and churchmen worried that much broader reform might begin. Rumors of plotting for a military coup led leaders of the Republic to transfer several high-ranking military officers to remote postings, the aim being to make communication and coordination between them more difficult. But it was not enough. The planning for a military rising continued.

The military rebellion took place on July 18, with the officers who organized it expecting a quick victory and a rapid takeover of the entire country. What the military did not anticipate was the determination of the Spanish people, who broke into barracks, took up arms, and crushed the rebellion in key areas like the cities of Madrid and Barcelona. At that point the character of the struggle changed, for the military realized it was not going to win by fiat. It faced a prolonged struggle against its own people and an uncertain outcome. Military leaders appealed to fascist dictatorships in Italy, Germany, and Portugal for assistance, and they soon began receiving men and supplies from Benito Mussolini, Adolf Hitler, and Antonio Salazar.

The 1936 Spanish election had already been widely celebrated as a great victory in progressive publications in Britain, France, and the United States. In the midst of a worldwide depression, the military rising was thus immediately seen as an assault against working people's interests everywhere. But the rapid intervention of German and Italian troops gave a dramatic international character to what might otherwise have remained a civil war. Almost from the outset, then, the Spanish Civil War became a literal and symbolic instance of the growing worldwide struggle between fascism and democracy. Indeed, the Republic, the elected government, perceived the country as being invaded by foreign troops. By the time the pilots of Hitler's Condor Legion reduced the Basque's holy city of Guernica to rubble the following April, many in the rest of the world had come to share that opinion as well. The Spanish Civil War became the great cause of the 1930s.

First published in *Sunday Worker* (January 16, 1938).

"Smiles and Blood"

First published in *The Alarm Clock* (1938).

"García Lorca"

García Lorca: Federico García Lorca (1898–1936) was Spain's most prominent twentieth-century poet and one of the major poets of the century worldwide. Murdered by the Nationalists at the beginning of the war, he became a symbol of the spirit of the Spanish Republic, in part because his death fused loss and aspiration, betrayal and solidarity, death and longing from the outset. The poetic memorial service for García Lorca started almost immediately after his death in August 1936, continued heavily for more than a decade, and sustained itself intermittently through the rest of the century. Elegies for Lorca were among the central and inescapable categories used to construct the war's intelligibility and its continuing power in the experience and memory of the Left.

First published in the *Brooklyn College Observer* (December 1940).

"Barcelona Celebrates Three Years of Franco"

Barcelona: Barcelona is the capital of the province of the same name as well as the autonomous region of Catalonia. Spain's primary port, it was the capital of the Second Republic from November 1937 and the object of intense bombing (as many as twenty raids per day) by the Nationalist air force. As the stronghold of the CNT, Spain's large anarchist union, and the POUM, Spain's radical anti-Communist Marxist party, Barcelona was involved in particularly intense conflict with the Republican factions, leading to the "May Days" (May 3–8, 1937) street fighting. Barcelona fell to Franco's Nationalists on January 26, 1939.

Franco: Francisco Franco y Bahamonde (1892–1975) was born into a naval family in Galicia and would rise rapidly through the ranks of the Spanish military. He was posted early in his career to Morocco, where he became commander of the Foreign Legion, and where he developed a reputation for ambition, authoritarianism, and ruthlessness. One of several leaders in the insurrection, his political maneuvering and military success gained him sole command of the rebel armies on October 1, 1936. He headed a dictatorship, particularly brutal at the outset, from 1939 until his death in 1975.

First published in 'Til the Grass Is Ripe for Dancing (1943).

"Guernica"

Guernica: On April 26, 1937, more than forty German aircraft of the Condor Legion appeared over Guernica, a historically important but militarily insignificant Basque town of seven thousand. Within a few hours most of the city center was in ruins and over a thousand civilians were dead. Its fame enhanced by Picasso's painting protesting the bombing, this raid has become one of the signal events of the war.

First published in Thru Our Guns (1945) as part of the sequence "The Triumph of Icarus."

"Tidings from Spain"

The poem was written in response to news of student and labor unrest in several Spanish cities, the first such news divulged since Franco took power.

First published in the Village Voice, June 7, 1962.

"Barcelona"

Ramblas: This is the street in Barcelona leading down to the harbor. It is a major shopping area.

First published in The Source (October 1978).

"Madrid: Coming Home"

Madrid: The capital of Spain, Madrid is located at the geographic center of the country. The inhabitants of the city stormed the military barracks and in hand-to-hand combat saved the city for the Republic in July 1936. The International Brigades were thrown into combat in Madrid and the government moved to Valencia. Madrid was the focus of several failed Nationalist attempts to capture the city. Madrid finally fell to the Nationalists in the last days of the war. The city became a symbol of the organized resistance to fascism and, along with García Lorca, was a major focus of wartime poems around the world.

Coruña: This is a province in northwestern Spain, facing onto the Atlantic. It was Franco's home province. Both the city of Coruña and the province as a whole fell to the rebels within days of the war's opening.

León: A province in northwestern Spain, León was largely taken by the rebels shortly after the war began, in part because a large group of Republican miners had left to help defend Madrid. Until March 1937, however, several thousand guerrillas fought the rebels in the León mountains.

Valladolid: This is a politically conservative province (and capital city) in north-central Spain, where Nationalists gained control and murdered about nine thousand citizens judged to be Republican sympathizers.

Guadarramas: Madrid is situated on a plateau 750 meters high and is encircled by the Guadarrama mountains to the north.

El Cid: El Cid (ca. 1040–99) was the great popular knight of Spain's chivalrous age, a figure of both history and legend. He is the central figure of stories told about Christian Spain's struggle against occupying Moslem forces. El Cid's exploits are celebrated in the twelfth-century "Poema del Cid," perhaps the oldest monument of Spanish literature.

"*No Pasaran*": This rallying cry—"They shall not pass"—was raised by the people of Madrid early in the war as Franco's armies threatened their city. This phrase came to represent the fighting spirit of the people of the Republic.

First published in *riverrun* (Spring 1979).

"*Sevilla: July 18th*"

Sevilla: Spain's fourth-largest city, Sevilla is the provincial capital in the province of Seville in southern Spain. During the war, it was a Nationalist stronghold and the site of relentless executions of citizens on the political Left.

Bizet: Georges Bizet (1838–75) was a French composer whose operas include *Carmen* (1875), which is set in Spain. In popular culture, Carmen has long been a figure for the pure, unmediated spirit of Spain.

Byron: George Gordon, Lord Byron (1788–1824) was a British Romantic poet.

"*But to the girdle* . . .": Kramer quotes two lines from act 4 of William Shakespeare's *King Lear.*

Guardia Incivil: This refers to the Spanish Civil Guard, a paramilitary force established in 1844 to police rural Spain. Often brutal, its members were frequently feared and hated by the communities in which they served.

Falange: The *Falange España de las JONS* was a Spanish political party founded in 1933 by José Antonio Primo de Rivera. Often identified as a fascist party, it stood for an authoritarian and centralized Spain and for Spanish nationalist traditions. It sided with the rebels during the Civil War and was forcibly merged with the Carlists to form a new political party, the *Falange España Tradicionalista*, controlled by Franco.

Arriba España: This phrase ("Long Live Spain!") was originally the Falangist salute used at public meetings and when greeting fellow members. It became a general rallying cry for the fascist forces.

"there's hell . . .": Kramer again quotes two lines from act 4 of Shakespeare's *King Lear.*

July 18, 1936: This was the date of the Nationalist rebellion against the elected Spanish government.

Murillo: Bartolomé Estaban Murillo (1617–1682) was a Spanish Baroque religious painter.

Leal: Juan de Valdes Leal (1622–1690) a Spanish Baroque painter, was noted for moralizing subjects like that of his *Allegory of Vanity.*

Andalusian: This refers to a person from Andalucía, a large agricultural region in south-central Spain, portions of which were captured by Franco early in the war.

"The Song of the Civil Guard": This refers to one of Federico García Lorca's most famous and politically pointed poems, a savage and devastating attack on the Guardia Civil.

First published in *riverrun* (Spring 1979).

"Granada: The Rose"

Granada: The province by this name is located in southeastern Spain on the Mediterranean. Its capital, also named Granada, was captured by the Nationalists early on, while the rest of the province was the site of considerable military conflict thereafter. The nationalists instituted a reign of terror to suppress the working classes there. García Lorca was murdered outside Granada in August 1936.

Alhambra: This is a Moorish palace overlooking the city of Granada.

Albaicin: Albaicin was the only section of the old quarter in Granada that was spared from demolition when Isabel and Fernando drove out the Moslems.

Fernando (Ferdinand) (1452–1516), founder of the Spanish monarchy, and Isabella (1451–1504): The king and queen of Castile and Aragon. Their reign was marked not only by the conquest of Grenada in 1492, ending Moorish rule in Spain, and by support for Christopher Columbus's voyages to the New World, but also by the Spanish Inquisition. They are entombed in Grenada.

Valdés: José Valdés Guzmán was the fascist commandante in Granada. He was the officer most responsible for García Lorca's death.

José Antonio: José Antonio Primo de Rivera was the founder and leader of the right-wing Falangist party. He was executed by firing squad on November 20, 1936, thereafter becoming a fascist martyr and eventually a cult figure. A statue of him is located in Granada across from García Lorca's window.

Acera del Casino: This is García Lorca's street in Granada, just off the Puerta Real and across from the Avenida José Antonio.

First published in *riverrun* (Spring 1979).

"Málaga: A Prayer"

Málaga: This significant port city on the southern coast of Spain was taken by the nationalist army on February 8, 1937, after the Republicans abandoned the city without much of a fight. Some of the most brutal reprisals of the war took place immediately afterward.

First published in *Carousel Parkway* (1980) and translated into Yiddish by M. [Maurice] Kish in 1982 as "Malaga: a tfilleh."

"Córdoba: Nocturne"

Córdoba: This is the capital of the Córdoba Province in Andalusia, about 150 miles east of Sevilla. Like most cities in Andalusia, Córdoba fell almost immediately to the fascist rebels when the uprising started in July 1936.

Alcázar: This refers to the Spanish Army's fortress-like school for infantry officers, site of a dramatic siege in the opening months of the Spanish Civil War. Nationalist soldiers were barricaded in the fortress until relieved by Franco. A frenzy of executions followed, as wounded Republican militiamen were killed in their hospital beds. Thereafter the fascists treated the Alcázar as virtually a religious shrine.

Maimonides: Moses ben Maimonides (1135–1204) was a Spanish-born Jewish rabbi and scholastic philosopher.

Lucan: Marcus Annaeus Lucan (A.D. 39–65), a Roman poet, was born in Spain.

Seneca: Lucius Annaeus Seneca (ca. 4 B.C.–A.D. 65), a Roman dramatist and philosopher, was the leading Roman intellectual figure of his time. He was born of a Spanish family.

Gabirol: Solomon Ben Yehuda Ibn Gabirol (ca. 1022–1058) was one of the leading figures of the Hebrew school of religious and secular poetry during the Jewish Golden Age in Spain.

First published in *Midstream* (February 1981).

"Granada"

First published as "Granada: First Sleep" in *Pikestaff Forum* 5 (Spring 1983).

"Madrid: The Ghosts of Its Defenders"

First published in *Pikestaff Forum* 5 (Spring 1983).

"Barcelona: The Last Night"

Catalan: This is the primary language in the province of Catalonia, the region in northeastern Spain bordered by France on the north and the Mediterranean on the east. Catalonia, and its capital, Barcelona, have traditionally sought independence from the rest of Spain. Autonomous during the war, it was the site of many significant battles, particularly during the last year of the war. The fall of Barcelona to the Nationalist armies in January 1939 meant the war was essentially over. The Catalan language was a symbol of the desire for regional independence. Franco banned its use during his reign.

First published in *North Atlantic Review* (Summer 1990).

"Madrid: July 1978"

Goya: Francisco de Goya (1746–1828), perhaps the quintessential Spanish painter of his age, was often counted the founder of modernism in Spanish painting. His work often reflected the violence of contemporary events. Kramer refers to three paintings, *The Shootings of May Third 1808, Saturn Devouring His Children,* and *Witches' Sabbath.*

First published in *Indigo* (1991).

"Granada: First Showing"

Sacromonte: This is a valley in Spain famous for its caves and its abbey.

Gary Cooper and Ingrid Bergman: These actors starred in the 1943 film version of Ernest Hemingway's Spanish Civil War novel *For Whom the Bell Tolls* (1939). Only after Franco's death was the film shown in Spain.

First published in *California Quarterly* (1991).

"Córdoba"

First published in *Indigo* (1991).

PART 13: RUNES, RIDDLES, AND DARKNESS

"The Flowers of Georgia O'Keeffe"

First published in *Roll the Forbidden Drums!* (1954) and set to music by Diana Arnow (1979).

"His Something"

First published in the *New York Times,* July 4, 1960.

"Lesson"

First published in the *New York Times,* May 17, 1961.

"Lines on a Museum Postcard"

First published in *Adelphi Quarterly* (Summer 1962).

"Midsummer"

First published as "Nocturne" in *Poet Lore* (Fall 1963) in *Rumshinsky's Hat* (1964) as "Midsummer."

"Air for Bagpipe"

First published in *Lyrismos* (Spring 1969) as "From Carlisle North to Edinburgh" and then in *On the Way to Palermo* (1973) as "Air for Bagpipe."

"The Redwing's Cry"

First published in *Modern Poetry Studies* (Winter 1974).

"Falling Asleep"

First published in *Wind/Literary Journal* (1982) as part 1 of "Suite" which also includes "Now," "Composition," and "After." Titled "Falling Asleep" in *In Wicked Times* (1983) and untitled in *Indigo* (1991) as part 2 of "Episode."

"Night Thoughts"

First published in *Pikestaff Forum* 10 (Spring 1991).

PART 14: POET'S WORK
"Neruda in Hiding"

Pablo Neruda (1904–73) was born Neftalí Ricardo Reyes Basoalto in a small town in central Chile. His life and work would end up shaping not only the course of Latin American poetry but also the emerging political consciousness of the region. He achieved literary fame early on, as his *Twenty Love Poems and a Song of Despair* (1924) became a bestseller. Only three years later, he joined the Chilean consular service. In the course of his life, he would take honorary diplomatic posts in Burma, Ceylon, Java, Singapore, Buenos Aires, Barcelona, Paris, Madrid, and Mexico. He was also a Marxist, a Communist, and a relentless advocate for the poor. This placed him in conflict with several governments, so that he managed repeatedly to be treated alternately as a distinguished public figure and an outlaw. At the time Kramer's poem was published, Neruda was essentially a fugitive in his own country, living underground because the regime of President González Videla was seeking to punish him for his protests against its repression of striking miners in 1947. Indeed, he had been elected senator of the Republic in 1945. Yet he had to flee the country in 1949, not returning until 1952, after the anti-Videla forces were victorious and the order to arrest leftists was rescinded.

He first began using the pen name Pablo Neruda in 1920, finally adopting it as his legal name in 1946. His range of poetic styles was unusual, from the surrealist *Residence on Earth* (1933), with its intimations of emerging political violence, to the impassioned wartime advocacy of the Spanish Republic in *Spain in My Heart* (1937), to the monumental *Canto General* (1950), a Marxist rereading of Latin American history deeply committed to social justice. Neruda knew García Lorca well and was powerfully affected by his murder. At the end of his life, he was equally devastated by the murder of the Chilean president Salvador Allende and the military coup led by the reactionary General Pinochet. Among other tributes to Neruda is a poem by Muriel Rukeyser, "Neruda, the Wine."

First published in *The Golden Trumpet* (1949) and set to music by Pete Seeger in 1967. Translated into Urdu by Adeeb Suhail in *Auraq* [Karachi] (November–December 1993).

"Singing"

First published in *Masses and Mainstream* (April 1953).

"Threnody" and "The Widower"

A threnody is a meditation upon death, a deeply poignant lamentation that is more despairing than an elegy.

"Threnody" first appeared in the *New York Times* on July 21, 1956, while "The Widower" first appeared in the *New York Times* on October 8, 1958. The poems should be read as a linked pair.

See the introductory essay in this book for details and context.

"And I Looked, and, Behold, a Whirlwind"

Kramer wrote this poem in reaction to the extraordinary proliferation of family bomb-shelters throughout the United States.

First published in the *Village Voice*, June 21, 1962.

"Dialogue"

First published in *National Weekly Poetry-Letter* (April 16, 1962).

"The Count"

First published in *The Lyric* (Summer 1962).

"To Himself"

First published in *Carleton Miscellany* (Fall 1963).

"Sunday Morning"

First published in *Rumshinsky's Hat* (1964).

"The Swan"

Boris Pasternak (1890–1960) was the child of prominent Jewish residents of Moscow. His mother was a famous concert pianist, his father a teacher at the Moscow School of Painting. The family home entertained such guests as the German poet Rainer Maria Rilke, the Russian novelist Tolstoy, and the Russian composer Sergei Rachmaninoff. Initially a music student, Pasternak switched to philosophy, which he studied at Marburg University in Germany. His first volume of poetry appeared in 1914; shortly thereafter, he found himself doing World War I service as a private tutor in a Ural Mountains chemical factory.

Then came the Russian Revolution of 1917. Pasternak saw the need for fundamental change in the Soviet Union and supported the revolution. He even wrote experimental poems on revolutionary themes. But as socialist realism came to be increasingly demanded in the 1930s Pasternak, among many other writers, would come to be denounced as an aesthete. And indeed Pasternak, though deeply concerned with how history impacts individual lives, and thus no aesthete in Western terms, was reluctant to urge unthinking service to the state. Interestingly, the main characters in his novel *Doctor Zhivago* spend much of their effort trying to insulate themselves from the forces of history—both the Russian Revolution and the civil war that followed it.

During World War II Pasternak did compose patriotic verses. Most poets did so out of the passionate need to save their country from Nazi aggression. But after the war he began work on his great novel. *Doctor Zhivago* was probably finished in 1955, but Pasternak was no longer permitted to publish his work in the Soviet Union. He mounted a false campaign to block its translation and publication abroad—one carefully calculated to assuage the authorities but to fail—and the novel was smuggled out of the Soviet Union and published in Europe. Awarded the Nobel Prize in 1958, Pasternak was compelled to refuse it. Unlike so many of his contemporaries, Pasternak did not die in the Gulag, yet his work was suppressed and he had to live in fear amidst public attacks. It was not until 1987, years after his death, that he was rehabilitated. Only then could *Doctor Zhivago*, considered by some the greatest Russian novel of the century, be published in his own country.

In 1964, the year Kramer published "The Swan," Pasternak's *Poems 1916–1959* was issued in the West.

First published in *Bitterroot* (Fall 1964) as "For a Distant Poet (for Boris Pasternak)." Kramer wrote the poem upon the publication of *Doctor Zhivago* outside the Soviet Union. In *The Burning Bush* (1983) as "The Swan" with the middle stanza omitted.

"To the Countrymen of Alfred Kreymborg"

Written two weeks earlier, after Kramer's last visit with his dying friend and mentor, this poem was included in *The Villager*'s memorial article titled "In Memoriam: Alfred Kreymborg." For biographical information, see the note for "Alfred Kreymborg's Coat," page 331.

First published in *The Villager* (August 18, 1966).

"Not Being Yevtushenko"

Yevgeny Yevtushenko was born in 1933 in the town of Zima in Irtutsk, which is in Siberia in the former Soviet Union. He went to Moscow in 1944 and there studied at the Gorky Institute of Literature from 1951 to 1954. His literary career has been a mix of celebrity, compromise, and eloquent witness, all conditioned by the shifting tides of Soviet policy and censorship. Two of his poems suggest the relevant contradictions. The 1961 "Babi Yar" courageously attacked both Nazi and Soviet anti-Semitism, linking both to the impulses underlying the Holocaust. Frequently read aloud in the Soviet Union, it gained him fame both there and abroad—indeed he appeared on the cover of *Time* in 1962—but it was not actually published in his own country until 1984. Similarly, "The Heirs of Stalin" was issued in *Pravda* in 1961 at a moment when the dictator's legacy was receiving public critique, but harsher political powers then prevailed, and the poem was not reprinted for a quarter of a century. Yevtushenko's freedoms were withdrawn early in the 1960s, when he was denounced as "the head of the intellectual juvenile delinquents," then restored. Thereafter the regime permitted him extensive travel, in part to showcase its purported openness. As he became an increasingly public poet in his own land, however, reading before large audiences, he sometimes opted for a bombastic style not equal to the quality of his best work. Then he was denounced as a collaborator by dissidents in the USSR and by conservative western commentators like William Buckley. All these contradictions are echoed in Kramer's poem.

First published in *Midstream* (June 1969).

"To the White Minority of South Africa"

First published as part 3 of "For Benjamin Moloise, Hanged in Pretoria Prison," in Blair Allen, ed., *Snow Summits in the Sun: A Different Anthology of Poetry and Prose Poems* (Cucamonga, Calif.: Cerulean, 1988).

"Paul Celan"

Paul Celan (1920–70) was born Paul Antschel in Czernowitz (later Chernovtsy, when the region was incorporated into Ukraine), a small town in Romania. The child of German-speaking Jews, he acquired several languages early on, among them Romanian, French, and a basic understanding of Yiddish. During the war, he also studied Russian. In 1938, he studied medicine in Tours, France, for a year, but returned home just before World War II began. The area was occupied by Soviet troops in 1940, but the following year the town was overrun by German and Romanian troops, and the area's Jews were gathered into a ghetto. In the summer of 1942, Celan's parents were deported to an internment camp in Transnistria. There his father died of typhus, and his mother was killed with a bullet in the neck. Celan himself escaped arrest until he was pressed into forced labor building roads in Southern Moldavia. The Romanian labor camp was dissolved in 1944 and Celan returned to his home province of Bukovina, now once again occupied by Soviet troops. He managed to leave illegally in 1947, spending a year in Vienna and then settling in Paris for the rest of his life. In 1947, he adopted the pseudonym Celan, an anagram of the Romanian version of his last name, Ancel.

In Paris Celan began to study German, becoming a lecturer in German literature at the École Normale Supérieure in 1950. Through all this time, he was haunted by his Holocaust experiences. He was also harassed by an accusation of plagiarism leveled by the wife of a German poet, an accusation that ultimately added an element of paranoia to his mental life. The strains of his personal and historical experience contributed to a poetry that often shapes fragmented diction and syntax to achieve a dark music. His poem "Fugue of Death," one of the century's major Holocaust poems, opens with an invocation of the "black milk of daybreak," an image perhaps appropriate only to a world in which one wakes to horror. Increasingly tormented, Celan leaped off a bridge into the Seine and drowned in May 1970.

First published in *Regrouping* (1997).

Aaron Kramer Bibliography

POETRY

The Alarm Clock: Poems. Privately printed, 1938.
Another Fountain: Poems. Privately printed, 1940.
'Til the Grass Is Ripe for Dancing. New York: Harbinger, 1943.
Seven Poets in Search of an Answer: A Poetic Symposium. New York: Bernard Ackerman, 1944.
Thru Our Guns: A Group of War Poems. Privately printed, 1945.
The Glass Mountain. New York: Bernard Ackerman, 1946.
The Thunder of the Grass. New York: International, 1948.
The Golden Trumpet. New York: International, 1949.
Thru Every Window! New York: William-Frederick, 1950.
Denmark Vesey and Other Poems. Privately printed, 1952.
Roll the Forbidden Drums! New York: Cameron and Kahn, 1954.
A Ballad of August Bondi. Privately printed, 1955.
The Tune of the Calliope: Poems and Drawings of New York. New York: Thomas Yoseloff, 1958.
Moses: Poems and Translations. New York: O'Hare, 1962.
Rumshinsky's Hat and House of Buttons: Two Collections of Poetry. New York: Thomas Yoseloff, 1964.
Henry at the Grating: Poems of Nausea. New York: Folklore Center, 1968.
Ghosts. Oakdale, N.Y.: Dowling College Press, 1970.
On the Way to Palermo and Other Poems. South Brunswick, N.J.: A. S. Barnes, 1973.
O Golden Land!: A Travelog in Verse. Oakdale, N.Y.: Dowling College Press, 1976.
The Dance. Port Jefferson, N.Y.: Street Press, 1978.
Carousel Parkway and Other Poems. San Diego, Calif.: A. S. Barnes, 1980.
The Burning Bush: Poems and Other Writings (1940–1980). New York: Cornwall, 1983.
In Wicked Times. Arlington, Va.: Black Buzzard, 1983.
In the Suburbs. Winterville, Ga.: Ali Baba, 1986.
Indigo and Other Poems. New York: Cornwall, 1991.
Border Incident: Poems. [translated into Russian] St. Petersburg, Russ.: Journal Neva, 1996.
Majestic Room. [translated into Bulgarian] Sofia, Bulg.: PAN, 1996.
Regrouping. Northport, N.Y.: Birnham Wood, 1997. [posthumous]

PROSE

The Prophetic Tradition in American Poetry, 1835–1900. Rutherford, N.J.: Fairleigh Dickinson University Press, 1968.
Melville's Poetry: Toward the Enlarged Heart: A Thematic Study of Three Ignored Major Poems. Rutherford, N.J.: Fairleigh Dickinson University Press, 1972.

Neglected Aspects of American Poetry: The Greek Independence War and Other Studies. Oakdale, N.Y.: Dowling College Press, 1997. [posthumous]

ANTHOLOGY

On Freedom's Side: An Anthology of American Poems of Protest. New York: Macmillan, 1972.

TRANSLATIONS (OR, AS INDICATED, WITH SUBSTANTIAL CONTRIBUTIONS)

The Poetry and Prose of Heinrich Heine. New York: Citadel, 1948. [Kramer provides 110 of 162 poetry translations]

The Teardrop Millionaire and Other Poems. New York: Manhattan Emma Lazarus Clubs, 1955. [translations of Morris Rosenfeld]

Songs and Ballads: Goethe, Schiller, Heine. New York: O'Hare, 1963.

Rainer Maria Rilke: Visions of Christ: A Posthumous Cycle of Poems. Boulder, Colo.: University of Colorado Press, 1967.

The Poetry of Heinrich Heine. New York: Citadel, 1969. [Kramer provides 110 of 162 translations]

Poems of Abraham Reisen. Oakdale, N.Y.: Dowling College Press, 1971.

A Century of Yiddish Poetry. New York: Cornwall, 1989.

All My Yesterdays Were Steps: The Selected Poems of Dora Teitelboim. Hoboken, N.J.: KTAV, 1995.

God Hid His Face: Selected Poems of Rajzel Zychlinshy. Santa Rosa, Calif.: Word and Quill, 1997. [Kramer provides 35 translations]

The Last Lullaby: Poetry from the Holocaust. Syracuse, N.Y.: Syracuse University Press, 1998. [posthumous]

SELECTED RECORDINGS

Serenade by Aaron Kramer. Folkways Records, 1957. Kramer reads fifteen of his own poems and four poems each by fellow "Poets of New York," including Alexander F. Bergman, Maxwell Bodenheim, and Morris Rosenfeld. Pamphlet accompanying album contains a short biography of Kramer; a photograph by Irving Karmin of Kramer reading to the blind; texts of all the poems; biographical notes on Bergman, Bodenheim, and Rosenfeld written by Kramer; and twelve art reproductions later published in *The Tune of the Calliope* (1958) as are all the Kramer poems.

Serenade was reissued in 1995 by the Smithsonian Institution's Office of Folklife Programs and Cultural Studies as Folkways Cassette Series 09703. The Smithsonian's goal is to keep each Folkways recording in print "in order to ensure that its sounds and the genius of its artists would continue to be available to future generations."

On Freedom's Side: The Songs and Poems of Aaron Kramer. Freneau Records, 1974. The recording includes excerpts from Kramer's Westbury concert of March 3, 1973. Kramer introduces and reads his own and selected poetry. The songs are performed by Viki Ann Diamond, Joan Fishman, and Karl Finger. Also includes "Neruda's Death," Kramer's elegy for the recently deceased Chilean poet, set to music by Pete Seeger. Recorded and mixed by Cue Recording Studios, New York City, N.Y. Issued December 1974.

The Emperor of Atlantis. Comp. Viktor Ullmann. Lib. Peter Kien. Trans. Aaron Kramer. Vermont Symphony Orchestra and Chorus. Cond. Robert DeCormier. Arabesque, 1996. Arabesque Recordings CD Z6681. See Donald Gilzinger Jr.'s introduction to "The Emperor of Atlantis (Der Kaiser von Atlantis)" in *Theatrical Performance during the Holocaust: Texts | Documents | Memoirs,* ed. Rebecca Rovit and Alvin Goldfarb (Baltimore, Md.: Johns Hopkins University Press, 1999) for details about Kramer's translation of Kien's libretto and Kerry Woodward's musical transcription of Ullmann's score.

ONLINE BIBLIOGRAPHY

A comprehensive two-hundred-page Aaron Kramer bibliography, compiled and maintained by Donald Gilzinger Jr., is accessible online at <http://www2.sunysuffolk.edu/gilzind/akbib.htm> (accessed September 21, 2003).

Index of Titles

AARON KRAMER (1921–97) was the author of *The Alarm Clock* (1938), *Denmark Vesey and Other Poems* (1952), *Henry at the Grating* (1968), *Carousel Parkway and Other Poems* (1980), and numerous other books of poetry. His poems appeared in *Kenyon Review* and *Icarus*. He is the editor of *On Freedom's Side: An Anthology of American Poems of Protest*.

CARY NELSON is Jubilee Professor of Liberal Arts and Sciences at the University of Illinois at Urbana-Champaign. Among other books, he is the author of *Repression and Recovery: Modern American Poetry and the Politics of Cultural Memory* and *Revolutionary Memory: Recovering the Poetry of the American Left* and the editor of *Anthology of Modern American Poetry* and *The Wound and the Dream: Sixty Years of American Poems about the Spanish Civil War*.

DONALD GILZINGER JR. is a professor of English at Suffolk County Community College in Selden, New York. He is Aaron Kramer's bio-bibliographer and has written about him in such collections as *The Second First Art* and *Theatrical Performance during the Holocaust*.

The American Poetry Recovery Series

Collected Poems   *Edwin Rolfe; edited by Cary Nelson and Jefferson Hendricks*
Trees Became Torches: Selected Poems   *Edwin Rolfe; edited by Cary Nelson and Jefferson Hendricks*
Palace-Burner: The Selected Poetry of Sarah Piatt   *Edited and with an introduction by Paula Bernat Bennett*
Black Moods: Collected Poems   *Frank Marshall Davis; edited by John Edgar Tidwell*
Rendezvous with Death: American Poems of the Great War   *Edited by Mark W. Van Wienen*
The Wound and the Dream: Sixty Years of American Poems about the Spanish Civil War   *Edited by Cary Nelson*
Collected Poems   *Don Gordon; edited and with an essay by Fred Whitehead*
Complete Poems   *Claude McKay; edited and with an introduction by William J. Maxwell*
The Whole Song: Selected Poems   *Vincent Ferrini; edited and with an introduction by Kenneth A. Warren and Fred Whitehead*
Wicked Times: Selected Poems   *Aaron Kramer; edited and with a biographical essay by Cary Nelson and Donald Gilzinger Jr.*

The University of Illinois Press
is a founding member of the
Association of American University Presses.

Composed in 9.5/13 Utopia
with Utopia display
by Jim Proefrock
at the University of Illinois Press
Designed by Paula Newcomb
Manufactured by Thomson-Shore, Inc.

University of Illinois Press
1325 South Oak Street
Champaign, IL 61820-6903
www.press.uillinois.edu